Money and Banking

This book focuses on the core issues in money and banking. By using simple applications for anyone who understands basic economics, the lessons in the book provide any student or reader with a background in how financial markets work, how banks as businesses function, how central banks make decisions, and how monetary policy affects the global economy.

Money and Banking is split into sections based on subject matter, specifically definitions and introductions, financial markets, microeconomic issues, macroeconomy policy, and international finance. It also covers:

- derivative and currency markets
- the microeconomics of banking
- trade and currency movements
- asymmetric information and derivative markets
- the future of financial markets and their participants.

By providing a mix of microeconomic and macroeconomic applications, focusing on both international examples and open economy macroeconomics, this book reduces the minutiae seen in competing books. Each chapter provides summaries of what should be learned along the way and why the chapter's topic is important, regardless of current events. For under-graduate business, economics or social science students, this book is a concise source of information on money, banking and financial markets.

Robert Eyler is Professor and Chair of Economics at Sonoma State University, and has been a visiting scholar at both the University of Bologna and Stanford University. He has a PhD in economics from University of California, Davis, USA.

Money and Banking

An international text

Robert Eyler

Routledge
Taylor & Francis Group

LONDON AND NEW YORK

First published 2010
by Routledge
2 Park Square, Milton Park, Abingdon, Oxon, OX14 4RN

Simultaneously published in the USA and Canada
by Routledge
270 Madison Avenue, New York, NY 10016

Routledge is an imprint of the Taylor & Francis Group, an informa business

Typeset in Times New Roman by
Keystroke, Tettenhall, Wolverhampton
Printed and bound in Great Britain by
TJ International Ltd, Padstow, Cornwall

British Library Cataloguing in Publication Data
A catalogue record for this book is available from the British Library

Library of Congress Cataloging-in-Publication Data
Eyler, Robert.
Money and banking : an international text / Robert C. Eyler.
p. cm.
Includes bibliographical references and index.
1. Finance. 2. Monetary policy. 3. Banks and banking. 4. International finance. I. Title.
HG173.E979 2009
332–dc22
2009014859

ISBN10: 0–415–77546–9 (hbk)
ISBN10: 0–415–77547–7 (pbk)
ISBN10: 0–203–86845–5 (ebk)

ISBN13: 978–0–415–77546–5 (hbk)
ISBN13: 978–0–415–77547–2 (pbk)
ISBN13: 978–0–203–86845–4 (ebk)

To Chérie and Lucíana

Contents

Figures

Tables

Case studies

Symbols and abbreviations

ε = expectation superscript

ℓ = script "L" used for "liquidity" in "liquidity premium"

Σ = summation sign in formulae

β = beta, or a regression coefficient, or the financial term "beta", or the reaction of expected inflation to a change in unemployment

Δ = change in the associated variable

π = profit

$\dot{P}$ = inflation rate

γ = forecast coefficient for expected inflation

α_p = slope of the Taylor Curve

¥   = symbol for Japanese Yen

£   = symbol for British Pound

dp   = default premium

tp   = taxation premium

ℓp   = liquidity premium

cpp = currency and political premium

Preface

This text is being written at a time where financial upheaval, across all markets and economies, has become prevalent in the news and pervasive in everyday life. For theoretical economists, money and banking is the underpinning of macroeconomic analysis, where policy is tied to macroeconomic variables and economic logic. For empirical economists, data flow in all directions from these markets, especially financial markets, such that knowledge of econometrics turns these data into a playground of fanciful hypotheses and assumptions about the differences between causality and correlation. The world's financial trauma of 2007 to the present (at least 2009) was foreseen by economists in scope, but not in scale or speed of effects. As I wrote this text, I was forced to reconsider many of the included topics. A book that should have easily flowed from class notes of over thirteen years of teaching money and banking, reflections, research, and discussions with other economists and professionals in these markets became difficult to write and assemble.

My classes have been populated by students who wanted to find jobs in advising, banking, insurance, and other financial jobs. They come in with a large range of backgrounds; some actually work in banking and are completing their education, while others are day traders and feel they have seized some greater knowledge of a gambling house that anyone can play in regardless of age. While I assume that most students come into my classes with some basic knowledge of both economics and finance, I am shocked at the lack of basic financial literacy of the average college student. However, once they are exposed to the connections between financial decisions and economic logic, students generally make the turn toward becoming better thinkers about both their own decisions and their abilities to advise and work for others to pursue maximum profit. I also want to thank Terry Clague, Robert Langham, and the staff at Routledge for their hard work on my behalf.

I want to thank many people who assisted with the writing of this text. I had three student assistants at Sonoma State University. Shane Holt, Charles Mutunga and Sinead McElligott all provided reference work and engaged in website research. Frank Howard Allen Realtors provided funding for these assistants. My colleagues in the Economics Department and the Department of Business Administration at Sonoma State provided invaluable discussions and answers when needed to elucidate pedagogical concerns I had.

I also need to thank two teachers of mine at California State University, Chico. Without John Orr and John Eckalbar, I would have never become an academic and not had the chance to enjoy these years teaching students about monetary theory, policy and its importance to our everyday lives. I owe them a large debt I could never finance.

1 Understanding money

Introduction

Money has been identified as the root of all evil, something that talks, and the ether upon which commerce takes place. In the modern world economy, money in a cash form has become less important. But money itself continues to symbolize power, authority and an ability to consume. This text has three major goals. To enhance the reader's financial and economic literacy is the first and foremost goal. Financial crises come and go, and have depths that are sometimes shallow and other times deep and very depressing. They are natural occurrences of markets gone wrong, of business cycles becoming disrupted by unforeseen events, and of bad policies. Understanding why policy takes place, how the markets are formed in the first place and why equilibrium is a natural pull for human interactions is important to understanding the economy from all angles.

The second goal is to understand the importance and necessity of developed economies to embrace less-developed ones. While this is not a text about economic development, it is one of how economies interact with each other financially. International finance takes place in global markets, connecting diverse institutions and economies to each other because of comparative advantage. The natural tendency to trade delivers a natural tendency to provide financing. This connection provides readers and students of money and banking with the tools to analyze both domestic and international events as economists do.

The third is to illuminate the importance of economics. Economists are generally physicists trapped in the body of a historian, political scientist, sociologist or psychologist. As a result, economists tend to put mathematical formulae and geometric figures to almost all human interactions and thoughts. Concepts of opportunity cost, insurance, central banking, net interest margin, spreading versus hedging risk, the difference between fiscal and monetary policy, and international finance are interconnected and make the world go round. This text begins with defining money and ends with the future of the markets for money, including central banking and monetary policy.

The essence of money

Money, for all of its pundits and pursuers, is the ether upon which commerce flows. It is critical to understand the origins of money and why it is used in economic transactions to fully understand economics as a science. Money's genesis follows the beginnings of civilization. Regardless of money's state as coinage, commodity or otherwise, the use of money provides efficiencies in trade. The logical alternative is barter, an economic system where two parties agree to make a transaction from a double coincidence of wants. The classic example is Jack and the Beanstalk: Jack trades two cows for three magic beans. While Jack may agree that two cows are worth three magic beans, he may be the only one of that opinion beyond the owner of the magic beans. Think of how inefficient that is in the aggregate! In a barter system, markets are made with every single transaction, as time is wasted determining the value of a good or service in each trade. When money is used as a medium of exchange, two cows may seem far superior in value than the three beans to a market full of buyers. What happens if Jack throws those beans into the ground and nothing comes up?

In a monetary economy, the double coincidence of wants is eliminated, and market activity determines prices for all goods in terms of how much money the seller asks in exchange for the good and how much money the buyer is willing to pay, a classic interaction of supply and demand from economic principles. A seller asks for certain prices, thinking about other goods to be purchased with revenue from the sale; the buyer pays only what he feels the goods are worth, and naturally does this by comparison to alternatives. The idea of opportunity cost, the cost of the best forgone alternative, is a major part of understanding why barter does not work as efficiently and why money is a much better medium for exchange. There is an additional cost of barter which does not exist with money. But money also has its costs, and those help shape the definition of what is accepted for all debts public and private.

The definition of money

Money is, at its foundation, a medium of exchange. This text uses a definition of money that also eliminates certain financial assets from being considered money. To be considered money, an entity must have the following four characteristics simultaneously:

- Medium of Exchange: money eliminates the double coincidence of wants under barter;
- Unit of Account/Standard of Value: all goods, services, and financial assets within an economy are priced in terms of the currency;
- Store of Value: money is an asset because money has value or explicitly earns income; and
- Standard of Deferred Payment: all debts, public and private, are priced in terms of the currency.

The medium of exchange characteristic is specific to being the lubricant between buyers and sellers, eliminating barter. Monetary economies came from a natural evolution of society. We will see later that differences between currencies around the world, and sometimes within an economy unified politically otherwise, were at one time set to a certain value of gold such that the relative prices of goods were basically the same in any country. Economists still consider "barter terms of trade", or the relative export to import volumes of goods exchanged between two countries. Karl Marx discussed an economy without money as a "natural economy". Marx suggested that a barter economy is not necessarily distinct from a monetary economy, simply a part of it. A coincidence of wants is still needed, but money allows for the use of credit to facilitate transactions. Both goods and credit can be priced in the same terms when a monetary economy is present. We will see soon how important credit markets are to economies and why money also makes those markets more efficient.

The unit of account function is tied directly to the medium of exchange function. All goods, services, and financial assets inside the economy should be priced in terms of that currency. This provides consistent, up-to-date information about prices to markets. This function also eliminates the guesswork in determining the value of goods in trade, either domestic or international. The supply and demand for cows determines cattle prices; the supply and demand for magic beans determines their price. Both are priced in terms of the local currency. With money, they now trade for each other using the accepted medium of exchange: Jack sells his cows, uses money from the proceeds to buy the magic beans. In modern economies, the unit of account function also regulates the domestic money supply. As more money enters the economy, via the economy's central bank, the more currency it takes to buy the same goods, reflected in increasing prices; this characteristic provides a natural barrier to the central bank printing currency without limits.

The store of value characteristic is not the most newsworthy, but in fact could be considered the most important. It is here where the difference between debit and credit cards shows its face. Both are media of exchange and both represent standards of value. Your debit card may be considered money in that funds are transferred directly from your checking account to the grocery store account where you purchased items. When you use your credit card as a medium of exchange, you create a liability, a debt to be paid later. Your credit card company pays the store, and then you pay the credit card company when your bill arrives. The beauty of a credit card is that it saves money on lost income earned from having to constantly use interest-bearing accounts to make purchases, if used correctly.

Finally, the standard of deferred payment function is a simple extension of the unit of account function to also cover debts. If you buy a car using a loan, the loan should be paid back in terms of the local currency. Both the lender and borrower know the financial terms of paying back the loan. The interest rate then becomes the dominant factor in debt repayment, as the interest payments are also in terms of the local currency. When paid this way, the lender docs not take any chances in losing value simply by currency exchange, or through a barter-style transaction.

Measuring money

Once you understand the definition of money, a natural question may be: what types of assets are considered to be money, given this definition? The US Federal Reserve defines money in the following three ways, with a fourth measure for close money substitutes or Domestic Non-Financial Debt (DNFD) or sometimes symbolized as L.

M_1 is the label for cash and its closest substitutes. These include currency in circulation, bank reserves held at the central bank and in bank vaults as cash, checking accounts that do not bear interest and those that do, traveler's checks, and money orders. The monetary base is equal to currency (cash in your pocket, e.g.) and bank reserves. This measure has some history concerning monetary policy.

M_2 includes M_1 and adds interest-bearing accounts that are highly liquid. These additions include individually held savings, money market mutual fund, and Certificates of Deposit (CD) accounts under $100,000 in value, and what are known as overnight ForDom (foreign checking accounts denominated in domestic currency) accounts and overnight repurchase agreements. A repurchase agreement is a contractual, short-term loan of cash from one bank to another where securities flow as collateral. The repurchase takes place when the borrowing bank buys back the securities for more than their original amount. Because these assets are generally cash or cash equivalents, these repurchase agreements include interest-bearing cash held in this form.

M_3 includes M_2 and larger, institutionally held accounts. Savings, money market mutual fund and CD accounts held by institutions or worth more than $100,000 held by individuals are M_3 accounts. Also, ForDom accounts that are savings rather than checking accounts and repurchase agreements that conclude after one day are also M_3 specific accounts. There is a difference in liquidity between M_2 and M_3 accounts that goes back to the idea of the interest rate as an opportunity cost; in general, the differences between each of the above monetary measures is based on liquidity differences. In 2006, the tracking of M_3 was abandoned by the Federal Reserve, who claimed that the cost was too large to continue collecting the data.[1]

These monetary aggregates are the main measures of money used by central banks. Since the late 1970s, the United States and most of the larger economies of the world have concentrated on M_2 for policy-making purposes.

The market for money

Markets are defined by supply and demand. If you have not taken an economics course for some time, this section should act as both a brief review and an introduction to how the market for money works. The supply of money is typically seen as an upward sloping "curve", defining all the combinations between the price and quantity of money. Supply is the willingness and ability to produce a good or service. Money supply comes from the central bank of an economy first and foremost. A question that is often asked is: don't banks supply money as well? In fact, they do. Banks do so in such a way that makes an upward supply curve intuitive and analogous to the supply of any other good. Banks supplying more money occurs as a movement along the supply curve: when the interest rate increases due to increases in demand, banks have larger incentives to release more funds for use because profits rise. That is contrasted with a shift of the supply curve, which is a parallel movement of the supply such that there is more money supplied at every price.

- Banks change the quantity of money available at each interest rate, given a money supply.
- The central bank changes the amount of money supplied, regardless of the current rate of interest.

The central bank also functions as the regulator of financial markets in most countries. Because the central bank controls both the supply of money and key interest rates, regulating the financial markets provides further oversight and consumer protection against problematic practices or potential financial crises.[2] The demand for money is where the interest rate acts as the "price" of money. When the rate of interest falls, the quantity of money demanded increases, which is a movement along the demand curve. The basic idea, which will be expanded on later in the book, is that when interest rates fall as a result of monetary policy changing money supply, consumers face a lower opportunity cost of holding cash. As a result, theory suggests that consumers will hold more cash. Policy can then change incentives toward holding cash and toward the consumer choosing to make purchases or not.

The consumer may also demand more cash, regardless of the interest rate. When consumer confidence increases, for example, consumption rises and pushes interest rates up for two reasons. First, consumers want to demand more goods and services and demand more money at every rate. This bids up the rate of interest because there is a shift in the demand curve. Second, money is scarcer because the current supply of money is not changing in total as the demand is changing. This scarcity bids up the rate of interest to reflect a relative scarcity of money.

The interest rate as an opportunity cost is the major element of the consumer's decisions, but also of policy. When the interest rate decreases, it is less expensive for the consumer to demand money and thus demand goods. It is also a lower opportunity cost to demand money because the interest borne on money in the bank is now less. This is a simple example of a portfolio adjustment, or a shift of the consumer's assets from one form to another. Opportunity cost drives markets, and the market for money is no different.

- The demand for money represents the willingness and ability to use money, and acts in many ways like consumption.
- Changes in consumer income are why money demand shifts mainly.
- The interest rate is the price or opportunity cost of demanding money, which makes the money demand curve downward sloping.

Governments want to monitor the amount of money in circulation and other, cash-equivalent assets such that it regulates financial institutions and its own central bank in the provision of currency. The household uses money for consumption rather than having to trade one possession for another. Banks get involved in monetary economies because people do not necessarily want to store their money at home; the bank contractually stores the money safely, pays interest or both. The interest rate binds banks, consumers and opportunity cost together.

The household, made up of workers, is the centerpiece of macroeconomics. The bank is considered a financial intermediary, linking those who want to save money to those who want to borrow. The household saves when it does not spend or consume as much as it made in income. The bank provides a way for the household to put money some place for later use. The bank will take the money and invest it for a rate of return. Investment banks, which provide financial products for households to convert their cash into assets for a larger rate of return, are also financial intermediaries. The classic bank is a depository institution, where the investment bank is a financial institution. Both are set up to do similar business: make money with your money where the difference is profit. Insurance is similar. Households pay premiums to insurance firms to avoid paying in full for unforeseen calamities. Holding an insurance policy is like saving. You pay now to have money available for consumption later. In sum, these institutions make up the financial markets.

The role of risk

Banks are specially constructed to engage in financial transactions and regulated to do so. We will see later that the microeconomics of banking include many regulations on both banking and finance dictating the provision of financial services. The information that banks or other financial institutions gather is used for profit. Most regulations are in place to protect the consumer while not hindering the specific firm's ability to conduct its business. Banks are the central focus of financial regulation; however, as the financial markets have evolved, so have regulations and institutions.

For many economics and business students, banking is a possible career path. Other financial markets hold mysteries and wealth that students read and dream about, heard in the news constantly, seen in popular culture everywhere. Risk is the main reason why any financial institution exists. The institution provides a service which helps reduce risk for the client and takes advantage of risk for the firm's profit. In the case of banks and insurance, profit is made because people try and avoid paying for risk. Banks and insurance firms make profits from diversification. In finance, the famous relationship between risk and return can be exploited to its maximum potential. However, prudent financial advisors recommend a strategy that is also diversified and not subject to huge risks, both good and bad. We study stocks, bonds, options, futures, swaps, insurance, pensions, etc., because of their ultimate links to banks and money. These transactions and markets somehow involve money and interest rates. We will see later that the interest rate exists in most decisions, maybe all of them. Interest rates dictate the decision to buy a home as much as the decision to start a war. It is the reason you get up in the morning and go to bed at night. This book and course centers on how the interest rate involves itself in the lives and decisions of all entities, most specifically the financial markets and their institutions.

Case study 1.1 Monetary and fiscal stimulus: does it matter?

Beginning in September of 2008, the Federal Reserve became very aggressive in its use of monetary policy by lowering the central bank's target rate for loans between banks, called the Federal Funds Rate target. The US Treasury Department facilitated "bailout" funding for financial institutions that were deemed likely to go bankrupt. Amidst rapidly falling stock prices, newspaper headlines about the role of greedy banks in what is now know as the "subprime" crisis, and a widespread fear of depositor illiquidity, the Federal Reserve began a process of over $700 billion of funding that reached both big and small banks by January 2009. This bailout package also came after direct tax rebates for US taxpayers in 2008. The bank bailouts provided banks with funding to stimulate lending for homes and businesses, create incomes, support real estate prices, increase tax receipts, and increase asset values to generate enough business for banks and revenue for the government to more than pay the bailouts.

In early 2009, the Federal Reserve dropped its target rate for interbank lending to between zero and one-quarter percent. This was the lowest cost of funds in decades, and made loans between banks virtually free in many cases. Monetary policy had hit a floor concerning new, direct actions, as nothing else could credibly be done. The focus now turned to a federal stimulus package that newly elected President Obama suggested would pull the American economy (and potentially the world) out of recession. On 9 February 2009, a new spending package to be funded by a mix of new government debt and new money printing was signed by the newly elected president. Its total was estimated at $789 billion dollars, and had seven foci of spending (approximately 84.7 percent of the total):

- **Health care**: $141.3 billion
- **New tax credit**: $116 billion
- **Infrastructure**: $90 billion
- **Education**: $87 billion
- **Energy**: $86 billion
- **Alternative minimum tax relief**: $71.2 billion
- **Aid to the poor and unemployed**: $68.1 billion

With all this spending, macroeconomic theory is now tested to empirical heights unseen to date. While John Maynard Keynes may be applauding from the heavens about these policies to stem the recessionary tide, Milton Friedman is probably shaking his head and wagging his finger across from Keynes.

Monetarism is the idea that the use of monetary policy for business cycle support will not work. In contrast to followers of John Maynard Keynes, who generally believed that the use of policy was necessary to both support recessions and restrain booms, Monetarists resurrected the classic models of macroeconomics with the belief that markets are the way economies move forward and solve their problems. Milton Friedman, an economist who became the face of Monetarism, suggested that all inflation episodes are the result of monetary expansions. That quote was rephrased to suggest that all recessions were begun by monetary contraction to defend against a boom's natural inflation. If current monetary policy around the world, not just in the United States, proves to have little effect on economic outcomes, does this vanquish Keynes's followers and provide evidence for Monetarism to be resurrected? Many developed nations follow a Keynesian style of monetary policy, where cyclic output and inflation in economies are tempered by policy changes in a discretionary manner. This discretion allows for easy switching between pursuits of inflation control and attempts to boost output. Monetarism has a simple rule: do not change the money supply more than the inflation rate your economy wants per year. However, Monetarism has a bit of checkered past itself, specifically in the last major recession of the post-war period, the stagflation of 1979 to 1982 (McCallum 2008).

Keynesian policies are being employed as of early 2009, following the American example in many nations. Coordination of policy between nations makes testing Monetarist or Keynesian ideas difficult, but if monetary policy provides nothing by inflation, and federal stimulus provides jobs and growth, many questions may be asked about the use of central banking outside the Monetarist idea of inflation consistency in lieu of fiscal measures. This was the legacy of Milton Friedman on economic policy. This book provides examples and cases of using Keynesian policies, but the discussion of monetary rules versus discretion in later chapters suggests this debate is alive.

Why study monetary economics?

Many of you reading this book may be taking this course because it is needed for a business administration degree. Others of you are economics majors and others are simply taking the course for fun. In any case, you must have some economics before taking this course. This book relies heavily on a strong knowledge of supply and demand, in the context of economic models. All phenomena in the business world, from accounting for bolts at a hardware store to a zoo's marketing plan, have an economic foundation.

This book is written with the idea that the normal student reading this text has recently taken principles of macroeconomics, microeconomics or both. This book relies on light microeconomic ideas and heavy macroeconomic policy and modeling. The more important course for the understanding of this book is introductory macroeconomics. Macroeconomic policy, specifically why monetary policy works the way it does, the different theories of international finance, why government deficits have a meaning in the financial markets, all come from macroeconomics. If you are wondering why you took basic macroeconomics, the later chapters of this book show you why. This book is light on fiscal policy's role in macroeconomics. It is also very heavy and expansive, for obvious reasons, on the monetary issues.

Ideas such as opportunity cost are central to your understanding all economic phenomena, and this is why economics courses are so necessary in a business education and the backbone of this course. The ideas inside this book bring to light issues in financial markets and macroeconomic policy that make working in these markets easier and more fun. In fact, there is an example in this book on how to make a risk-free profit! That itself is worth taking the course, I think!

Layout of the text

This text is meant to be less encyclopedic and more topical than competing texts. The book has five major sections. The book is split into three sections based on the chapter's subject matter. The first section is definitions and financial markets. The second section is microeconomic issues concerning both banking and the central bank's relationship with banks, consumers and firms. The final section is about macroeconomic policy and international finance. The breakdown of each of these sections is below. An introduction to money and its market is followed by a general description of the loanable funds market, generally bond market issues. Risk, as both a concept and an entity, is discussed before equity markets are compared and contrasted to bond markets. This includes housing markets. Finally, derivative markets and their connections to the underlying assets that make them derivatives rounds out the first section.

The microeconomics of banking comes after an accounting for cash flows and the structure of a bank. The optimal allocation of bank assets is the thrust of how the interest rate dictates the bank's profitability. The next microeconomic issue is the consumer. How consumers demand money, from holding cash in a wallet to taking a loan and saving money, is the next chapter, followed by how the central bank manipulates the money supply by estimating demand's reaction to the new supply. As you can guess, the economy's central bank can limit your ability to get more money easily, which involves the interest rate.

Chapters 9 through 13 encompass the macroeconomic analysis in this text. The goods market is where physical goods and services are traded, and where demand must equal supply at all times. We will see that inventories held by firms also have a place in this course, and in fact are a major portion of what we later refer to as real investment. This idea of real investment versus financial investment involves linkages between microeconomic decisions made by financial institutions and macroeconomy policies and flows the central bank attempts to control. One of the major constraints on a central bank is fiscal policy, which is briefly discussed. The macroeconomic market for money leads into a discussion of how the open macroeconomy works with the exchange rate. When you understand the open macroeconomy, you have in your hands the same theoretical tools used by the central banks around the world. We will see that the IS-LM model is a powerful and intuitive way to look at macroeconomic policy and phenomena. This combination, including international finance, is what makes up international macroeconomics. The final two chapters of the book wrap up many ideas concerning policy choices and consequences, and the potential future of central and private banking.

The chapters end with chapter summaries, key terms and questions for students. Please refer to these throughout the book's use as a way of summarizing the material.

Key terms

1 Derivatives: assets, such as futures, forwards or options, which have a value derived from the value of an underlying asset.
2 Diversification: spreading risk by purchasing many different types of assets.
3 Double coincidence of wants: two parties must have a simultaneous want for a good another party wants to sell and possess a good the same party wants to buy.
4 Liability: a financial position in which the party owes.
5 Medium of exchange: an excepted method of payment for debts public and private.
6 Monetary base: the sum of currency in circulation and bank reserves at the domestic central bank.
7 Opportunity cost: the cost of the best foregone alternative.
8 Portfolio adjustment: changing the composition of assets held in a portfolio of investments.
9 Real investment: the purchase of new plant and equipment, housing or inventories.
10 Repurchase agreements: a contractual transaction in which a seller of an asset has the right or obligation to buy back the asset after its sale at a specified price on a given date.
11 Risk: the price of uncertainty.
12 Standard of deferred payment: the currency or unit of account for all debts.
13 Store of value: an asset, or something that generates income.
14 Unit of account: a standard of value, an accepted way to measure value.

Questions and problems

1 Define money by stating and explaining the four characteristics of something called money that must hold simultaneously.
2 Define opportunity cost and explain why the interest rate can be considered the opportunity cost for consumption.
3 Why would the interest rate also be considered a cost of saving? Explain.
4 Explain what diversification is meant to achieve in terms of risk.
5 Why would risk and reward be positively related, i.e., as risk rises, so does the potential reward?
6 Explain what a bank is in your own words.

Websites

A history of the American Currency: http://www.frbsf.org/currency/index.html.

Interest rates and financial markets

Introduction

Interest rates represent prices of every economic action because they represent both opportunity costs for the use of goods, services and inputs and connect time periods to each other. The sacrifice of consumption today must come with a reward, and consuming today must have its cost. There are many interest rates, one for every asset that exists. The "price" of an asset is in part determined by an interest rate. Interest rates are used in business plans to discount the future, as income to those who have deposited money, purchased stocks and bonds, and to those who make a loan. It is a cost to those who borrow, the cost of consuming more than you can afford at a given time. It is also the cost of not buying something that could produce income. We can summarize the interest rate's definition generally in four ways:

- The revenue from lending or not consuming;
- The cost of borrowing or consuming;
- The opportunity cost of holding money as cash; and
- A measure of time preference concerning consumption.

Interest rates come in many forms, all with the same basic set-up. An interest rate includes measures of risk, both general and very specific. When you borrow money, the rate at which you borrow is the nominal rate. This rate is the stated interest cost or return of a financial investment. There is also a real rate, but what separates the two? The difference between nominal and real variables in economics has to do initially with inflation, or purchasing power erosion, and other risks. In its most basic form, a nominal interest rate has the following equation:

$$R^\varepsilon = r + P^\varepsilon \tag{2.1}$$

where R^ε is a nominal rate, r is the associated real rate and P^ε is the expected inflation rate. Equation 2.1 assumes the only risk to be inflation. The best way to think of the real rate of interest is what the lender wants to receive as revenue, less the calculated risks. The nominal rate is the sum of the real rate and the "expected" inflation rate, which is a calculated guess and not the actual inflation rate. When a lender provides a loan, the lender must make conjectures concerning what the risk of future inflation may be. Unless the interest rate is allowed to adjust with new inflation information, the lender bears that risk directly; when inflation rises without the nominal rate changing, the real value of her loan gets smaller. Both the borrower and lender make decisions based on their individual assessment of the real rate of interest. Even though the borrower writes a check every month to the credit card company based on a nominal rate, the lender is seeking protection of the real rate as the driving force behind providing credit. If all the expected risks play themselves out as predicted, the borrower and lender pay and receive the real rate respectively.

We will discuss later the difference between fixed and variable rates of interest, but keep in mind that few assets, real or financial, can circumvent the risk of inflation. Inflation is also a representation of time in financial markets, specifically eroding nominal income and wealth.

Defining interest rates

The cost of borrowing

This is the classic role we think of interest rates playing in finance, an explicit cost of consuming beyond one's income or wealth by choice. As a corollary, it is also the opportunity cost of consuming, regardless of the entity being a net consumer or not. A net consumer is a household that both consumes and saves, but consumes more than its income in net. If one consumes anything, there is lost interest revenue from saving the resources otherwise; however, financial leverage may be a decision because the cost of debt is less than the return to savings. Households are willing to bear this cost, however, at some level because of necessity and because of satisfaction or utility otherwise, an issue discussed in more detail in Chapter 9 concerning money demand.

The revenue from lending

The only way a household can borrow money is if there is someone willing to lend the money, a function of the revenue derived from lending; the benefit from saving with interest. The interest rate provides an incentive to save more, and saving implies that interest is being paid. Suppose you have two bank accounts, one that is your checking account that you use for household expenditures. The other is a savings account which bears interest. While you are not consuming the entirety of your checking account, it is technically not part of your savings because the money does not bear interest. In Chapter 9 when money demand is discussed, this distinction is clearer, but think for now that what distinguishes savings from consumption is whether money earns interest or not.

The cost of holding money

Something we will explore in depth when we talk about money demand later is the idea of the interest rate as the opportunity cost of having cash in your pocket. This relationship between the quantity of cash or liquidity demanded and the interest rate is of key importance to a great deal of macroeconomic theories but also to monetary and fiscal policy in practice. The way consumers react to changes in interest rates paid on their cash holdings changes the demand for goods and services, as well as the demand for lending. However, for now the idea is simple: the interest rate is the opportunity cost of holding money in your wallet rather than in an interest-bearing account or investment.

Measure of time preference

It is this definition that links the three above and binds them in the household's eyes. When you chose to consume more than your income, or consume with credit rather than paying in full, you are making a choice about your time preference to consume. The interest rate is a measure of how people prefer to consume with respect to time: if the interest rate falls, there will be marginal changes in consumption based on a smaller cost of credit. Certain households which initially would save, say $1000, now spend $100 of that $1000 and save only $900. They still save a certain amount, but it is less. The lower interest rate has triggered an incentive for them to spend on credit, or prefer to spend now than later in time.

The cost of borrowing falls in the previous example, providing an incentive to borrow. Certain lenders must provide the loan, thus they see the interest rate as the revenue from lending, and want to take advantage of it. Finally, the borrower must demand cash in order to spend, thus the cost of holding money must also be going down at the same time, and intuitively it does. The interest rate is all four of these ideas simultaneously, and must be for financial markets to work correctly. We will see later that the interest rate's measure of time preference characteristic makes the entire economy work correctly.

There are different assets available at different rates of interest categorically, including the loans one can take and make. As we continue, we will see there are two sides to each lending story, and that each side is driven by risk. On the borrower side, the risk resides in money's use. Will the project, home, car, or clothing purchased on credit "pay off" versus the purchase of a financial asset? On the lender side, the risk is based on the borrower's ability to pay back the loan, and the protection of the real rate of return the lender is seeking in the first place. Will the loan be paid off? The loanable funds market is our first step to understanding these relationships better.

Things to remember

The four definitions of the interest rate are:

- The revenue from lending
- The cost of borrowing
- The opportunity cost of holding money
- A measure of time preference

Types of risk and specific interest rates

Like any other market, the supply and demand for loans determine the amount of a loan and the interest rate to be charged. Loans generally are individualized, as even similar loans can be a little bit different from one another. What factors help to determine the interest rate in the lender's mind? The real interest rate and its preservation is the lender's focus. Any perceived risk the lender foresees becomes part of the nominal interest rate charged to protect the real rate. The following are asset-specific risks that add to the borrower cost of taking a loan specific to the borrower.

Default risk

This is the most obvious risk in loans, representing the inability to pay back the loan. It is difficult to say how any individual bank looks at different borrowers from this perspective, but every bank does. This risk is also known as counterparty risk. Households and firms may be less likely to default because there are social stigmas against personal bankruptcy, and the cost of displacement from one's car, home or business can be very traumatic. Default risk is normally assessed by gathering borrowers' financial data and calculating the expected chance of default from factors other than borrower choice.

Credit scores help to reduce the uncertainty in assessing default risk. A credit score is a number calculated based on a borrower's credit history. Credit scores accelerate the decision-making process for a lender, awarding points based on a credit report. The specific borrower's score is compared to that of other potential borrowers with similar credit profiles, much like a bond rating. With this information, lenders can predict how likely someone is to repay a loan and make payments on time. The credit score most commonly used is from Fair Isaac and Company (FICO). This FICO score ranges from 350 to 850, where 22 pieces of data about a borrower are assembled for that score; income is not a factor taken into consideration. Each of the three major credit bureaus (Experian, Equifax and TransUnion) worked with Fair Isaac in the early 1980s to come up with the current scoring method used in the United States. Credit scores are used worldwide, but generally are the result of a statistical model, specifically a logistic regression, which predicts the probability or odds of the borrower paying back the loan.

Taxation risk

The interest income derived from a loan is taxable in most cases, at all levels of taxation. For example, interest paid by a homeowner on a mortgage is income to the loan owner, and their profits will be taxed. Most assets generate taxable income. Certain government loans, especially in the United States, do not have national-level tax assessed on derived income. Municipal bonds, debt securities issued by a city or metropolitan area, generally provide income not taxable at any level. These types of bonds are the foundation of what are known as tax-sheltered investments, where income is taxable in certain ways. While default risk is difficult to assess, this taxation risk is much easier to calculate.

Liquidity risk

This type of risk is a major issue, and encompasses most day-to-day risk. If you were to purchase a corporate bond in Australia, issued to help finance the building of a firm's micro-processor plant, you may wonder how easy it would be to turn that bond into cash while you owned it. Like any other financial asset, liquidity risk comes from the probability a market may not exist for this bond when its owner is attempting to sell it, or the cost of selling it is high. There is a risk that you will not be able to easily convert (find a buyer for) your asset on the secondary market to convert into cash. The expected profitability of the investment dictates its liquidity risk. If the return on the bond is in question, for whatever reason, the liquidity risk rises.

Currency and political risks

Investments made outside one's country may have risks above and beyond those mentioned above because of currency fluctuations or the instability of a government or both. Buying a bond issued from a British food processor is less susceptible to political risk than buying bonds from an Argentine security alarm manufacturer. Both companies may be equally sound financially, but the political risks in Argentina are historically higher than in the United Kingdom. For this reason, the lender should expect to receive a higher nominal rate of return on the Argentine bond to compensate. We see later the importance of currency risk to how exchange rates are determined and fluctuate; currency fluctuations can erode profit pursued by international investors based solely on interest rate differentials. This risk increases the rate of return necessary for investors to make that purchase. While the risk may be small in certain cases, the risk still exists.

Case study 2.1   Risk and inflation: the case of Zimbabwe in 2008

As with other hyperinflations, a mix of negative political events, poor economic policies and bad luck coincided to buckle and collapse the Zimbabwe economy in 2008. The sub-Saharan African nation had seen modest economic growth between 2003 and 2007, albeit with ever-rising inflation; the confluence of inflation pressure and political problems became a major economic collapse. On 29 March 2008, Zimbabwe attempted national elections for both new presidential and parliamentary leadership. The current president, Robert Mugabe, who has ruled since independence in 1980, ran against Morgan Tsvangirai, the leader of the opposition party. Though the election was in favor of Morgan Tsvangirai, the results were withheld for several weeks and civil war slowly began. In September of 2008, a power-sharing deal was brokered to allow Mugabe to remain in power and for Tsvangirai to also rule; parliamentary seats were filled based on the election results as well. In February 2009, Tsvangirai was sworn in as the prime minister.

Long-standing economic problems began to affect Zimbabwe in 2007. There was a general drought, which forced food prices to rise rapidly, and policies that attempted to freeze food prices met with little success. Second, the white farmers who remained in Zimbabwe were forced off their lands and new price regulations were introduced to control the beginnings of runaway inflation. Race aside, the farmers who were removed from Zimbabwe included relatively efficient producers of basic foodstuffs. With a drought and inefficiency in food production walking side by side, pressure on food prices increased even more quickly. Third, to pay for its debts, the Mugabe government began to print money as Zimbabwe's tax base and ability to borrow were shattered by a humanitarian and financial crisis easily seen by world financial markets. As in most hyperinflation episodes, an expansion of the money supply exacerbated runaway inflation. The printing press ran wild through most of this decade, providing fuel for inflation pressure. With no viable government debt and a broken infrastructure, government spending was paid for by money printing. In 2006, Z$250,000 was replaced with Z$250. Because the new Zimbabwean (Z) dollars had no backing economically or politically to control its value, this "conversion" to a new currency was an exercise in futility. In January of 2009, Zimbabwe introduced a 100 trillion dollar banknote. With an 80% official unemployment rate and hyperinflation, Zimbabwe's economy looks much like the economies of post-war Germany.

Zimbabwe has a history of poor economic choices, wild politics and systemic problems concerning food, disease prevention and links to terrorism. Some blame South Africa for its current economic problems; Mugabe believes a conspiracy has taken place between most of the developed world and South Africa to topple his regime. However, this episode is classic hyperinflation: internal economic and political problems cause all prices to rise, exacerbated by uncontrolled monetary expansion due to the loss of Zimbabwe's tax base and other automatic stabilizers. As much as this problem seems political, it became economic very quickly (*The Economist*, 11 March 2009).

Summary of risks

These risks are additional costs the borrower must pay in order to compensate the lender to protect the real rate of interest sought by investors. We can add these to Equation 2.2 and make a complete picture of the nominal rate of interest in any financial market.

$$R = r + \dot{P}^\varepsilon + dp + tp + \ell p + cpp \tag{2.2}$$

where dp = default premium
tp = taxation premium
ℓp = liquidity premium
cpp = currency and political premium

Notice there is a "premium" or additional rate of interest for each of the risks mentioned above. We will see in Chapter 3 that the evolution of risk in an asset can be generalized into a term structure of interest rates. Given the basics of how interest rates are viewed by the lender, let's look briefly at specific interest rates, and think about why one interest rate differs from others.

Specific interest rates

Most economics texts use a general idea of the interest rate rather than picking a specific rate. We will look at six categorical rates below and assume other rates lie among these.

The discount rate

This is the rate at which the central bank of an economy lends to banks domestically, or to all banks under the central bank's domain if the domestic regulatory structure is more comprehensive. In the United States, the discount rate (DR) was at a time only for use by Federal Reserve System member banks. The Monetary Control Act of 1980 changed that to hold for any bank operating in the United States. In 2006, the Federal Reserve reversed the Federal Funds Target Rate/Discount Rate relationship to make the discount rate 0.5% greater than the Federal Funds Target Rate. If a bank seeks a loan from the discount window, there is now a penalty involved. Discount rates exist where a central bank exists. Not all countries have a functioning interbank loan system, and as such central bank functions are done by other central banks in these situations.

The interbank rate and target

Central banks, when their financial system allows it, do not want to be bothered with continuous requests for loans from banks that have overnight cash needs. An interbank market specifically joins together banks willing and able to lend and borrow to keep the central bank out of the transactions implicitly. It is important to distinguish between the interbank target rate, if one exists, and the actual interbank rate. In some countries, they are one and the same, set by monetary policy. Some confusion exists between the discount and interbank target rates. The discount rate may or may not change as a result of policy, which also holds for interbank rates. The key is to recognize that these rates compete and substitute for each other. We will see later the importance of an interbank rate to banking as a business. The London InterBank Offered Rate (LIBOR) and the Federal Funds Rate (FFR) are examples of such rates.

Government securities rates

Government debt securities, bonds that represent a government's attempt to finance its spending, exist in most countries. US Treasury securities come in three major versions, with many different types in each category. First is the Treasury bill, or T-bill. This is the most famous of the three, and is normally used to illustrate government debt. However, the distinguishing feature of the T-bill is its maturity length. T-bills are short-term securities and mature in one year or less, which makes them money market securities. These securities are used as bridges between cash shortfalls from tax collection cycles or a need to raise cash quickly, much like commercial paper for corporations. The T-bill's role in the financial markets is a critical one. For now, think of a T-bill as the government's short-term debt option, but only one of three debt options.

Second is the Treasury note, or T-note. The T-note is a medium-term bond that the government uses to finance projects with 1- to 10-year timeframes. The most important role of the T-note to the American financial markets is its connection to mortgage rates, specifically 10-year government debt. Most banks and mortgage lenders use the 10-year T-note rate as a base rate of interest, the real rate of interest plus an inflation premium. From there, lenders add risk premiums.

The T-bond, government debt with fifteen years or more to maturity, is historically seen as the government's "mortgage". Financial markets have generally contracted their purchases of long-term securities from both firms and governments due to higher debt-to-asset ratios, and escalating debt use by consumers, which puts firms and governments further at risk. The main use of the T-bond has been as the foundation of the US Social Security Administration's pension plan for American workers. In fact, the US government, in different agencies, holds the majority of US government-issued debt.[1]

Government debt securities worldwide have a similar structure to the US market. The risk-free characteristic of these securities originating in larger countries leads to their high demand. The rates of interest on this debt act as baseline nominal rates for all other bonds and loans issued for different maturity dates in major economies.

Why? The rationale is that the lender incurs an opportunity cost by lending to households and firms, rather than to the government, which can tax citizens and print money. The consumer can only liquidate assets to pay off debts, refinance, or work more. The only risks which financial markets see concerning government debt from industrialized nations are to the real rate of return on the loan through inflation. For this reason, which we investigate at length later, financial markets consider government debt to be risk-free.

The prime rate

The prime rate also has a significant role in financial markets, generally tied to the domestic interbank rate or the LIBOR by a fixed difference or spread. The prime rate is what banks initially use to assess risk to most businesses for lines of credit, or for long-term debt to finance projects or real investment. If you were to start a business, the rate of interest for your debt would probably start with the prime rate and move up from there. The prime rate is the basis of credit card interest rates, normally set at the prime rate plus approximately ten percent. Such a rate means that the credit card provider believes that the average consumer is more risky, at almost ten percent more than are low-risk, large companies as an opportunity cost. If you pay off your credit card every month, these companies make no income from you.

Mortgage rates

When purchasing a home, the borrower is bombarded with options to help finance the purchase. However, the interest rates you may have to choose from are few. Mortgage markets have changed a great deal over the last 30 years, changing the way consumers "shopped" for a home loan and also how the financial markets provide credit. There are many options, ways to refinance, take equity lines of credit, and combine all your debt into one large, monthly payment; it seems very confusing. The mortgage itself is a loan to acquire real estate. Mortgages exist for office space, a factory, or a retail store. The key here is that the money borrowed is to buy real estate. As mentioned above, mortgage rates generally follow the 10-year T-note rate in the United States. The mortgage rate is an important rate because it is used to finance real asset purchases, providing the owner with a roof over his/her head and hopefully appreciation in value. It is possible to borrow either fixed or variable rate loans.

Fixed rate loans lock the interest rate such that it does not change over the loan's life, protecting the borrower against inflation risk (which exposes the lender to that inflation risk instead). Even if your mortgage is purchased by another bank on a secondary market, the terms and cost are the same to you. The main reason why fixed rate loans are attractive to consumers is that fixed payment. If you borrow $250,000 at six percent interest for 30 years, your monthly payment is approximately $1500 per month. That never changes for the entire 30 years. If inflation erodes the value of money such that one dollar buys a tenth in 25 years of what it buys today, you still pay $1500 a month (which in the scenario above means you pay the equivalent of $150 in monthly mortgage payments before any tax breaks).

Variable rate mortgages allow banks to shift inflation risk onto borrowers, especially borrowers who are more risky or willing to take such a risk to gain access to credit. The interest rate and monthly payments react to new inflation information. Typically, variable rate mortgages have lower initial interest rates with respect to fixed rate mortgages. That initial rate may hold for a few years, and then allow the bank to change the rate upward if inflation conditions warrant the shift. The global financial crises beginning in 2007 were partially from homeowners experiencing higher interest rates as their monthly payments were reset for adjustable rate mortgages. This forced some homeowners to sell due to higher risk of default and profit-taking, exacerbating a downturn in home prices already pressured by profit-taking from fixed-rate borrowers, tightening credit conditions, and cyclic movements downward in real estate.

A loan's characteristics (amount of loan, type of home, location of home, etc.), including the borrower's credit and other financial characteristics (net wealth and current income typically), help the bank determine the loan's interest rate. In all of the above cases, the lender needs to be assured that the real rate of return is secure by estimating the risks.

Venture capital rates (junk bonds)

The late 1990s saw the resurgence of venture capital in the midst of equity market rallies worldwide. Venture capital funds are typified by investing in something other than physical capital, investing in a business venture or entrepreneurial idea. Investors, looking for pathways into burgeoning technology sectors, were willing to part with billions of dollars to provide entrepreneurs with the capital necessary to create new products. As of January 2008, $1.1 trillion of junk bond debt was owed or outstanding in the United States' financial markets; junk bonds are also known as below-investment grade debt. Bond ratings help investors determine the riskiness of corporate debt, much like a credit score helps lenders determine good individual borrowers.

Bond ratings

Typically debt is "rated" by financial institutions to provide a quick way of gauging potential bond investments. Where lower-risk, government bonds and large corporate debt issues are given extremely high ratings, junk bonds are given the lowest rating. It is much like a grading system, and can affect the specific bond market's liquidity greatly if changed. For example, a movement from a BBB rating to a BBA rating can change the bond market quickly to lower prices because of a perceived higher rate of return. To illustrate bond ratings and their meaning, Standard & Poor's has the following ratings:[2]

AAA and AA: high credit-quality investment grade
AA and BBB: medium credit-quality investment grade
BB, B, CCC, CC, C: low credit-quality (non-investment grade), or "junk bonds"
D: bonds in default for non-payment of principal and/or interest

For corporations debating the use of debt to fund a project, this bond rating is of major importance. If Standard and Poor's gives a BB or lower rating, the liquidity risk of the bond issue rises greatly, forcing firms to pay higher interest rates to sell the bond initially. BBB grades and above are the target for most corporate debt, and that bond rating can change due to new events concerning the borrowing firm. This links directly to default and liquidity risk as discussed above.

In summary, interest rates differ from one investment to another based on differential risks. The 10-year Treasury note rate acts as the floor rate for many long-term investments because it lacks the risk premiums of investments that are similar to each other in terms of maturity. While the inflation risk is the same for investments with the same maturity date, the other risks, as explained above, deliver higher risk expectations to the investor. The key is expected risk, as all investors make conjectures about the future. Financial analysis uses a basic mathematical formula to assess an investment's current value based on expected risks and the expected cash flows to come from investment purchases. The last section of this chapter focuses on the time value of money idea called present value.

Case study 2.2 The LIBOR

Credit cards are a natural part of almost every developed economy, used by both businesses and households. One large uncertainty about credit cards is what interest rate is really being charged. In some cases, the rate is fixed for a short time, but almost all credit cards are simply variable rate loans. In the United States, the credit card rate is based on the American prime rate. This is the rate charged by banks to their best commercial customers. Sometimes the rate is the London InterBank Offered Rate or LIBOR. As discussed in this chapter, the LIBOR is a version of the Federal Funds Rate (FFR) for short-term, interbank lending worldwide. The LIBOR acts as an international gauge for the cost of money at banks. Estimates suggest that over $150 trillion in assets use the LIBOR as either the explicit rate of return or as an index to adjust rates. Many credit card companies, including bank-issued credit cards, use the LIBOR as the base rate of interest because it measures the worldwide opportunity cost for lenders; instead of providing you with a credit card, the bank could lend to a large bank anywhere in the world at the LIBOR and be guaranteed that rate of return. When your credit card rate is LIBOR plus ten percent, the additional ten percent measures consumer debt riskiness on average and the LIBOR fluctuates with the market for interbank lending.

The LIBOR is also part of an increasingly infamous measure of risk in financial markets called the "TED" or the "Treasury-Eurodollar Differential" spread, where the spread is the difference between the three-month government debt yield in the United States and the three-month LIBOR rate in dollars (Eurodollars). When this spread rises, it is a signal of growth in the US macroeconomy; the spread is a signal of expected inflation. The purchase of government debt, specifically from the United States government, over lending to commercial banks is an indicator of shifting attitudes toward risk in financial markets away from banks. Academics are still mixed about the TED spread's ability to predict recessions, but the importance of the LIBOR as a rate that reflects general riskiness in banking is showcased daily in how government debt is traded. Figure 2.1 shows that spread.

Watching the LIBOR alone may provide many details as to the direction of the economy through the eyes of the financial sector, something to consider through the remainder of this text and course. Figure 2.2 on page 20 shows the LIBOR movements since 2000. One can see from this figure than as the recession after the 11 September 2001 attacks took hold, the LIBOR dropped significantly only to rise again after growth began again in 2004. The wild movement between 2007 and 2009 shows the financial market's confusion.

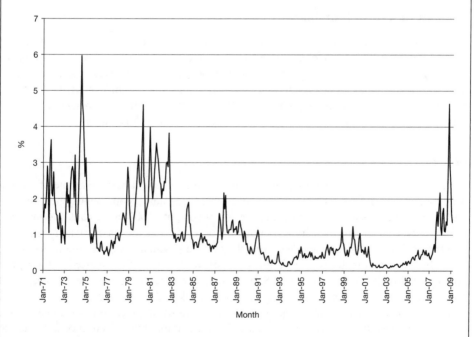

Figure 2.1 TED spread, Jan 1971 to Jan 2009.
Source: Economagic.com.

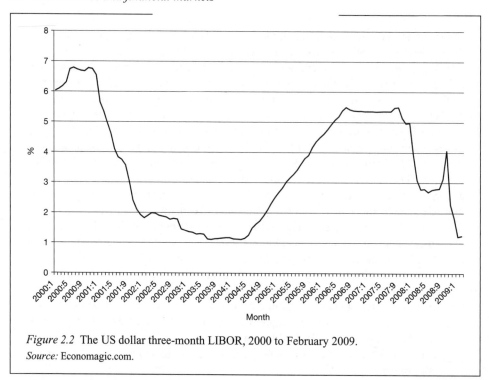

Figure 2.2 The US dollar three-month LIBOR, 2000 to February 2009.
Source: Economagic.com.

PV analysis: the basis of finance

You may have had some basic introduction to the idea of present value (PV) in the past. The concept is very much related to the interest rate as a measure of time preference. If you save today, you expect to get interest and principal (your original investment) back at a future date. What you invest today to receive the interest is the present value of that asset, according to your expectations. We investigate three different ways to formulate present value, then state the reason this formula is used and its meaning in finance and economics.

The basics

The easiest way to understand the present value idea is to take a basic example of putting away money in a savings account for one year, where the interest compounds one time only when the savings account is one year old. Let's say you put $1000 in the bank for one year, and the interest rate is five percent. Compounded only one time means that when the money is in the bank for one year, they determine the interest payment they owe the investor one time when the bond matures. The future value of the $1000 at 5% invested today equals $1050: principal ($1000) and interest ($50). The value of that same investment today is, of course, $1000, the amount of money you put in the bank in the first place.

Now let's take the other angle. Suppose you wanted to know the current value of $1050 in one year. Suppose further that you needed at least a nominal rate of return of 5 percent to ensure a real interest rate based on your assessment of the expected risks. For example, if you expected inflation to be 2 percent, the real rate of interest you would earn at a nominal rate of 5 percent is 3 percent. By making at least 5 percent on the investment, given your calculation of risks, you will earn at least a t3 percent real rate of return. Today's value (again assuming annual, one-time compounding) would be $1000 = PV. Regardless of the perspective, the answer is the same, which brings us to an algebraic statement of the present value in its simplest form.

$$PV = \frac{FV}{(1+R^\varepsilon)}$$ (2.3)

where PV = present value, FV = future value, and R^ε is the expected nominal interest rate on the specific investment, assuming annual compounding and a one-year investment. If you plug in the above numbers, you will see how it works. The denominator in this equation is known as the present value discount factor because it discounts or reduces the future value to a smaller, present value. As investment risks rise, the nominal rate of interest should rise, forcing the present value to fall. This simple relationship is the basis of why an inverse relationship exists between bond prices (the cost of buying debt securities to the investor) and the bond's effective rate. A bond may pay a stated interest rate, but may deliver a different interest rate based on its current market price. As the expected risk rises for a bond, its present value falls, which reduces the maximum price the investor is willing to pay for the bond. By purchasing the bond at a lower price, given the bond's face value to pay the investor, the effective interest rate the bond pays will rise and compensate the investor.

Compounding and its effects

Compounding interest provides two benefits to the investor. First, it tracks the true cost of liquidity, as rapid interest payments reduce long waits to receive cash flow payments; also, interest income can be immediately reinvested instead of waiting to gain access to the income. Compounding comes in almost any frequency you like: yearly (as shown above), semi-annually, quarterly, monthly, weekly, daily, continuously, etc. However, the actual gain in interest compounded continuously from that compounded yearly is small as a percentage. A good exercise is to look at the interest rates on accounts that compound at different frequencies. All else equal, the liquidity risk is lower in more frequent compounding, and thus the interest rate should be slightly lower. Equation 2.4 generalizes the present value calculation to include higher frequencies of payment periods than annual and the effects of compounding on annualized interest rates. In this equation, the index i represents the number of payment periods and m represents the number of times in one year the interest compounds. If the investment compounds quarterly, m is equal to four. If there are 30 years, with 12 monthly payments, as in the typical, 30-year mortgage, $i \cdot m$ equals 360 at the maximum.

$$PV = \sum_{i=1}^{n} \frac{FV_i}{\left(1+R^\varepsilon/m\right)^{i \cdot m}}$$ (2.4)

Once you understand the basics of present value, a general statement can be made about the way the PV equation works for more complex investments (stocks and bonds with compounding or multiple income sources), and understanding the economic meaning of PV to an investor. Suppose you buy a ten-year government debt security, with annually compounding interest of 5%. The bond's face or par value is $1000. This means you will receive $1000 the day the bond matures in ten years. This means $1000 is the future value of the bond, principal plus interest. The present value of this bond should be less than $1000, and most of the time it is less.[3] The present value formula in Equation 2.5 is just slightly different than Equations 2.3 and 2.4 above.

$$NPV_{Bond} = \sum_{i=1}^{n} \frac{Bond\ Interest\ Payment}{(1+R)^i} + \frac{FV}{(1+R)^n} \tag{2.5}$$

$$NPV_{Bond} = PV(Interest\ or\ cash\ flow) + PV(Face\ Value)$$

The NPV concept is in many ways the foundation of finance. The comparison of initial cash flows, or the current cost of the asset, as compared to its expected revenue in terms of present value permeates most financial analyses.

Something to consider: the meaning of PV in financial markets

The present value of an asset represents what the investor is willing to pay for an investment at the maximum level, given the investor's expected nominal rate of return. If you were offered an investment opportunity that paid you 5% for one year by paying $1000 in one year, what would you pay for that investment? If you pay more than $952.38, you lose return because the cost is too high; if you pay less than $952.38, you gain even more because you paid less than you had to pay. It is simple economics: buy as low as possible. However, as we will see in the next chapter, there are a lot of investors looking at the same investment and the financial market is a market for this reason: everyone is looking to buy low and sell high, thus the markets gravitate to the price that delivers close to or equal to zero profit as a whole above the real rate of return. The PV analysis indicates what you should be willing to pay at the stated interest rate. The riskier the rate, the higher the rate of interest, the lower the PV, the lower price you are willing to pay due to the higher risks.

Summary

The interest rate is the cost of borrowing, the revenue from lending, the cost of holding money in your pocket, and a measure of time preference, when you should consume or save. It is also a measure of risk in its nominal form, as investors see risks from inflation, possible default on the investment, lack of liquidity, income lost to taxes, and currency and political problems in international investments. Different rates of interest exist for investments with similar timeframes due to differential risk. For example, one-year US Treasury Bills are considered risk-free, while one-year junk bonds are considered high risk. While the real rate of interest and the inflation risk may be the same in both securities, additional risks are definitely higher in the junk bonds because we cannot see the future perfectly. Some junk bond issues pay their high interest payments and succeed. Many do not. Expectations play a huge role in financial markets, as we will see in the next chapter and beyond.

The idea of present value is a major concern in the course, as it is the backbone of asset valuation in finance. Regardless of the type of investment, the calculation of PV provides a way to price investments, and gives the investor a maximum price of entering an investment with contractual cash flows and rate of return. However, the investor must think about his or her own risk in truly evaluating the risk of any investment, as junk bonds have very low prices, but their high risk means you may not get you principal back. The key is that as the interest rate changes, the PV calculation on assets changes as the financial markets shift their beliefs about the investment's riskiness. Chapter 3 expands on the concept of risk in economics and finance.

Key terms

1 Asset: an income-generating item, both physical and financial.
2 Commercial paper: a short-term debt instrument used to supply cash flow to large businesses.
3 Counterparty risk: the risk that the other side of a financial contract will not fulfill the contract's obligations.
4 Credit score: a weighted average of risk characteristic for a borrower, FICO for example.
5 Discount window: the place where central banks lend money to private banks.
6 Effective interest rate: the percentage spread between the cost basis of a bond and its face value, or the difference between the face value of an asset and its cost basis, divided by its face value.
7 Face or par value: the stated amount of principal and interest due when a bond matures.
8 Financial leverage: using financial assets to both borrow and lend in an attempt to profit from the difference in rates of return and cost of capital.
9 Fixed interest rates: an interest rate that is fixed over the life of the bond.
10 Future value: the value of cash flow at a later date.
11 Logistic regression: the use of binary variables as explanatory variables in a statistical analysis.
12 Money market: the financial market for assets that mature in one year or less.
13 Mortgage brokers: financial intermediaries that specialize in linking borrowers and lenders for mortgage loans.
14 Nominal rate: the market rate of interest on a loan.
15 Present value discount factor: the denominator in the present value calculation.
16 Prime rate: the rate that a bank's lowest-risk, business customers receive.
17 Real asset: a physical, non-human entity that generates income from its existence.
18 Real rate: the nominal rate of interest less the inflation rate and other risk premiums, if they exist for an asset.
19 Risk-free asset: an asset which has risk premiums valued at zero.
20 Social Security: a social assistance system that provides income to retired workers, much like a pension plan.
21 Spread: the difference between two interest rates, usually one as revenue and the other representing cost.
22 Tax-sheltered investments: financial investment in which the taxation risk is lower or zero based on the income derived from the asset being less taxable or non-taxable.
23 T-bond: a long-term government debt security in the United States.
24 Term structure of interest rates: the way in which short-term and long-term interest rates for similar assets are related.
25 T-note: a medium-term government debt security in the United States.

26   Treasury bill (t-bill): a short-term government debt security in the United States.
27   Utility: the satisfaction derived from an action taken.
28   Variable interest rates: interest rates that fluctuate, generally due to new inflation information, over the life a bond.
29   Venture capital: financial investments provided to entrepreneurs to fund new ideas or ventures.

Questions and problems

1   Explain the difference between the nominal and real rate of interest on an investment.
2   If all assets derive income taxed in the same way, would a taxation premium exist? Explain.
3   Discuss one difference between the discount rate and the interbank rate in an economy with both.
4   Why would a government issue debt of different maturities? Explain.
5   Government debt securities issued by large economies with stable governments and long histories have debt that is considered risk free. Why? Explain.
6   Explain why inflation is good for certain borrowers and for certain lenders, but not those in the same transaction.
7   Explain the economic intuition behind the mathematics of present value.
8   Why does real investment differ from financial investment? Explain.

Websites

Australia: http://www.rba.gov.au/FinancialSystemStability/Statistics/index.html and click on "Financial Markets".
China: http://www.pbc.gov.cn/english/diaochatongji/tongjishuju/ and click on the appropriate year.
Euro Area: http://www.ecb.int/stats/money/aggregates/aggr/html/index.en.html and choose the appropriate rate category.
For descriptions of rates: http://www.newyorkfed.org/education/diff_rates.html.
India: http://www.rbi.org.in/scripts/Statistics.aspx and choose the report and frequency of data appropriate to your question.
The algebra of finance: http://www.algebra.com/algebra/homework/Finance/.
United Kingdom: http://www.bankofengland.co.uk/statistics/ and select "Interest and Exchange Rates".
United States: http://www.federalreserve.gov/datadownload/.

3   Risk and risk aversion

Introduction

A popular game show, which originated in the Netherlands with the name "*Miljoenenjacht*", asks players to choose one of 26 briefcases. Each case has an unknown amount of money within it. The player knows the possible amounts of money in the cases, and is hoping for a large value inside the case they choose. The object of the game is to pick and thus eliminate cases in such a way that the remaining money amounts, which become better known with each subsequent player choice, provide the player with a large expected value of winnings. At specific intervals, a "banker" offers the player money to purchase their initial case choice and end the game. In theory, the offers should follow the expected value of winnings as cases are chosen. The lower the offer versus the expected value of the remaining cases, the less likely the player will stop pursuing the higher value cases that remain. In theory, as a reaction to the banker's offer, the player assesses the expected value of the remaining case amounts versus the bank's offer. The player decides to take the offer or continue playing, taking or not taking the deal. This game show is known as "Deal or No Deal" in the United States and elsewhere for this reason.

Though simple, this game is a great lesson for students of financial economics. The player chooses an asset (the initial briefcase), which has an expected value of $131,477.50 given each of the cases has an equal probability of 1/26 of being chosen first. As the player chooses cases to open, the expected value of the unknown amounts reflects changing probabilities. The constantly evolving expected value affects the basis of the bank's offer. At each offer stage, the player must weigh the latest offer against a quick calculation of the remaining expected value, and decide whether the gamble (continuing to play for an unknown amount) exceeds the offer's certain value. If the player is provided a banker's offer less than the remaining expected value of unknown case amounts, theory suggests the player should not take the offer if it is significantly under the board's expected value. The banker is careful not to approach this value too early, providing the player with incentives not to take the offer. Watching the game show a few times shows that the banker generally baits the player by offering amounts far below the expected value at any given time, providing the player with the incentive to continue playing and not take the deal.

The concept of risk aversion is at the heart of this game.[1] In Chapter 2, the idea of risk was introduced, where interest rates for specific financial markets provided investors with information about the relative risk of one asset to another. When allocating assets in a portfolio, an investor must think about exposure to risk against otherwise certain outcomes. This chapter is outlined as follows. First, risk is discussed in terms of expectations and the acts of speculation and arbitrage. Ideas of information asymmetries versus perfect foresight are compared to understand why risk exists in financial markets and where certain entities in transactions can take advantage of their monopoly position concerning information. Next, the concept of risk aversion explains why financial decisions are made and portfolios are allocated in specific ways. Portfolio allocation is of major importance to any financial institution and their clients/investors, from banks to pension funds to hedge funds to an Individual Retirement Account (IRA).

This chapter also looks at moral hazard and adverse selection as categorical ways information is asymmetric in financial markets. From the market for lemons to banks rationing credit, these concepts have changed the way financial markets are analyzed. Finally, the international aspects of risk, including currency and political risks as introduced in Chapter 2, are expounded upon further. It is important that students understand that with the globalization of trade comes a globalization of financial markets and an expansion of taking and spreading risk among many countries, which may or may not exacerbate pressure on financial institutions worldwide.

Famous and infamous dichotomies

Financial markets provide specific assets to meet specific needs. This section discusses market dichotomies. Financial assets may be a mix of these submarkets; for example, a home is a capital market asset, sold on a spot market, but may or may not be a primary or secondary market asset. If the home is an existing home, it is sold on a secondary market; if it is a new home, the market is primary. The characteristics of these markets may be very similar, but slight differences in perceived risk change the value of the investment to different investors. The interest rate applied, or the asset's expected rate of return, also reflects its market characteristics.

Capital versus money market assets

Capital market assets have more than one year to maturity. Examples of such assets are corporate stocks, automobiles, homes, and debt securities that mature in more than one year. In Chapter 2, we discussed how interest rates account for time in a simple way using inflation risk. Other risks may rise over time due to problems in forecasting further and further into the future, augmenting default, liquidity and currency/political risks. The money market includes assets of less than one year to maturity. These assets are generally cash or cash equivalents, where the assets are short-term debt, a bridge between a current cashflow shortfalls and a new surge of cash directly. Typical examples are short-term government debt, short-term corporate debt and commercial paper. The differentiating factor and what determines differences in risk is time to maturity.

This market dichotomy can be confusing because the name of each submarket is deceptive. When you buy a bond, you are really lending someone money, as discussed in Chapter 2. However, the length of that loan is variable for many different reasons. Simple reasons include the different contractual lengths of loans, from a six-month loan, buying a television on credit, or borrowing through a 30-year home mortgage. Any loans to be paid in full, both principal and interest, in less than or equal to one year's time are technically money market bonds. Bonds that are due after one year or more are not considered to be for cash but for different uses, especially the purchase of physical assets or capital, hence the name "capital market". Corporate stocks, or equity market securities, are considered capital market assets not for how long the investor intends to hold the asset but for the assumption that the purchase of these equities represents the purchase of capital by the issuing firm. Stocks are purchased with the theoretical belief that they will be held forever, even if held for only a few hours in reality.

Primary and secondary markets

Primary markets are where financial assets are first sold, or initially available. A primary transaction in financial markets is typified by an initial public offering or IPO. In the late 1990s, the IPO became synonymous with financial riches, booming portfolio values, and the most attention at the next cocktail party for brilliant financial tacticians and strategists of all kinds. Since 2002, IPO activity has all but ground to a halt. The main players in an IPO are large investment banks, firms that leverage client funds; money is made by the investment bank from a spread, or the difference between their cost of funds and revenue generated. If a company wants to go "public" and become a corporation by having public ownership through the availability of stock, the easiest way is to find an underwriting bank to act as the middle person in the transaction. The highest bidding brokerage house gets a certain sum of stocks, potentially millions of shares, at a certain price. The brokerage acquiring the IPO believes that when these shares are sold to the public, the difference in revenue and cost per share will be significant and positive. Profit is, as always, the driving force behind a firm underwriting (funding) such a purchase.

Spot vs. future markets

The spot market is the current market for an asset today. The future market for assets is much more complex, and is a derivative market. Future markets run on contractual arrangements between buyers and sellers to complete transactions at a future date. The price of a future market asset is a contractual price, where both the buyer and seller agree to respectively purchase and sell the underlying asset. Since the trade takes place in the future, the underlying asset's spot price is unknown when the contract details are finalized. As each side of the transaction pursues mutual profit, the two parties agree to a price that both the buyer and seller see as their individual best guess to deliver profits greater than zero the day the contract is executed. When the contract is executed, and fulfilled by both sides, the buyer and seller compare the contract price to the spot price the day of the contract's execution to determine the contract's profitability. If the buyer purchased the asset through the contract at a price higher than the current spot market, the buyer lost money by paying too much. The reverse is true for the seller: if the buyer pays too much, the seller got more than the spot market provided, and thus made money.

Spot and future markets create both financial winners and losers, of course, but they do so in very different ways. Futures are a type of derivative asset because the contract's value depends on that of the underlying asset (the commodity or financial security to be traded at a later date), which changes from day to day. When you buy a stock, for example, you do not know whether you will make money or lose money: time needs to elapse before you can make that judgment. In a derivative asset, time is yet another factor to consider. Only when the contract is executed will who won versus who lost be completely determined. The contract's existence separates these two markets.

The Chicago Board of Trade (CBOT) was the original market in the United States for such futures contracts. Such markets also exist in London, Tokyo, Sydney, and Dubai.

Suppose a farmer harvests grain in July, like all the farmer's neighbors. When the harvest takes place, the farmer is unsure what the spot market price will be, because the spot price depends on many unknown factors: weather, crop disease, import competition, the farmer's own crop's yield, etc. All parties know what the historic prices are and could forecast loosely what the price of grain is likely to be. However, some farmers will want to ensure an amount of revenue through a contract. The concern is not so much forecasting market prices as trying not to lose from fluctuating grain prices. It is likely they will guess wrong and could have made more on the spot market had they waited, but it is also likely that they could have made less revenue.

Futures contracts ensure the farmer of a certain price if a certain quantity is delivered. There is another side to this process. The party buying the grain must agree to the farmer's price or no one will engage with the farmer in this contract. The CBOT was set up to find both buyers and sellers for standardized (futures) and non-standardized (forwards) commodities contracts, eliminating the search cost for all parties involved and centralizing these contracts' operations. The grain buyer must perceive profit from the contract to agree. Profit rules the game, and a negotiation process takes place to deliver a "market" price for grain far before the harvest takes place. It is likely that the spot price on the day the contracts and grain delivery is due will be very close to the future price in the contracts.

Commodity markets also showcase another interesting aspect of future markets. Suppose you were a grain buyer and you wanted to buy 100 bushels of August grain for $100 per bushel. Suppose it is July 1 today. The future contract is set and now you wait. You are a commodities broker, living in TriBeCa on Manhattan Island. While you sit in your loft watching world financial markets on television, the day inches closer when this contract will expire and needs to be executed. If you do not sell your obligation to someone who really wants the grain and not just profit off the grain price fluctuations between July 1 and the execution date in August, a truck will arrive and double park on your lower Manhattan street to dump 100 bushels of grain in front of your apartment building. The options market was developed to provide a way to release one side of a future or forward contract if liquidity otherwise did not exist.

In conclusion, the spot and forward markets are arenas where investors can invest in many different ways, but the two markets fundamentally follow each other. The futures and forward markets act as predictors of the future spot market for an asset or commodity, as investors try to profit from contracts set now to exchange assets later. This dichotomy is also very important for foreign exchange. Dichotomizing between speculation and arbitrage provides further light on how risk is taken and how these market dichotomies define risk.

Case study 3.1   Enron and California's continuing budget deficits

California is considered to be the eighth largest economy in the world; if California was taken away, the remaining 49 states in America would be the fourth or fifth largest economy. California's large economy demands a large amount of primary products. Fortunately, for Californians, food is not an issue in general. Energy and water are issues instead; California has a wide variety of climates and subsequent energy needs. Winters in California can bring a great deal of rain, or little at all. In 2009, for example, many areas of California are worried about drought.

In 2000, as in preceding and subsequent years, there was also a worry about energy during the summer; many of California's homeowners trade natural gas demand for electricity as they turn on air conditioners to beat the heat. This worry turned into a energy crisis, where the ability to acquire additional energy from outside California was monopolized by a firm that would soon after find itself as a case study of unethical behavior in accounting and finance and toppled by its own risk.

Enron was an energy company that at first produced and sold energy. Enron developed into an energy exchange firm, buying and selling energy contracts like any other commodities brokerage. As an institutional investor, Enron attempted to use its information advantages and resources to influence market prices for profit. In late 2000, California's already deregulated energy market became slightly less regulated. By the end of the 1990s, the expectation of lower energy prices from a competitive, deregulated market gave way to market manipulation by firms such as Enron. Electricity providers were, however, mandated to provide energy to the transmission grid; only the production and subsequent sale of excess energy was allowed to be competitive and subject to market forces. Demand increased for energy in California through the 1990s, as California's economy grew alongside the macroeconomy. The limits on pricing that came with deregulation provided disincentives for suppliers to increase domestic production (inside California) and forced energy providers such as Pacific Gas and Electric (PG&E) to purchase energy outside the state.

Knowing that deregulation forced this importation of energy onto the California economy, Enron took advantage of the situation and began to manipulate spot prices for energy in such a way to profit from their positions in future contracts. The future contracts would focus on purchasing large amounts of energy, and then cause a short-age on the spot market. The spot price outside California increased, and Enron could sell the energy purchased through the futures contracts at higher spot prices. The revenue made from this deal would then go immediately into purchasing more energy in the futures market, causing an exacerbated shortage.

Two events took place in 2001 that toppled two organizations. First, California's governor at the time, Gray Davis, reacted slowly to the energy pricing and delivery problems. As a result of his inaction, California endured rolling blackouts, where part of the power grid was shut down for a certain amount of time, followed by another part of the grid, and so on. This hurt an already buckling economy in California. The sharp increase in prices increased expenses for the state and for its businesses, increasing the state's budget deficit. After 2001, Gray Davis attempted to get an increased vehicle license fee (VLF) into law, partially to make up for some of the deficit caused by the energy crisis of 2001. This action forced consumers to initiate a recall of the guber-natorial seat. Arnold Schwarzenegger, a motion picture actor and budding politician, became California's governor in 2003 on a platform of repealing or "terminating" the VLF increase. In November 2003, the VLF was repealed. Due partially to this repeal, and a broken budget and political system, the California budget has been in deficit every year since; California's government faces a deficit through the 2009–10 fiscal year that is over $40 billion as of February 2009.

Enron, through the manipulation of spot and future prices for energy, was partially to blame for a budget deficit that remains in California's budget and still costs California's residents and businesses money every year. A film called *Enron: The Smartest Guys in the Room* from 2005 is recommended to the reader.

Case study 3.2 A partial explanation of hedge funds

The subprime crisis of 2007 and the subsequent financial issues worldwide put a hot light on financial markets, specifically on entities known as hedge funds (Chan et al. 2006). The name is somewhat deceiving, as these funds normally do not engage in true hedging strategies but instead use financial instruments such as futures, forwards, options, and other derivative assets that are built for hedging to create more profit (and thus taking more risk) opportunities. Chapter 5 discusses these types of assets in more detail. Not all hedge funds are built on risky assets per se; some funds use fixed income assets as the basis for their investments. The following list from Chan et al. (2006) provides almost every mix of strategy available:

- *Convertible arbitrage*. Notice arbitrage in the name, which suggests a mix of positions in the same asset or company. Generally, it is long in a company's convertible bond and short in its common stock. Positions generate profits from the bond income and the short sale of stock to protect the original investment.
- *Dedicated short-seller*. Maintenance of a net short position as opposed to complete short positioning. Short-biased managers take short positions in mostly equities and derivatives. The short bias of a manager's portfolio must be constantly greater than zero to be classified in this category, as long positions are mixed to hedge. This is a spread rather than hedge position generally.
- *Emerging markets*. As many emerging markets do not allow short selling or offer viable derivative products to engage in a hedge, this is just like a portfolio choice to purchase equity positions in emerging markets. Many brokerages have such instruments, which look like a mutual fund in a mix of businesses in places such as India, China, Singapore, Argentina, and other markets.
- *Equity market neutral*. This investment strategy exploits equity market inefficiencies and usually involves being net zero in the same country's markets. Well-designed portfolios typically control for industry, sector, market capitalization, and other exposures (ibid., p. 78).
- *Event-driven*. This strategy captures price movements generated by pending corporate events. Obviously, the financial crisis of 2007 and beyond signals more events in the future as banks and other financial institutions continue to falter. There are three popular subcategories in event-driven strategies: risk (merger) arbitrage, distressed/high-yield securities, and Regulation D (ibid.).
- *Fixed-income arbitrage*. This was a popular category for many institutions, as mortgage-backed securities and counterparty risk swaps live in this category. Fixed-income profits come from price differences between related securities that bear interest and thus provide income. Global markets are used to generate returns with low risk.
- *Global macro*. This is another popular category. Using a mix of positions in international markets as influenced by major economic trends and/or events, trades are made to take advantage of slow reactions to changing world events and news. The portfolios of these funds can include stocks, bonds, currencies, and commodities in the form of cash or derivative instruments (ibid.).

- *Long/short equity.* This is classic spreading of risk through mixed positions in multiple companies across multiple markets with a focus on equities. Long/short equity funds tend to build and hold portfolios that are substantially more concentrated than those of traditional stock funds (ibid.). This is really the core of hedge funds historically, as they are "hedging" within a large market portfolio (not necessarily as we defined it in this chapter by holding multiple positions in the same stock). This strategy is why hedge funds have the name they do.
- *Managed futures.* This strategy invests in listed financial and commodity futures markets and currency markets around the world; the managers are usually referred to as commodity trading advisers, or CTAs (ibid., p. 79).
- *Multistrategy.* Here managers use many strategies and reallocate funds between them in response to market opportunities, which also includes funds employing unique strategies.
- *Fund of funds.* A "multi manager" fund will employ the services of two or more trading advisers or hedge funds who will be allocated cash by the trading manager to trade on behalf of the fund (ibid).

In short, hedge funds are really another method by which investors can have their money managed, and, as with any other "fund", the inherent risks should be considered.

Things to remember

There are three major market dichotomies:

- Capital versus money markets (based on time to maturity)
- Primary versus secondary (based on chronology of transactions for an asset)
- Spot versus future (based on when the transaction is agreed to take place).

Speculation versus arbitrage

Speculation is simple: a wager. Gambling casinos are classic clearinghouses for speculation activity as entertainment. In financial economics, speculation is simply risk exposure of any kind. This can be as small as buying 100 shares of Microsoft stock and borrowing 99 shares the same day to be sold on the same day in the future, or buying junk bonds or penny stocks or holding money in your pocket. Financial transactions are generally speculative to some extent because risk is inherent in most economic transactions.

The level of risk exposure determines the investor's potential reward. Risk exposure can also determine the level of potential losses of principal. In some transactions, when an investor borrows money or securities in an attempt to profit further from risk, the loss of the loan's value can mean the pursuit of the investor's assets beyond original principal to pay the loan back. The loan amount and interest payments are what ultimately bound the potential losses; if you borrow $100,000 worth of stock from your brokerage, and that stock loses all its value while in your hands, you are liable for $100,000 plus interest in the loan, not any more than that.

Arbitrage is technically the state of not speculating; it is also a word that describes taking advantage of asset price differentials in two or more markets for riskless gain. In this book, arbitrage will be discussed in a slightly different context. Arbitrage is the act of reducing risk exposure, where full hedge arbitrage is the act of eliminating asset-specific risk completely. The futures market above is an example of this more complex financial exercise. A simple example provides a way to think about arbitrage in action.

Suppose an investor holds an asset, say 100 shares of Google (GOOG) stock. The investor believes the price of GOOG will fall from its present level. Instead of selling the 100 shares and taking accumulated profit to date, the investor borrows 100 shares of GOOG on margin (assuming the investor has enough wealth to be provided the loan). Now the investor both owns and owes GOOG simultaneously. Any gains from owning the original 100 shares from this point forward are eliminated by parallel losses in what is owed (as the price of GOOG rises, the asset position rises in value while the liability position grows in cost). The reverse is true if the price falls: what the investor owes on the borrowed stock will fall in value, which is an implicit gain; the originally held stock will lose value simultaneously as the parallel loss when prices fall.

Reduced risk exposure is theoretically achieved by "hedging" or betting against an asset's gain by taking another position in assets that historically move in the opposite direction to the original asset's value. However, this is not hedging in the sense of arbitrage, nor is it hedging at all. When playing casino games, the outcomes are deterministic, or known; the actual results are unknown, but happen with a certain probability. By betting on one outcome, the gambler is exposed to risk; by betting on all possible outcomes, the investor reduces risk, which reduces the available rewards. True risk exposure is measured by how an investor holds a mix of positions in the same asset.

Positions in assets

There are three ways investors can position assets. The first is to own the asset in net, or be long in the asset. This is the typical way assets are held; the risk is the asset's price falling and the potential reward is from the asset price's increase. The second way to position an asset is to be in a net liability position, or be short. Being short means you want the asset's price to fall so you owe less money back to the lender. If the price rises, the value of the debt the investor owes also rises. However, most short positions are seeking to sell the asset immediately and then buy it back at the perceived lower price, keeping the residual after interest payments as profit. The final position is a net zero position, or a full-hedge arbitrage position. Holding an equivalent long and short position means the risks have been eliminated, as have the rewards. When we discuss foreign currency markets, the rationale behind full-hedge arbitrage transactions will be clearer.

Table 3.1 shows the possible investment positions and the wager on the underlying asset's price when taking such a position.

Table 3.1 Positions and expectations

Net position	Price expectations
Long	Price increase
Short	Price decrease
Net zero	Price stable/indifferent

Risk aversion

While speculation assumes a gamble, financial theory suggests that most investors will not take a gamble if an investment of equivalent value also exists. The concept of risk aversion, the level of reluctance an investor has toward an uncertain outcome versus a certain outcome, is a reflection of how the investor views risk exposure. A simple example of investment opportunities helps. Suppose you are offered a guaranteed $105 in one year for a $100 investment today. This suggests a five percent nominal rate of return to the $100 that is riskless, a certain outcome. You are also offered the following array of possible outcomes. You could lose your principal with 25 per cent probability. You could also make your $100 back with 50 percent probability. Finally, you could make $220 with 25 per cent probability. The expected value of the second investment opportunity is found by multiplying each dollar return by its associated probability:

$$(\$0 \times 0.25) + (\$100 \times 0.5) + (\$220 \times 0.25) = \$0 + \$50 + \$55 = \$105.$$

There are three risk attitudes you could take toward this choice between assets. The first is to be risk-averse, where you would take the certain outcome of $105 rather than the gamble with has an expected value of $105. Financial theory suggests most people are risk-averse, taking a sure thing versus a gamble. This idea comes from the assumption that investors perceive diminishing returns in terms of risk exposure. The more risk an investor takes, the less satisfaction is gained with each additional amount of risk. You may also be risk-neutral, indifferent between a gamble and a certain outcome with the same expected value. Finally, you may be risk-loving, where you are willing to take a gamble instead of an equivalent, certain outcome and risk the principal payment to seek the $220 with 25% probability. The "Deal or No Deal" game discussed at the beginning of this chapter is a game based on using risk aversion to the banker's advantage. If the banker gives a relatively low offer, the player is less likely to take the deal because the risk is worth the reward. When the banker's offer approaches the expected value of the remaining cases, the player is more likely to take the deal. This assumes the player is risk-averse.

Risk aversion and financial markets

Our current example of two investments provides some insight into financial market behavior. The first insight is that investors, given equivalent expected values of investment choices, are likely to go with certain outcomes rather than gambles. If we think in simple terms about borrowers and lenders, lenders are risk-averse and borrowers must recognize that in each specific loan. If the borrower is unable to guarantee a positive financial outcome for the lender, the borrower must be prepared to provide a larger expected value than a riskless or certain outcome of an equivalent value otherwise. As a result, the borrower must pay a higher rate of return to attract lenders. That difference between the return on a gamble and on a certain outcome for the same initial investment is known as the risk premium. In Chapter 2, we briefly discussed specific types of risk premiums for bonds. If the investor perceives risks above and beyond the level that is considered inflation risk only, it is a signal that a larger rate of return is needed to provide incentives for the purchase of riskier assets.

Portfolio allocations and risk

An asset portfolio is a collection of income-producing investments. Most people diversify in a portfolio, or hold a mix of assets. There are two approaches to portfolio risk, however. One is spreading risk, or diversification. Holding a mix of assets means the investor simultaneously holds a mix of assets and risks. As a result, the risk to holding a specific asset is reduced or spread against the risk of other assets; also, there is less risk taken in any one asset. The other approach to portfolio risk is hedging risk, where holding multiple assets is meant to directly reduce the risk of specific assets. For example, holding a position in two different assets that are assumed to move in opposite directions with market fluctuations is one form of hedging risk, so long as the inverse relationship between the two assets' returns holds over time.

However, true hedging is when the investor holds opposite positions in the same asset, not two assets where the historic data suggest they move in opposite directions as a result of a price increase on one of the assets. For example, suppose you held a bond and a stock, and the data suggested that as the value of the stock increased, the bond's value decreased. This example of hedging assumes that the historic data will continue to hold into the future. In contrast to that example, when the investor holds a long position in a bond and a short position in the same bond, the bond's price increasing is a gain to the long position and a loss to the short position. How much of each position held determines the level of hedging done by the investor and the level of risk exposure.

Things to remember

There are three types of risk aversion:

- Risk-averse (certain outcomes favored over gambles for same average return)
- Risk-neutral (indifferent between certain outcome and gamble)
- Risk-loving (favor the gamble over certain outcomes for same average return).

Summary

As we move into analyzing equity markets in Chapter 4, risk is seen as simply the investor's cost of seeking profit. When the investor perceives risks in assets, the investor attempts to buy risky assets at the lowest value possible. The lower the purchase price, the higher the potential for profit. On the other side of the transaction, the seller of a risky asset is attempting to maximize the sales price. Each side must convince the other that mutual risks are covered by the negotiated price. Risk aversion describes the investor's attitudes toward risk. An investor could be risk-averse, which is the typical case, risk-neutral or risk-loving. These attitudes are for comparing equivalent returns on an asset with no risk versus assets with risk. The risk-averse investor would rather take the certain outcome versus the gamble with the same expected value, the risk-loving investor prefers the gamble. The risk-neutral investor is indifferent. Dichotomies in financial markets exist between money and capital markets, primary and second markets, and spot and future markets. The dichotomies help investors assess risks and also profit from risk exposure and use the markets against each other for profit. The capital and money markets are separated by time to maturity of the asset. The primary and secondary markets are separated by the number of times the asset has previously traded hands. In later chapters, the dichotomy between spot and future markets becomes more important for two reasons. A large volume of financial transactions now take place on future markets for commodities, currencies, and financial assets. One can both speculate, increase risk exposure, or arbitrage risk, where risk exposure is reduced using either the spot or future markets.

Risk exposure is determined by the investor's willingness and ability to spread or hedge risk. An investor can hold three possible positions in an asset to hedge risk. The investor can be long in the asset, or own more of the asset than is owed. The investor can be short in the asset, or owe more than is owned, or hold equal values of equity and debt in an asset. When investors borrow financial assets, they believe the price of the asset will fall and they will pay back less than they borrowed; the residual of this transaction is profit. Spreading risk is having long and short positions in different assets, using those positions to reduce the risk of any one asset's return on investment. The investor's portfolio of assets, or group of specific investments, may also have hedged strategies within it. A typical hedge is holding two assets whose returns move in opposite directions to one another; this is really more like diversification than the true economic meaning of hedging risk. When the investor holds long and short positions in the same asset, hedging is truly taking place as there is no uncertainty about the inverse relationship between the positions. Chapter 4 expands the discussion of the types of assets held by investors to discuss equities, the stock, and housing markets.

Key terms

1   Arbitrage: the act of reducing risk in a speculative position, or buying in one market and selling in another for profit.
2   Capital market: the market for securities that mature in more than one year.
3   Deterministic: the outcome is known.
4   Equity market securities: financial assets that represent ownership.
5   Expected value: the weighted average.
6   Forwards: non-standardized contracts for transactions at a future date for a specified price and quantity.
7   Full-hedge arbitrage: the act of eliminating all risk in a speculative position, or holding equivalent long and short positions simultaneously.
8   Futures market: a market for contractual transactions, where the contracts specify a date, quantity and price to be exchanged in the future.
9   Futures: contractual transactions in the future for a commodity or financial asset where both sides of the contract are obliged to fulfill their sides of the agreement.
10   Initial public offering (IPO): the first transaction for a financial asset, usually associated with a firm first seeking or augmenting its equity.
11   Investment banks: financial intermediaries that specialize in connecting firms to those seeking equity investment, or in providing investment services to any entity.
12   Long position: owning an asset.
13   Margin loan: a loan to purchase financial assets based on the level of the investor's portfolio.
14   Monopoly: a market structure in which there is one seller of the good, service or asset.
15   Net zero position: full-hedge arbitrage.
16   Options: contractual transactions in the future for a commodity or financial asset where one side of the contract is obliged to fulfill their side of the agreement due to the payment of an option premium by the side that retains the right to fulfill their side of the contract.
17   Portfolio: a set of assets, which can be a mix of long and short positions.
18   Risk attitudes: the possible ways humans view risk-taking.
19   Risk-averse: a risk attitude where the entity views the certain outcome for an expected rate of return as providing more utility than a gamble with the same expected rate of return.
20   Risk-loving: a risk attitude where the entity views the certain outcome for an expected rate of return as providing less utility than a gamble with the same expected rate of return.

21   Risk-neutral: a risk attitude where the entity views a certain outcome and a gamble over the same expected value indifferently.
22   Risk premium: the additional rate of return sought by investors to compensate for additional risk in making an investment.
23   Short position: having a liability.
24   Speculation: the act of gambling or exposing oneself to risk.
25   Spot market: the current market for a good or asset.
26   Spreading risk: diversification.
27   Stock: the name for a share of equity or ownership in a firm.
28   Underlying asset: the asset being traded in a futures, forward or options market.

Questions and problems

1   Define the three attitudes toward risk and why the definition of being risk-averse makes intuitive sense.
2   Describe an asset that is sold on the secondary capital market and is a futures asset.
3   Explain the difference between spreading and hedging risk in terms of speculation and arbitrage.
4   Describe how an investor would hold an arbitrage position in an asset, in terms of full-hedge arbitrage.
5   Why would the interest rate on a corporate bond have a higher risk premium than government debt in a developed nation? Explain.

4 Equity markets, stock markets and real estate

Introduction

The stock market, where ownership in companies is bought and sold, is a market where you must have a license or pay someone with a license to buy and sell assets for you. Securities brokers are such people, and are paid a commission for their services. There are three general ways firms can set up their ownership: sole proprietorships, partnerships or corporations. Corporations are companies that issue certificates of ownership, known as shares, and use equity markets to finance real asset purchases initially. Suppose you were a partner in a computer software company. You and your partner decide you need more office space for your employees. Your firm has three ways it can finance this expansion. The firm can use its retained earnings, or the accumulated profits the company has hopefully made and accrued over time. Second, your firm can also take a loan from a bank or find some debt instrument to gain access to cash and pay interest and principal over time. Finally, your firm can expand equity and find new partners who will help finance the expansion as trade for partnership, or go public and expand ownership through the equity market.

This initial choice to go public is where the primary market comes into play. You announce to the world that you are entertaining bids from brokerage houses for your IPO, and the wheel begins to roll. Decisions you need to make if you decide to go public include the amount of common stock you will offer and whether you will offer preferred stock. Common stock is the classic type of stock market asset; it is traded with a value changing every day on the secondary market. It is considered common because each stock has ownership and voting rights, but only has the privilege of receiving dividends if paid; dividends are a disbursement of retained earnings by a firm. A firm is not obliged to pay common stockholders any dividends at all.

This chapter looks at the pricing of equity positions, mainly stock prices. The parallel to bond pricing is made. The Capital Asset Pricing Model provides a method of estimating the expected rate of return, and ultimately the present value discount factor, for any capital asset. This model is generally used for stock pricing. A brief discussion of housing markets expands the definition of equity, where portfolio allocations and management complete this chapter.

Stock market indices

Before we tackle the issue of stock market pricing, let's first look at something you are likely to recognize. The news focuses on the equity markets. Individual stock prices and movements may be highlighted, but the focus is constantly on an amalgamated value of stocks in different indices. An index number revolves around a number, generally 100, the value in a base period.

Table 4.1 DJIA composite stocks, June 2009

Company	Ticker SYM	Company	Ticker SYM	Company	Ticker SYM
Alcoa	AA	Home Depot	HD	Merck & Co.	MRK
American Express	AXP	Hewlett-Packard	HPQ	Microsoft Corp.	MSFT
Boeing	BA	IBM	IBM	Pfizer Inc.	PFE
Bank of America	BAC	Intel Corp.	INTC	Procter & Gamble	PG
Caterpillar	CAT	Johnson & Johnson	JNJ	AT&T Inc.	T
Cisco Systems	CSCO	JPMorgan Chase	JPM	Travelers Cos.	TRV
Chevron Corp.	CVX	Kraft Foods	KFT	United Technologies	UTX
DuPont	DD	Coca-Cola	KO	Verizon	VZ
Walt Disney Co.	DIS	McDonald's	MCD	Wal-Mart Stores	WMT
General Electric	GE	3M	MMM	Exxon Mobil	XOM

The Dow Jones Industrial Average, or DJIA, is such an index. Thirty stocks make up this index; the DJIA is a weighted average of the combination's value. These stocks are chosen and also replaced based upon their role in the overall financial markets as leading indicators of specific industries. Table 4.1 shows the most recent stocks that make up the DJIA.

DJIA is just one of many such averages; every major investment bank, local newspaper, and pop financier worldwide follows some variation of a stock index for information about the equity market's overall movement. Other indices include the NASDAQ, Standard and Poor's 500 (SP500), Russell 2000, Wilshire 5000, and many others. The NASDAQ is probably the best index to use as a comparison to the DJIA. The NASDAQ market was introduced as an Automated Quotation system (the AQ in NASDAQ), facilitating trades and market information through the use of computers. As computer technology developed at a rapid rate, so did the number of firms dealing in that technology; the NASDAQ became the index which tracked high-tech firms. The NASDAQ was in the spotlight during the late 1990s boom and the subsequent market adjustment early in this decade. Just like the DJIA, the NASDAQ composite is a weighted average of stock prices, a little over 3000 stocks. This has every stock on the NASDAQ exchange represented and is a market capitalization or value-weighted index; the NASDAQ Composite is driven by the dollar value of stocks on the NASDAQ market.

In England, they watch the DJIA and NASDAQ indices, but have their own index called the FTSE 100, named after the Financial Times. In Germany, it is the DAX; in France, the exchange and index are known as the CAC; in Tokyo, it is the Nikkei; in Hong Kong, the market is the Hang Seng. All these indices track market movements without having to observe specific stocks. Alternative theories of how stock pricing should take place, and fundamentally what a stock's price signals to its potential buyer and its current owner, are discussed later. Let's investigate the fundamental idea behind a stock price and see how it relates to interest rates and to present value.

Equity market pricing

There are millions of theories as to why equity prices fluctuate. Many are based on conjecture and luck rather than research and economics. Of course, conjecture and luck have some merit: both are virtually costless. Research and education about the markets cost money and time; any cost incurred in predicting the markets reduces rates of return. The Firm

Foundation Theory of equity prices is our focus here. This basic theory states that the price of stock is a function of four fundamental characteristics of a company. The first two foundations are the expected dividends to flow from the firm and the expected growth rate of the stock's price. Both of these are cash flows to the investor, acting as proxies for interest payments that do not take place with stock but would take place from lending. The other two foundations are the perceived company-specific and market risks. The company-specific risks include default, liquidity, taxation and currency/political risks from Chapter 2. The market risks are primarily inflation, but could include some political risks that are market-wide and not specific to any firm. Notice that all four foundations are either expected or perceived. The lack of perfect information and knowledge augments stock price and overall market volatility.

We will call the first two foundations numerator foundations, reflecting the expected cash flow from the stock. The expected cash flow from any security is its future value, or FV, as discussed in Chapter 3. The price of the stock is, therefore, the present discounted value of the expected cash flows while owning the stock. These flows are determined by past performance, maturity level of the firm, corporate policy and history toward dividend payout, and other factors that may have little tangibility. Risk assessment and diversification lead investors into portfolio analysis and other ways than conjecture to determine the correct nominal interest rate to discount the future value of the stock. As we build the basic stock price formula, there are different ways to look at risk premiums that investors seek as they assess the denominator foundations.

The price of a stock changes from day to day because the market for a stock changes its valuation of that company every day, based on new expectations of dividends, future price growth or risks. Both the numerator and denominator foundations in the following present value formula potentially move every day.

$$P_{Stock} = \sum_{i=1}^{n} \frac{ECF_i}{(1+R^{\varepsilon})^i} \qquad (4.1)$$

where ECF is the sum of the expected dividend payout and growth of the stock price in dollars, and R^{ε} is the nominal interest rate. Comparing Equation 4.1 with Equation 2.5 shows similarities to the valuation of a bond or any other asset. When you buy a stock, you expect to receive some cash flow at a later date. That future value is discounted to tell you how much these future cash flows are worth today. To pay more is a bad deal; to pay less is great. The largest problem is figuring out how to value the expectations. For now, Equation 4.1 summarizes the Firm Foundations Theory of stock pricing.

Cash flow expectations drive this pricing formula, in stark contrast to bond pricing, where the only uncertainty was the expected nominal interest rate; the numerator foundations add a second element of uncertainty not within the bond market. Notice that the investor takes into consideration the risks involved in holding the stock versus alternatives, or the opportunity costs, which adds up to the expected nominal interest rate in the denominator. Preferred stock has more information, and thus marginally less uncertainty, but the timing of the payments still remains a mystery. Bonds contractually set the timing and amounts of cash flow to the bond holder, while common stock does neither. In search of more information, we start with a very famous model called the Capital Asset Pricing Model or CAPM. This model helps to determine the risk premium on a specific stock beyond a risk-free alternative in a way that provides insight into the bond market pricing of Chapter 2.

Things to remember

Like bonds, stock prices are an inverse function of the risk in holding the stock. As the opportunity cost in holding the stock rises (higher risk), or as the expected cash flows from the stock falls (higher risk), the stock price falls.

The Capital Asset Pricing Model

The CAPM is a model that predicts the nominal rate of return used to discount future cash flows to a capital asset. A capital market asset, for example a firm's stock, faces both systematic (non-diversifiable) risk and idiosyncratic or diversifiable risk. When an investor adds a firm's stock, let's call it stock **k**, to a portfolio, the investor risks having the entire portfolio's expected return change for the better or worse. Assessing stock **k**'s risk versus the remainder of the stock market (diversifiable) and risk-free (non-diversifiable) alternatives is a major part of using the CAPM. The CAPM is a simple linear combination of the risk-free rate and the estimated, weighted spread between the return on a market portfolio of assets and the risk-free rate. The weighted spread represents the risk premium, the additional risk added to the risk-free rate because other assets face asset-specific risks. If an investor held a diversified portfolio of assets that pays the average market return (for example, the return to the SP 500 or the Wilshire 5000), the investor would want a return that exceeded the earnings of simply buying risk-free assets for the same money. Consider our discussion of risk aversion in Chapter 3. For the same level of investment, risk follows reward; for a risk-averse investor, the price of a risky asset must fall to reflect additional risk or no incentive exists to purchase the asset.

For students who have basic statistical knowledge, specifically regression analysis, the key to the CAPM is the coefficient that weights the spread between the risk-free and market rates of return by the volatility of the asset in question versus the market's volatility. In financial economics, this is the famous "Beta" (β_K). In regression analysis, the relationship between a single independent variable and an associated dependent variable provides a "slope" coefficient. In the CAPM, β_K is such a coefficient. This estimation of stock **k**'s expected return does involve error, and let's assume that the error term is zero on average for now.[1] A constant term is also included in this equation, which has the following, general form:

$$y = \alpha + \beta x + \varepsilon \qquad (4.2)$$

where y is the dependent variable, x is the independent variable, and ε is the error term. Using known data for x and y, regression analysis provides an estimate of the coefficients, α and β; where α is the constant term and β describes the relationship between x and y. In terms of the CAPM, assume that α is the historic risk-free rate of return (R_{RF}), which is considered to be a constant when stock **k** is purchased. Assume further that y is the historic return on stock **k** (R_K) and that x represents the spread between the historic return on a market portfolio of assets (R_{MKT}) and the risk-free rate of return (R_{RF}) or the constant, α. Renaming the variables in Equation 4.2 to match these assumptions, we have Equation 4.3:

$$R_K = R_{RF} + \beta_K(R_{MKT} - R_{RF}) \qquad (4.3)$$

As the market spread rises in value, the required rate of return on stock **k** also rises with some multiplier effect, based on the value of β_K. β_K is assumed to have a value between zero and infinity for the stock picked at random, where zero means the stock's historic returns do not move with the market spread and thus need no risk premium. For larger β_K values, stock **k**'s reactions to a growing spread are larger and more volatile. The larger the value of β_K, the larger is the risk of purchasing stock **k** versus the purchase of a portfolio of assets that provide the market's historic rate of return on average. The link to regression analysis is the way β is calculated, which is the same as any other regression coefficient.[2] Once β_K is determined, the investor can forecast the rate of return necessary to compensate against risk taken by purchasing asset **k** rather than making a more diversified purchase or buying a risk-free security.

Integrating estimates of R_K into the stock pricing formula

The estimate of R_K takes place by changing the weighted spread and then solving for the resultant change in asset **k**'s rate of return in Equation 4.3. This is the estimate of a minimum rate of return necessary to cover current risk evaluations. Plugging this value into Equation 4.1 for R^ε provides the sum of the asset-specific and market risks faced by the investor by choosing to purchase asset **k**. Notice, holding all else constant, as the value of R_K rises, the investor will reduce their valuation of the stock's price to compensate against the new risks. As R_K falls, the valuation of the stock's price rises. Later in this text, we will discuss in more detail the role of the central bank in determining financial market outcomes. If we assume the central bank uses risk-free assets as a way of manipulating financial market and macroeconomic activity, the CAPM provides insight as to why other asset prices follow monetary policy and its manipulation of risk-free markets. If the central bank buys risk-free securities, the rate of return on risk-free securities falls to reflect higher asset prices caused by the central bank's demand for these assets. As that rate falls, the spread between R_{MKT} and R_{RF} rises, but the constant terms also falls. How the market reacts to the central bank's policy now partially determines the estimated return on asset **k**. The CAPM provides a framework that shows how complex these relationships between rate of return and alternative assets really are.

In summary, the CAPM is one of many tools to help investors understand the relationships in financial markets between alternative rates of return and riskiness of a specific asset's purchase. The similarity to regression analysis shows us that β_k is simple to find and has major implications concerning the financial markets.[3] Starting from the risk-free rate of return, the investor adds a risk premium, due to asset-specific risks and the opportunity cost of not investing in some other assets. Another asset class for investors is real estate, which has similar aspects to stock markets because of ownership, but is much different in terms of liquidity and use.

Housing markets versus stock markets

Housing markets are capital markets in which the investor purchases a tangible asset to own. Stocks are considered intangible assets because they are entitlements to tangible or real assets. Real estate has "real" in its title on purpose. Purchasing a home is a good portfolio choice for most investors for three key reasons. First, there is a limited supply of homes and land, which puts natural pressure on prices to rise in the long term as more homes are purchased. Stocks come and go with new and re-issues of stock from publicly traded companies, but there are only so many houses and developable parcels of land available. Second, buying a home circumvents the payment of rent. When we discuss different types of life insurance, the insured either owns or rents the insurance. This is true for homes as well.

When you rent, you are simply paying to occupy another party's asset and have no claims to the asset's value; as a renter, you are more likely to depreciate or reduce the asset's value faster than augment its value. When you own, you are both paying and being rewarded for any appreciation in the asset's value. Each payment of principal on a mortgage is a payment to claim the home's value, which is hopefully rising over time. Finally, there may be tax advantages to buying a home with a mortgage. In Europe, only a few countries allow such a mortgage interest deduction. They include Sweden, the Netherlands and Switzerland. France does not allow such a deduction yet, though it has been debated. The United Kingdom and Germany do not allow such tax deductions. In the United States, the ability to deduct mortgage interest is one of the foundational reasons to purchase a home.

A home or other real estate investments can reduce inflation risk. As inflation rises, the real value and return on stocks, bonds and other long positions are reduced. For the home-owner borrowing through a mortgage, the real cost of the remaining principal and interest payments both fall as inflation rises. Further, if a home's value should rise as fast or faster than inflation, the homeowner enjoys real gains on the home value as well.

Case study 4.1 Canada's housing market: a contrast to American markets?

Housing markets are generally regional. The market for single-family homes in Des Moines, Iowa, is different than in Omaha, Nebraska; these markets are different still from Buenos Aires, Argentina, and also Tokyo, Japan. Housing markets represent another asset that an investor can purchase within a portfolio. Much like Americans, Canadians have a regional market for homes, driven by many of the same economic and social factors. There has been much made of the American housing market in worldwide news, and looking at Canada's housing market provides some contrasts and similarities.

A recent report by the Canada Mortgage and Housing Corporation (CMHC) provides the state of this market as of October 2008. In Canada, housing markets are defined as those in Western Canada and then elsewhere. British Columbia in particular, where the city of Vancouver is located, acts as the driver of Canada's housing market. Alberta and Saskatchewan have grown impressively over the last few years, due to thriving oil markets, and the demand for housing grew alongside it. Manitoba, which separates Western and Eastern Canada, experienced modest housing demand in 2008. Ontario, Ottawa and Quebec, which are the major provinces of Eastern Canada, are more tied to the American economy than Western Canada. As a result their outlook is less rosy than their Western counterparts, but still not terrible.

Much like other housing markets worldwide, Canada's market is driven by major characteristics of housing supply and demand. From the CMHC (2008) report, these include (with their short- to medium-term forecast):

* *Mortgage rates*: likely to remain relatively low for 2009 and 2010
* *Employment*: at a historic peak in Canada at the end of 2008, but forecasted to contract in 2009
* *Income*: tightness in the labor market to drive up incomes in Canada

- *Net migration*: Canada continues to receive more people than it loses, and migration inside Canada is headed westward
- *Natural population increase*: declining birth rate due to an aging demography reduces demand for housing in the medium to long term
- *Resale market*: record level of units on the market, likely to put downward pressure on house prices in 2009
- *Vacancy rates*: rising rental demand from high immigration and rising gap between cost of homeownership and rentals. Rental demand to remain stable

Since the early fourth quarter of 2008, many changes have taken place to both Canada's economic outlook and its housing market. First, employment has contracted more quickly than anticipated. Incomes have also fallen. Primary product prices, especially oil, have fallen greatly from their heights in late summer 2008. All of these are negative influences on Canada's housing market; Canadian banks are still lending to potential homeowners and avoided the troublesome subprime markets versus American banks. The key idea from this case is that these factors affect the demand for housing in all markets. Canada, being a neighbor to the United States geographically, has seen a slightly better transition from growth to recession in the housing market, but as recession hits Canada harder, this relatively good forecast may be reversed in the next report.

Portfolio analysis

Housing, equity and bond markets are used by investors to both spread and hedge risk. How do these markets compare to one another? A simple answer to how these markets are related is that they follow each other: as the price of stocks rise, home and bond prices rise as well, as a reflection of consumers and firms augmenting spending and saving simultaneously, especially during an economic boom. However, it is also plausible to imagine that as stock prices rise, investors sell bonds to take advantage of higher stock prices. In that case, bond prices would fall as stock prices increased. It is also feasible that as stock and bond prices both decrease during an economic downturn, housing prices rise due to a movement from financial to real assets markets. When thinking about the investor's portfolio, we must consider all these possibilities; after this consideration, the inherent volatility and difficulty in predicting equity market activity is likely to be more apparent to the reader.

Substitutes and complements

Basic economic theory suggests that as the price of one good rises, there are effects on the demand for other goods based on how they relate to the rising-price good. For example, automobiles and tires are considered complements because they are consumed together; potatoes and rice may be seen as substitutes, as they are generally not consumed together but as alternatives. Ultimately, the relationship between the price of one good and the demand for another determines whether or not two goods are substitutes or complements. Applying this logic to the financial markets provides some insight into how difficult analyzing portfolios held by investors can be.

Assume bond prices decrease as interest rates increase. As bond prices decrease, bonds become more attractive to investors. If bonds and stocks are substitutes, the lower bond price should lead holders of equity to sell their current holdings of stock and buy the relatively less-expensive debt securities instead. This would force stock prices to fall, which stabilizes the bond-price driven sell-off in equities. If stocks and bonds are complements, as bond prices decreased, stock prices would rise. The ability to buy less-expensive bonds in a well-diversified portfolio may act as a catalyst for investors also buying stock to spread risk. Buying a home, for example, is generally seen as complementary to buying stocks or bonds.

Think about the bond and stock pricing formulas introduced to this point. As interest rates rise, both bond and stock prices should fall, holding all else constant. In a sense, these formulas assume that stocks and bonds are substitutes for each other: as prices fall in one market, the other market follows this price reduction in order to stay competitive. However, the financial markets are not that simple (neither are many goods markets). The substitution effect of a price change in one broad market is just one effect of that price change. There is also an income effect. If interest rates are rising, real income is falling. If stocks and bonds are treated as normal purchases, where their quantity demanded changes in the same direction as income, then as the price of bonds falls due to higher interest rates, the demand for bonds will fall due to the income effect. Stock purchases will also face this income effect; if they are substitutes for bonds, the substitution and income effects cause the quantity demanded for stock to fall as rates rise. If they are complements, stock prices may fall if the income effect outweighs the substitution effect. The problem is figuring out whether stocks and bonds are substitutes or complements, which may be intractable and the cause of much of the equity market's volatility over time.

Mutual funds

Let's consider the implications of this problem's intractability. If you knew, at all times, that stocks and bonds were substitutes, you could predict price behavior in one market by watching the other, assuming stocks and bonds were considered normal "goods". Most investors do not want to waste time reacting to every price change, hoping their suppositions of this relationship hold correct. Further, many individual investors do not want to spend the time picking individual stocks, bonds or other financial assets in order to spread risk. Mutual funds are investments that represent diversified portfolios. Generally, these funds are amalgams of stocks, bonds, real estate, or a mix of all these in an attempt to spread risk for the mutual fund investor. Classically, investors choose from funds with discrete aggressiveness toward risk (low, medium, or high), which come with parallel potential for growth and profit (as well as loss). Much of the guesswork about risk is eliminated using mutual funds, which makes them very attractive to average investors. Around the world, mutual funds have been developed to provide an easy vehicle for investors to purchase the stock of many companies, especially in emerging markets, without taking the risk of just one company at a time.

Mutual funds themselves have become more diversified over the years. One popular choice, which integrates residential and commercial properties, is a real estate investment trust or REIT. A REIT is a mutual fund of real estate, where the investor buys a share in a "firm", as with all mutual funds, and that share's value changes with the underlying real estate assets' changing value. For example, suppose a REIT had ten residential homes in it and each share was worth $100 on the current spot market. The price would rise from $100 per share as the aggregate property values increased and would fall as that aggregate value fell. Some of the properties may rise or fall, but the REIT diversifies the risk to more than one property and does so in the form of a mutual fund. It may not matter in the long term how a portfolio is assembled, as financial theory is built on two ideas that suggest the market return is only going to cover opportunity costs in the long run.

The Modigliani-Miller Theorem

In the late 1950s, seminal research papers on financial markets changed the way investments were viewed worldwide. The paper that is considered the beginning of modern financial theory was by Franco Modigliani and Merton Miller, called "The Cost of Capital, Corporation Finance and the Theory of Investment". The article appeared in the *American Economic Review* in June 1958. Modigliani and Miller suggested that in the absence of market frictions, specifically asymmetric information that could lead to either speculative or arbitrage profit, the cost of the firm financing its capital investment activities (the purchase of new plant and equipment, for example) was the same regardless of the mix of financing tools used. A paraphrase of this idea became known as the Modigliani-Miller Theorem in financial economics.

The further implication of that idea is on the investor. If the cost to the firm is the same, then the potential return to the investor is also the same. In competitive (the investor's speculative profits are ultimately equal to zero) and complete (no arbitrage profits are available by purchasing assets in one market and selling them in another, for example) financial markets, the investor will simply cover their opportunity costs. This leads to a long-run concept, a concept that has also been known as the Efficient Market Hypothesis (EMH). Apart from pure luck, the prices of financial assets already carry all the information available about the asset, and the errors made by investors in predicting the path of financial asset prices over time will simply average to zero (those who win are paid by those who lose). If information is complete in a financial market, asset prices deliver the information. The idea of a random walk of stock prices emerged from the EMH, and has been challenged many times, where a random walk is when the error in predicting an asset's price is white noise centered at zero. The biggest challenge in verifying the EMH has come from the data itself. The data suggest that there is an excess return on holding equity portfolios, which further exceeds the risk premium for equities on average. This is a mystery for financial theorists, known as the "equity premium puzzle". The puzzle suggests that the amount of risk aversion necessary for the consumption-based version of the CAPM (CCAPM) to replicate the data concerning the pricing of risk is so great that no human being would be that afraid of risk. As we will see in Chapter 5, the use of derivative assets can both insure and exacerbate risk, creating more volatility for all financial markets.

Case study 4.2 Mexico's stock market: más Tequila Crisis?

The Mexican stock market is set up in similar ways to other equity exchanges around the world. It is called *Bolsa Mexicana de Valores* or *Bolsa* or BMV. Like the New York Stock Exchange (NYSE), BMV is also a publicly traded company. There are over 130 companies listed on the BMV, including firms such as *Wal-Mart de Mexico*, Coca-Cola and Citigroup. The BMV also trades indices that can also be underlying assets for derivatives. Bonds, commercial paper and government debt, including American government debt, are also traded. As with other markets, share prices for Mexican companies have volatile price movements. Much of this movement is tied to Mexico's macroeconomic conditions and world financial market volatility. In stark contrast to markets such as the NYSE or the Financial Times Stock Exchange (FTSE) in London, the BMV is in a relatively under-developed nation that may or may not be an emerging market. Mexico's equity market history has recent episodes of investor flight from this market to pursue other, more stable markets. Heavy volatility in the BMV is considered to have partially triggered the Tequila Crisis of 1995. This story also underscored the importance of the exchange rate in investor decisions about purchasing emerging market equities or debt.

In 1991, the Mexican peso was unified from having official and unofficial exchange rates to having a solitary rate. The Mexican economy experienced rapid inflation at the beginning of the 1990s and the fixed exchange rate to the dollar was constantly devalued to fight the peso's eroding value; in 1993, Mexico introduced a new peso worth one thousand old pesos. Throughout 1993, there was relative stability in the peso as the demand for both Mexican stocks, including both budding communications companies and short-term government debt at high yields, supported the peso's international demand. With the devalued peso demanded alongside Mexican stock by foreign investors, waning investor confidence was exacerbated as 1993 came to a close due to uncertainty over how sustainable recent corporate tax rate cuts were and whether lower energy prices would help the Mexican economy prosper. The passage of the North American Free Trade Agreement or NAFTA provided a short-term boost to Mexican stocks, but political issues coupled with growing economic problems made this euphoria short-lived.

In 1994, political problems in Mexico began a spiral that would be further derailed by the Mexican stock market's exposure to foreign investors, who could easily pull out of these investments and purchase assets in more stable environments such as the United States or Western Europe. As political assassinations and new elections heightened uncertainty about the Mexican economy, serious doubt was cast about the long-term profitability of Mexican companies. Initially, the demand for the Mexican peso began to fall and with it the peso's value. The Mexican government used foreign reserves to support the peso, but that strategy soon became a currency crisis that ended with a rapid devaluation of both the new peso's and the BMV's value. This collapse of foreign investor confidence in Mexico spread itself to other economies, most notably Argentina. The Argentinean economy closely resembled its Mexican counterpart in terms of political problems and lack of commitment to its currency value. Where 1995 was a difficult year for the BMV, 1996 was a recovery year; the 1995 crisis is now known as the "Tequila Crisis". Di Tella et al. (2005) provide a great case study of the crisis.

Since the late 1990s, the BMV has continued to follow the Mexican economy's movements. Since 1999, Mexico's economy has been relatively stable. The political change over to the *Partido Acción Nacional* or PAN party ushered in a crackdown on vice and corruption between 2000 and early 2008. Starting in late 2008 and into 2009, the Mexican economy began to falter and with it growth in socioeconomic unrest. Figure 4.1 shows the movement of the BMV's main index, IPC or *Indice de Precios y Cotizaciones*, which has 35 stocks within it. This is compared to the Dow Jones, NASDAQ and S&P 500 indices below since 2000. Notice the rise and fall versus the American stock indices since 2000, which was a peak year for the American indices.

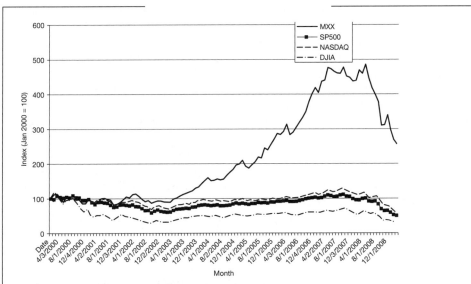

Figure 4.1 The BMV index compared to the DJIA, SP500 and NASDAQ 2000–Feb 2009.
Source: Yahoo! Finance, Accessed on 3 March 2009.

As can be seen, the Mexican stock market performed well through this decade, using the year 2000 as a starting point. This strong movement, and subsequent rapid decline, is probably a reflection of three issues. First is the political stability of Mexico; it began strong in this decade and is now eroding. Prosperity came with that relative stability, and now there is a two-pronged attack on Mexican stocks, as the political problems surrounding the drug trade, corruption and the domestic economy become unwound along with global recession. Second is how developed the Mexican economy really is; it began this decade seemingly emerging, and now has regressed. The peso's value is the third, and is likely to suffer versus the American dollar as Mexico attempts both fiscal and monetary policy supports for its economy. It will be another strange year for the Mexican stock market.

Summary

Equity markets are where financial investors purchase ownership in a firm or in a parcel of real estate, or finance a company via paid-in capital. Stocks are ownership certificates for corporations, and represent a share of a company. Common stocks are held by those seeking capital gains through prices rising and potential dividend income, where preferred stock is held by investors who want dividend income. Equity markets and their daily fluctuations are measured by indices, or some weighted average of stock prices in a specific portfolio of stocks. The Dow Jones Industrial Average and SP500 are two famous indices. The pricing of stock is similar to the pricing of bonds, as seen in Chapter 2. The investor assesses the risk of a specific stock, and seeks a nominal rate of return to cover against those risks and hopefully make a profit. The nominal rate of return discounts the future value of expected cash flows from the stock, the expected revenue from selling the security and expected dividend income. The present value of these expected cash flows represents the maximum price the investor is willing to pay to take on the risky return to the security.

The Capital Asset Pricing Model is a famous model of determining overall asset risk. This model adds a risk premium to the risk-free rate of return in financial markets based on historic characteristics of the average market return and the volatility of the asset in question versus the market's volatility. The more historically volatile the stock, for example, the larger the risk premium and thus the larger the expected nominal rate of return sought by the investor. Housing markets represent another capital asset purchase, and help investors diversify portfolios. The Modigliani-Miller Theorem and the Efficient Market Hypothesis both suggest that portfolio diversification may not matter in the long run, but taking risks will not improve the overall market.

Stock markets are volatile because investors must make expectations about cash flow and opportunity costs with a general lack of knowledge about the future. As compared with bonds, stock faces two categorical uncertainties: cash flows and asset-specific risks. The movement of both these expectations causes investors to constantly rethink portfolio allocations and risk exposure. Chapter 5 provides ways of insuring against that risk in derivative markets.

Key terms

1   Base period: the initial period in an index, usually normalized to equal one or 100.
2   Capital Asset Pricing Model (CAPM): a model that approximates the expected rate of return on an asset based on the asset's price history and the spread between the market's return overall and the return on a risk-free asset.
3   Commission: the percentage of a transaction paid to the broker or intermediary in the transaction.
4   Common stock: equity in a firm that has voting rights but not the right to receive dividends first.
5   Complements: goods, services or assets which are consumed together or whose cross-elasticity of demand is negative.
6   Denominator foundations: the present value discount factor, or the sum of the expected risks on a financial asset.
7   Dividends: the distributed retained earnings of a firm to its owners.
8   DJIA: the Dow Jones Industrial Average.
9   Income effect: the effect of a change in income on how two or more goods are consumed.
10 Mutual funds: financial assets that represent a pooling of other financial assets, usually a diversified pool of stocks and bonds.
11 NASDAQ: the National Association of Securities Dealers Automated Quotation system, an equity index.
12 Normal good: a good which experiences increasing demand when incomes rise.
13 Numerator foundations: the sum of the expected cash flows from an asset.
14 Preferred stock: equity in a firm which receives dividends first or accrues dividends when not paid at some rate of return.
15 Random walk: a random variable with a constant trend and deviations from the trend that are zero on average and have a constant variability; these are also known as unit root processes, where past values and trend dictate all the variables' movements on average.
16 Real Estate Investment Trust (REIT): a mutual fund made up of positions in real property.
17 Retained earnings: the earnings of the firm accumulated over time and not dispersed as dividends.

18 Securities brokers: financial intermediaries that specialize in providing investment services to purchase and sell financial securities.
19 SP500: the Standard and Poor's 500, an equity index.
20 Substitutes: goods, services or assets which are consumed as alternatives or whose cross-elasticity of demand is positive.
21 Value-weighted: weighting an index by the market value of its component parts.

Questions and problems

1 Explain why when the dividends paid by a firm increase, the firm's retained earnings fall.
2 What is the difference between a value and price-weighted index? Explain.
3 The stock price formula given in this chapter is simply a present value calculation. Explain that formula's meaning and an example result.
4 Explain why the stock price formula is specific to an investor and not a proxy for a market calculation.
5 Are stocks and bonds substitutes? Explain.
6 Are stocks and bonds complements? Explain.
7 Does a mutual fund spread or hedge risk? Explain.
8 What is the link between the consumption-based CAPM and risk aversion? Explain.
9 Explain the meaning of a random walk statistically.

Websites and suggested readings

Websites

Yahoo! has an easy-to-navigate finance page to investigate stocks:
  http://finance.yahoo.com.

Suggested reading

A Random Walk Down Wall Street, by Burton Malkiel (Norton, 2003), is a standard text for an overview of financial markets.

5 Derivative asset and insurance markets

Introduction

This chapter discusses what many consider a boring market (insurance) and a fun market (derivatives). Both markets have similar functions. Insurance policies are sold due to both legal requirements and financial prudence. Purchasing insurance reduces the risk exposure of insured parties from unexpected costs and events. For example, a home insurance policy protects against a fire consuming a home and the homeowner's belongings; the homeowner and insurance company have no idea whether a fire will break out in the home or the level of financial damage that will result. Further, neither party knows whether the homeowner will be culpable for a fire that leads to financial damage. Because humans are prone to error, insurance markets exist to minimize the risk of everyday life. Markets for insurance have sprung up for many unknowns, including alien abductions and earthquakes, regardless of how small the probability is of such future events occurring. The payment of an insurance premium provides incentives for insurance firms to "cover" another party against potential losses, sharing the risk by funding insurance over time. To the insured, the policy is a prepaid asset, used only under certain conditions. We see in certain examples below that insurance can be both a source of wealth and a prepaid asset simultaneously.

Investors can also insure themselves against lost profits or principal in financial investments. When investors own assets, they may not want exposure to large risks. For example, suppose an investor purchased Google (ticker: GOOG) stock at $280/share in 2005. The investor held GOOG and watched its value rise quickly over the next two years, making a profit on the stock price's appreciation. The investor realizes that remaining long in Google means an increased risk of losing some of those profits. The investor now may seek a way to insure the profits against a price decrease in Google. Financial futures, forwards and options are available for investors to enter a contract to exchange an asset at a certain date, price and quantity, ensuring a revenue or cost stream set contractually. Slight differences exist between futures and options markets, but both markets have the same basic mission: provide insurance against loss of profit in an asset, just like any insurance market. Speculation also occurs.

Derivative assets are financial instruments that derive their own value from an underlying asset's value. The value of a financial futures contract on GOOG will rise or fall as the current market value of GOOG rises or falls, depending on what type of futures contract it is, either a buy or sell contract. The basic details of these contracts are further discussed in this chapter. There are two key ideas that prevail throughout this chapter, acting as a mantra for budding financial economists to understand these markets:

- Insurance and derivative markets are built to reduce and not enhance risk, but must be used in a certain way to truly reduce risk

• There is always an opportunity cost with the choice to purchase insurance or enter a derivative asset contract

The next section lays the groundwork for understanding derivative markets, and we revisit classic insurance markets toward the end of this chapter. We see that classic insurance markets have similar principles to banking, providing a segue into Chapter 6's discussion of banking.

Derivative markets: commodity and financial futures

The first derivative markets insured against tulip harvest problems in the Netherlands in the late nineteenth century; there is also some evidence of futures markets in Japan around the same time.[1] Since 1975 in the United States, the Chicago Board of Trade (CBOE) has been a clearinghouse, much like the NYSE, for derivative asset transactions of all types. These markets were born from uncertainty in agricultural harvests, as farmers were willing to pay a transaction cost to enter a contract market with potential crop buyers before harvest to ensure the farmer's revenue stream.

Commodities futures

Commodity futures are contracts that oblige both sides of a transaction, buyer and seller, to purchase a tradable good (a commodity) at a certain date, price and quantity. Because of the uncertainty in agricultural harvests, contracts may contain quantity promises that could easily be invalidated. The legal aspects of the contract dictate what may happen if the terms are not fulfilled. Commodity forwards are non-standardized contracts that fit specific scenarios but use pricing information similar to the futures market, where futures are standardized contracts for set amounts of quantity at a certain time and price. For example, suppose a farmer tried to sell 1000 head of cattle using ten 100-head cattle futures contracts. If 375 of the cattle to be sold originally died, the farmer could sell four of the 100-head contracts to another cattle rancher and reduce the risk exposure in delivering the full 1000 head. In a forward contract, the farmer could agree to sell 1000, 625, or only 5 head of cattle, as long as there was a buyer on the other side flexible to the possible quantity level. Such flexibility would be written into the forward contract's terms because it is specific to two parties and not available on the open market otherwise.

There are four characteristics of futures and forwards we need to recognize. First, both sides are obliged to execute their side of the contract, or to sell their obligation to another party who then becomes obliged. Second, the contract price is determined by the supply and demand for the contracts versus the current spot market for the underlying commodity. Third, the date of contract execution (maturity date) is agreed to by both parties and generally not going to take place until that set date. It is possible, because a forward contract is not standardized, to add provisos concerning early execution where both parties agree to date flexibility; the contract price is partially a function of the distance to the execution date, which means date flexibility leads to some price flexibility. We learned in earlier chapters that the expected rate of return on assets should be an increasing function of time: the longer one holds an asset, the larger the expected rate of return from that asset. As investors wait longer periods, the risk rises for both sides. The fourth characteristic is that one side of the contract gains while the other side loses based on the fluctuations in the underlying asset's or commodity's spot market price. It is important to view this only from the perspective of the choice to enter the contract. Both may profit overall from either owning the underlying asset or from the contract, depending on the cost basis for each party. However, there is always an opportunity cost: one party's expectations were matched, while the other's was not. It is also possible that one party is hedging risk, which is the main function of the derivative markets.

Hedging or insuring against speculative risk

While futures and forwards sound speculative in general, these markets need not be speculative. Remember, we began this chapter by discussing insurance and the reduction of risk. The soybean farmer who enters a commodity futures contract on the "sell" side may be doing so to eliminate the risk in finding a market when the soybeans are harvested. Because the farmer is long in soybeans, the projected harvest of soybeans, the farmer may enter the contract to insure against price changes based on a large supply of soybeans coming onto the market during the harvest. The soybean customer, a tofu producer for example, enters the contract to ensure the soybean's acquisition cost. Because the tofu producer is going to buy soybeans one way or the other, the futures market may offer a better price than the current, expected spot price the date the contract is to be executed. The two sides of the contract have different viewpoints about the expected direction of market movements, which means one side is going to be wrong (assuming the future spot price is not exactly the same on the future or forward contract price).

From the farmer's perspective, the futures or forward contract acts as a hedge or insures against downward price movements by holding price at a contractually set level. The day the contract is agreed upon, the farmer knows the revenue to be received, assuming no contract violations. While the futures contract reduces some of the risk, it does not reduce it the entire way. Suppose soybean prices increased due to some general harvest problems, but did not affect this specific farmer. The farmer still delivered the appropriate amount of goods, but could have sold the soybeans on the spot market for more per unit. While the farmer still gained from executing the contract, the farmer could have made more profit. Thus, there is an opportunity cost. The tofu producer, in this scenario, makes an implicit gain if soybeans were purchased at the contract price if that price was lower than the spot market price the day the contract was executed. The implicit risks taken on both sides of this transaction reduce explicit risks. Without the contract, the farmer could have made more money, but may also have lost money. With the contract, the farmer is assured of a specific revenue stream, but is exposed to risks specific to the contract's value. The tofu producer faces the same problem concerning soybean acquisition costs in contract.

And a market is born. Financial futures and forwards work in similar ways. Instead of a physical asset, such as corn, soybeans, or gold as the underlying asset, financial derivative markets use stocks, bonds, funds, and other intangibles as underlying assets.

Case study 5.1 Weather derivatives

Can rainfall and the average temperature in a region or country be an underlying asset in derivatives contracts? There are markets for such contracts, called weather derivatives, where the entity writing the contract is attempting to hedge against an asset's value that is affected by unforeseen, adverse weather conditions (Speedwell 2009). For example, if a farmer's revenue is derived from crops that need a certain amount of rainfall to provide a full yield, the farmer can write a contract that protects against too little rainfall (or too much rainfall or both) reducing revenue. These contracts differ in many ways from insurance, as the weather derivative is not a contract based on the farmer's characteristics as much as on the farmer's belief about the weather in the farm's region. Insurance and hedging seem very similar on the surface, but insurance contracts are generally for low-probability events. One difficulty with weather derivatives is that there is no tradable, underlying asset. One cannot trade the rain, sunlight or snow. These contracts are structured much like option forwards, where the over-the-counter (OTC) markets trade the contracts; each contract is specialized or not a standard contract because each agreement is specific to the writer's needs and is an option where the entity seeking to cover themselves against adverse weather pays the premium to the entity assuming the opposite risk.

Each contract is unique because the underlying "asset" is usually an index specific to a region and a timeframe that suits the writer of the contract. The number of heating degree days (HDD) or the number of cooling degree days (CDD) can be an underlying asset, which are classic climate measures. HDD is the number of days that the average temperature is below 65 degrees Fahrenheit (18 degrees Celsius). The price for a weather derivative is typically calculated by adding the HDD values for a month and multiplying that sum by a certain amount based on how much coverage is expected by the option writer. There are multiple indices that calculate these degree days, and an example helps understand weather derivatives' uses.

For example, suppose Pacific Gas and Electric (PG&E), which is a provider of natural gas in California, is worried about the winter being unusually warm and thus the demand for natural gas will fall from current forecasts. PG&E can hedge against this outcome by purchasing a weather option which pays PG&E revenue in the event that the HDD in California exceeds the forecasts in a normal winter, assuming that HDD and natural gas demand are inversely related. Much like any other option, the option writer is hedging against the asset's value falling, where the "asset" in this case is the expected revenue from natural gas sales. If there are fewer HDD than expected, the contract pays nothing and PG&E loses their premium. If there are too many HDD, PG&E receives revenue from the party that received the premium and covers against lost natural gas revenue because homes were naturally warm.

The key problem is the pricing of these contracts because they lack a tradable asset underlying the deal. Because each contract is individually negotiated, the weather history and its volatility determine the contract value's variability and the option premium. The intriguing thing about these contracts is that the indices act in similar ways to financial assets. Following the Black-Scholes-Merton model, the volatility of weather can be used as a proxy for volatility in a stock price. Jarrow (1999) gives a great overview of this pricing with a relatively non-technical approach. This case suggests that acts of a higher power can lead to transactions of a higher order.

Financial derivatives

Suppose an investor held 100 shares of Costco (COST) common stock, and had purchased the stock at a cost basis of ten dollars per share. The stock price increases to 20 dollars per share, and the investor suddenly projects that the price will fall in a few months. To insure the ten dollars per share gain already in place (the difference between the current spot price and the investor's cost basis), the investor enters a financial futures transaction by contracting to sell 100 shares of COST at 20 dollars per share. Suppose further that a futures market existed for COST and 20 dollars per share was the current contract price. From the investor's perspective, they are guaranteed a ten-dollar per-share profit. Above we argued that this logic is somewhat faulty from an economic standpoint and is better seen as an accounting profit rather than economic profit of ten dollars. It is more important for now to recognize that the investor is insuring the accounting profit through two basic actions. First, the investor holds the underlying asset already at a cost of ten dollars per share (the long position). The contract (the short position), in the investor's mind, guarantees 20 dollars per share will be delivered for the 100 shares of XYZ, insuring the accounting profit of ten dollars. This mix of positions, holding the stock itself and a futures contract to sell the stock, is a "covered" position. The investor is covered against the risk of the stock's spot price falling; if the spot price of XYZ is greater on the day of the contract's execution, a larger gain by selling the stock on the spot market is possible, reducing the economic gain by executing the contract and selling at 10 dollars per share rather than a higher spot price. If the price of XYZ falls below 10 dollars, the loss in the spot market is made up through the contract. This is once again the insurance aspect of the derivative markets.

The example investor's complete position is a mix. From Chapter 3, being long in an asset means you own the asset. The investor owned the XYZ stock and wanted the price of XYZ to rise if that were the only position. Being short in an asset means the investor owes the asset to another party. In this case, engaging in the derivative contract on the sell side obligated the investor to sell to another party, in essence "owing" the other party 100 shares of XYZ for 10 dollars per share, regardless of the current market price of the stock. When the positions are mixed, a hedge takes place, as in the example above; when they are mixed perfectly, the positions are called a net zero or full-hedge position. The full-hedge position means the investor is exposed to zero risk, and thus zero gain from that point forward.

Once an investor chooses a net position, risk exposure is set by the position's price expectation. In certain circumstances, the investor may want to pay for the ability to walk away from the obligation otherwise in place with a derivative contract. Such a contract is priced in a similar fashion to other derivatives, but the payment to retain the right to execute or not execute the contract is an additional cost of a new derivative asset called an option.

Case study 5.2 Islamic interest and insurance: a different way of looking at finance

In Western financial markets, interest and insurance plays roles that market economists would say help markets work correctly. The role of interest is to penalize those who consume beyond their means, acting as the opportunity cost of that spending. Insurance is another aspect of opportunity cost; the insured entity is willing to pay for an asset now that they may never use, saving for an unknown event in the future. Insurance also makes markets work well by providing investors with a way to hedge against risk. Could the financial markets work the same way without these two attributes?

In Islam, where Islamic law dictates the way markets work, a concept known as *takaful* describes insurance. Chiu and Newberger (2006) provide a great overview. It is a community concept rather than an individual; *takaful* is pooled insurance where the common good is respected rather than wagering on uncertainty or looking at one's own profit possibilities in lieu of the group. Five simple elements of a *takaful system are*:

- there is no unlawful element of the contract;
- all business is conducted in good faith and with the common good in mind;
- cooperative risk sharing and mutual assistance are part of every transaction;
- a council exists to uphold these conditions and is appointed to ensure that business is done according to Islamic law; and
- Islamic law permeates every transaction.

Another difference from Western insurance is in terms of absolute insurance rather than relative measures of risk. In Western insurance, premiums are generally risk-specific; in Islamic insurance, the premium is the same for all similar transactions and there is a shared burden by all in the community who pool their funding to insure certain parties. Also, risk- and profit-sharing are foundations of Islamic insurance rather than a gamble by both sides as to when a financial calamity may befall the insured.

Concerning Islamic interest, there is a strong connection to the concepts of *takaful*. An essential feature of Islamic banking is that loans and accounts are interest-free. Interest payments are seen as a violation of Islamic law, as they are not in the common good by being potentially usurious. Islamic banking is about equitable wealth distributions rather than wealthy lenders charging interest and taking advantage of their wealth. Borrowers are seen as entering social rather than financial contracts for loans, which reduces the borrower's financial burden but increases social incentives to pay the loan back. It is this social pressure that acts like implicit insurance. Notice the connections to *takaful*. Profit-sharing acts as the alternative to competitive profits. The social contract in an Islamic loan is that the borrower shares income made in a cooperative way, and that sharing is a substitute for interest payments. The principal is paid back along with any profit-sharing for all who gave to the loan.

We assume that Western banking involves an individual person or entity that charges interest to make a profit throughout this text. The concept of profit-sharing is not completely at odds with Western banking, especially for publicly held financial institutions that pay dividends on a regular basis. The idea of charging interest is to compensate investors for opportunity costs. Profit-sharing can be analogous to interest where the opportunity cost is partially paid through the sense of community. The fundamental difference is the concept of community in terms of not holding the individual accountable for debts. Assuming the borrower acted in good faith with the loan, the lending entity pools that risk among community members with a motive of equitable distribution of income instead of profit maximization.

Islamic finance prevails in many countries, and many Western banks have recognized its growing significance worldwide. There are banks opening branches that focus on Islamic financial transactions or have Islamic windows at banks that are for *takaful* transactions (Islamic Bank of Britain 2009). Had the world used Islamic finance more comprehensively, could the financial downturn of 2007 and beyond been mitigated or avoided?

Things to remember

Futures and forwards are similar contractual arrangements to trade a financial asset or a commodity where both sides of the transaction are obliged to execute the contract. The contract stipulates the price, quantity and timing for the transaction.

The options markets: futures with initial cash outflow

An options contract is similar to a futures contract with one small twist. The investor that wants the contract to happen "buys" or "writes" the option and must pay the other party an option premium. This payment represents two characteristics of the transaction. First, the option premium releases the option buyer from the obligation faced in a futures or forward contract. As discussed previously, a futures or forward contract obliges both parties to make transactions, while the option provides just that: an option to execute the contract. Second, the option premium represents the opportunity cost of entering the contract from the other side. The party that received the option premium as payment receives cash in advance of the actual transaction, and must consider that payment a reduction of loss if the option is executed. The premium's value is determined by a mix of data, known as the options pricing formula. Three economists, Fisher Black, Myron Scholes and Robert Merton, all provided seminal contributions to the construction of this pricing formula. The three main components are the expected volatility of the underlying asset, the rate of return on a government debt security of equal length to the option, and the time to option expiration. Before we explore how these components affect the option premium, we need some more definitions of the options market.

Calls versus puts

There are two categorical ways to buy an option. The first is a call option, where the buyer of the option seeks to purchase the underlying asset in the contract. The put option is where the option buyer seeks to sell the underlying asset. For example, if a farmer wanted to sell soybeans and use an option, the farmer would buy put options on soybeans that "expire" in the month of projected sale. If an investor forecasted that the value of Costco stock (COST) would rise, the investor might want to buy a call option for 100 shares of COST at an expiration date of two months for a certain "strike" price. If COST rose as predicted, the investor would hopefully purchase COST shares at a price lower than the spot market in two months and then could sell the stock immediately on the spot market for a profit. An options contract can be executed at different dates from contract to contract and market to market. European options expire on a specific date; the decision to execute or not is made on that date. An American option is one where the contract may expire at any time, which is up to the option buyer. The buyer may decide the day after the contract begins to execute or may wait until the expiration date. These ways to construct an option's contract terms change the risk characteristics of both sides, and thus the ultimate contract price.

Pricing the option premium

If the underlying asset's volatility is relatively high, the option premium will rise in value depending on the volatility's direction. If the strike price is higher than the underlying asset's current market price, call options will have lower premiums and put options will have higher premiums; the reverse is true if the strike price falls. This is a reflection of the market's perceived risk in the contract. The higher the strike price is, the less risk to the seller of the underlying asset. In the put option, the reverse is true. At relatively high strike prices, the buyer of a put is at less risk and the party receiving the premium is at more risk, which demands a higher premium. If the rate of return on government debt rises, the premium rises in all contracts. Simply put, investors who would otherwise receive option premiums have fewer incentives to engage in those contracts versus investing in an asset that is considered risk-free. To entice the other side, the option buyer must pay more. Finally, the longer the expiration date is into the future from the current time period, the higher the option premium. The unknown makes waiting more risky, and the other party would seek compensation for that risk.

Options which expire sooner are less risky, and thus also have lower premiums than relatively longer-term options. The only caveat to that is for American versus European options. An American option is less risky to the option buyer because the option buyer controls both the choice to execute and timing of contract execution. For that second loss of control, the other party will seek compensation. Like futures contracts, an option's strike price is determined in a market setting. Multiple strike prices are available at different premiums. In sum, the more risky the contract is to the option buyer, the smaller the option premium. Table 5.1 contrasts and compares calls and puts.

Things to remember

Options are also contractual arrangements to trade a financial asset or a commodity. In this case, the party that writes the contract, or pays the option premium, has the right to execute while the other side of the transaction remains obliged. The contract stipulates the price, quantity and timing for the transaction.

Profiting on derivative assets

The making of profit in these markets is similar regardless of the market used. The costs are different for options markets because of the premium. We begin with the futures and forwards markets and then look at options.

Making profit in futures and forwards

Assuming the investor is speculating and not hedging, where profit is explicitly sought by the investor, profits are made as in any other transaction: revenue derived is larger than cost. However, the way futures and options profit is not as explicit as producing a good or providing a service. Profit is made in both implicit and explicit ways, the sum of which is the economic profit or loss. Suppose a farmer has costs of $100/bushel of delivering wheat to

Table 5.1 Calls vs. puts

Calls	*Puts*
Buyer intends to purchase underlying asset	Buyer intends to sell underlying asset
Buyer wants underlying asset to rise in current market price	Buyer wants underlying asset to fall in current market price

market, and enters sell contracts for wheat at $110/bushel for 1000 bushels. This futures contract is executable in two months. On the surface, the farmer will make $10/bushel or a total of $10,000 on the transaction. There are three additional costs the farmer must take into account. First are commissions. There will probably be transactions fees for the farmer to purchase the futures contract, and possibly to execute the contract. Suppose that the commission is two percent of the contract price, payable when the contracts are executed; suppose that there are 10 contracts at 100 bushels each for $110/bushel. This reduces the accounting profit to $7.80/bushel.

There is a second cost. The cost of waiting two months for the delivery of revenue means that the present value of that revenue must be compared to the present value of the costs to truly reflect the cost of time for engaging in this contract. If the farmer has already paid for the wheat, the revenue must be discounted. That will reduce the revenue from an economic standpoint, reducing the present value of the profits. A third cost is other opportunity costs in sum. Suppose the harvest goes exactly as planned for the farmer. However, the price of wheat falls and the contract price is higher that the market price in two months. Not only did the farmer make an accounting profit, but also extended that profit by choosing to use the contract to deliver the same amount of revenue that was otherwise not available on the spot market. The spot market for wheat, assume it was at a price of $105/bushel, still delivered an accounting profit, but not as much as the contract. On the other hand, suppose the spot price of wheat was $115/bushel instead. The farmer still has an accounting profit through the contract, but could have made more had the wheat been sold on the spot market instead. This is the insurance aspect of the futures/options markets. Since the farmer did not know what the future spot price would be, the contract insured against loss; by reducing the risk, it also reduced the potential gain.

In an options contract, however, the farmer buying wheat put contracts could have let the contracts go unexecuted, depending on how much the option premium was in the first place. The option premium is meant to compensate the party that may lose profit based on the option buyer's gain and subsequent choice to execute the contract. This is where the option is different from the futures/forward contract, based on the same foundations. There is a fourth cost, income taxes. Of course, this cost only exists if a profit is made.

Interest-rate swaps

Banks may use interest-rate swaps to change their risk exposure to adjustable interest rates. Suppose a bank has assets that pay revenue from fixed interest rate contracts, conventional mortgage loans. Further, suppose that the bank has costs based on variable-rate savings and money-market mutual fund accounts, such that costs change as interest rates rise and fall. The bank is better off in periods of falling interest rates and exposed to more risks as interest rates rise. Another bank may have the reverse problem, where revenues are based on adjustable-rate mortgages and costs are based on fixed-rate deposits.

These banks may find it advantageous to swap assets or liabilities to reduce their mutual exposure to interest rate changes. Through matching the principal exposed to interest rate fluctuations, the banks can match a certain percentage of their portfolio to similar interest rates. This principal, called notional principal, determines the "quantity" of dollars to be exchanged. The swap's value depends on the interest rate being paid on this notional principal. Both banks must agree to the swap, which implies that both banks must assume they individually gain from the transaction.

For both banks, the main advantage of such a transaction is to reduce risk and thus to reduce potential losses on both sides. Much like other derivative assets, banks would seek

Figure 5.1 The typical swap between depository institutions.

to hedge against the interest rate risk they face when they lend or fund themselves through liabilities such as deposits or loans. It is possible for a bank to speculate using swaps, where the bank may forecast adjustable rates rising and can take advantage of rising net interest margin for profit by trading fixed-rate for adjustable-rate assets. The primary problem with swaps is the potential default of assets purchased by either party. Figure 5.1 illustrates the typical swap between financial institutions.

Credit-default swaps: a bridge to insurance[2]

In the financial morass of 2007 to the time of this writing, one financial instrument that received a lot of press is the credit-default swap. Its name makes it sound like a variation on the swap described above. However, it is more like insurance than trade of assets and liabilities based on their interest rate structures. The credit-default swap is insurance paid by the owner of corporate debt to insure against default. In many ways it is like a long-term put contract, where an insurance premium is paid to a company, such as AIG, to buffer against risky lending. As a result of this financial innovation, many banks and investment firms were willing to lend in risky ways, where lenders could partially offset the swap's cost by augmenting the loan contract's rate. This allowed a further increase in lending, particularly risky lending, where the lender was not exposed to the risk directly because they, in a sense, held both a long and a short position in the loan. If the loan paid for the insurance premiums, the lender made a small profit while not exposed to default risk. Insurance companies wagered that defaults or losses would not happen in large magnitudes and simultaneously, which unfortunately did take place in 2007 and 2008. This is one way that derivative markets and insurance are very similar.

How insurance works

Insurance and insurance companies have been around for centuries. The market for such policies is similar to that for derivative assets in the way they are used. In the derivative markets described above, the purchase of a derivative asset changed the investor's position in the underlying asset. Life, auto, health, and casualty insurance in general (yes, even alien abduction or earthquake insurance) are similar instruments. Your life is not only your asset, but is also an asset to your family if you are a potential source of household income and wealth. Many people purchase life insurance because they do not know when they will die and want to provide for their family posthumously. Auto insurance insures the value of your car and your financial assets in case of an accident where you, another driver and potentially both cars are damaged. Health insurance protects your financial assets if you become ill, insuring you against a rising cost of health care or a health situation that is beyond your means to pay. General casualty insurance, insurance against an unforeseen event that causes the insurance holder a loss of financial assets, protects against that loss. The insurance itself is held as a policy, a description of coverage and amounts covered.

The insurance premium paid on a policy is the cost to hedge against a future financial calamity. This premium is similar to the options premium above; the insurance premium reflects opportunity costs; the premiums are how insurance companies hedge against the policyholder's riskiness, the risk the company faces in having to pay out on a policy. A market is formed as the insurance buyer is seeking to reduce the risk of unforeseen events and is willing to pay for that now without knowing the present value of losses later. The insurance company sells insurance assuming that the premiums paid on average will not exceed the average payout plus the policy's administrative costs.

Insurance markets for this reason are very interesting economically, and are very similar to commercial and investment banking. The model of the insurance firm with regard to profit is very simple. Suppose the Eagle Insurance Corporation (EIC) provided four types of insurance: home, life, auto and health. In each type of insurance, EIC wants to make a profit from every policy. EIC knows it will not, thus it must diversify insured parties by using certain characteristics. In doing so, the insurance company intends to make a profit on the average policy: for every additional dollar of insurance premium revenue, the additional cost of insuring that policy is less. EIC has economic incentives to continuing seeking clients until those revenues and costs are the same for the next policyholder insured.

Risk assessment is one of the most difficult tasks the insurance company faces. Actuaries assess the risk of potential clients and help price policies. Each insurance policy is a little different in how risk is assessed; but for each type the way the insured party can be risky is intuitive. For example, if you have been injured sky diving, your health, life and auto insurance may all rise because you now have a history of taking physical risks. Just like any other market, insurance companies face elasticity of demand issues in pricing and cannot arbitrarily set the price higher to receive more revenue. The policyholder's riskiness allows the insurance company to assess their elasticity of demand and engage in price discrimination. The insurance company charges different premiums to different policyholders based on their specific risk characteristics.

Theory suggests that the insurance company can increase profits by price discriminating, as those policyholders who are more risky have more to lose and are willing to pay a higher premium because they are inelastically demanding insurance (not responsive to premium changes in the insurance they demand because for them there are few substitutes). For example, life insurance may have different premium charges depending on the policyholder's age; older clients would pay more for life insurance because they are statistically closer to death. The insurance amount and current health status are also part of the risk assessment. The premium does not completely compensate for risk if risk is assessed incorrectly. When an insurance company assesses risk, it is apt to make mistakes based on a lack of information about the future. This asymmetry in information is a driving force in pricing insurance and in economics generally.

Asymmetric information in insurance markets

In the history of economic thought, one of the major splits among economists has been the use and availability of information by each side of a transaction. In Adam Smith's writings, his ideas implied a free flow of information in markets where price delivered all the necessary information. This became the basis for "Classical" economists who came after him to use such models to explain the dynamics and consequences of market activity. This assumption of perfect information helped economists to explain that market volatility was simply a transition from one "long-run" outcome to the next. For example, one could argue that recessions are times when consumers or producers lack information about the other, and they make their adjustments, the information becomes clear by their actions, and the economy surges toward the long run again during the subsequent boom period.

There are many, most notably John Maynard Keynes, who have argued that the assumption of perfect information does not work. His followers, named "Keynesians", suggested that if a lack of perfect information existed and persisted in markets, the long-run economic outcomes promised by Classical economics may never be achieved and should not be seen as a policy goal. Since the Great Depression of the 1930s (there were depressions before the 1930s as well, just none quite as large), there has been wide acceptance of a lack of perfect information that persists, regardless of market actions, which has become a foundation in economic theory, specifically in finance.

The insurance markets are a great place to apply the concepts of asymmetric information. Transactions with asymmetric information provide an advantage to the party with more information than the other. That information advantage represents a profit opportunity. For example, suppose you wanted to buy a used car. You meet the private party selling the car, a friend of the family. You look at the car, you drive the car, you listen to the sound system; you are very pleased. You ask how much the car is worth and you are told $5000. You perceive this to be a good deal, and you accept that offer. The next day when you pick up the car, it runs fine. Five days later, the car fails to start, and you find out it will cost $2000 to fix. It is possible the family friend had no idea that the car was about to fail. When you take the car into the repair shop, the mechanic tells you this car has been in a flood, and the electrical system will also fail very soon. He says you are lucky you did not die in a fiery car accident.

When buying a used car, the seller has an information advantage over the buyer. First, the seller knows the car, its tendencies and its history, at least while they own the vehicle. Second, the seller has incentives not to tell you everything about the car because that will increase the risk you face in purchasing the vehicle, which reduces the potential revenue from the sale. Regardless of the ethics, this incentive is the key to asymmetric information in markets. The incentive is profit, as always. There are two problems that a lack of perfect information about the future creates for insurance markets.

Adverse selection

Adverse selection is an information problem that refers to the buyer's screening process. In insurance markets, this problem can be seen in one of two ways. The first is to see it from the perspective of the insurance policy buyer. When shopping for car insurance, the buyer has myriad choices. Each company is about the same in price, deductible, and coverage. However, it is unknown how the insurance company will react to claims, call you back if help is needed, and change premium rates versus other companies. The buyer faces the problem of potentially choosing the wrong firm and receiving a "lemon" in return. Much like when a buyer goes to the used car market, some cars are lemons and some are not, even if they are the same price. For this reason, contrary to Classical economics, price may not carry all the information about markets to buyers and sellers. This problem was described by Nobel Prize-winning economist George Akerlof at the University of California, Berkeley.[3] Another application, one we will follow from here, is that insurance companies may face a problem in choosing potential clients. Insurance companies face the problem of not being able to screen good insurees from bad. For example, suppose you were an insurance agent and someone called you about buying a car insurance policy. You would want to know their driving record, criminal record if one existed, income level, family situation, age, and other details that may help assess the risk your company faces in providing this person with an insurance policy. You will never be able to ask all of the questions you need to completely or perfectly assess the risk. For that reason, you will not assess the information or have an ability to screen good from bad insurees perfectly. However, you will also struggle in separating them based on raising premiums. The insurance company cannot simply raise insurance premiums and price risk perfectly based on each insurer having different elasticities of demand. Insurance companies do price risk based on defined criteria, but on the market as a whole the insurance company cannot raise insurance premiums and spread that risk to good drivers. The good drivers will not buy the car insurance, unless legally bound to do so, if the premium is too high. This leaves only the bad drivers in the pool of potential insurance clients or those who inelastically demand insurance.

Moral hazard

Unfortunately, the adverse selection problem is not the only problem facing insurance companies. Once insurance is provided and the newly insured driver leaves the insurance office, the insurance company faces another information problem. Even if the insuree was deemed a "good" risk by the company's screening process, the insured driver may become a risky driver as soon as the insurance is provided. Moral hazard is defined as an incentive problem. The provision of insurance may skew the insured's incentives away from being a good driver to become less of a good driver based on the sharing of risk with the insurance company. It is now less costly to drive like a race car driver when insured, which implies profit to be made.

The inability of both the insurance company and the insured driver to predict the future leads to the moral hazard problem. The driver cannot know their own probability of an accident with certainty, only their own ability to avoid that accident as well as possible. Further, even actuarial tables cannot be perfectly certain; any change in driver riskiness that deviates from the actuarial assumptions leads to more risk for the insurance company. That risk will be internalized and spread among all insured drivers, increasing premiums for all; this is the market reaction of the insurance firms to this risk to reduce their own risk and force drivers to share in that burden. An expansion on both moral hazard and adverse selection takes place later in the book in the context of lending.

Things to remember

There are two information problems related to any transactions in which uncertainty about the outcome exists.

- Adverse selection is a problem of screening, or an inability to filter good risks (more likely to profit) from bad risks (less likely to profit) perfectly.
- Moral hazard is an incentive problem, or an inability to know with certainty how another party's incentives may change toward fulfilling their side of a transaction.

Summary

When hedging against uncertain financial outcomes, investors use derivatives and insurance markets. The future, forward and option markets are very similar. These are contract markets which set the date, price and quantity of trade for an underlying asset. The value of the contract, regardless of its form, derives its value from the underlying asset's price movements. If the contract becomes more profitable, the contract's value rises; if the contract's profitability falls, the contract's value follows. In the futures and forward markets, the contracts represent an obligation to each party involved. To remove your obligation, you must sell the contract to someone else; the profitability of that sale and the incentives to walk away from the contract depend on the contract's value as described above. An options contract, where an option premium is paid initially to reserve the right to execute the contract, provides more flexibility. The option premium pricing is based on the risk-free rate of return, the historic volatility of the underlying asset and the length of time to contraction expiration. The decision to execute the option contract or not depends on the spot market price of the underlying asset, and whether that spot market price allows some recovery of the option premium. If some of the option premium can be recovered, an incentive exists to execute to minimize loss. If none of it can be recovered, incentives exist to not execute to also minimize loss. Call contracts are controlled by the buy side of the option, while puts are controlled by the sell side. Interest rate swaps are another type of derivative market, where banks trade cost and revenue portfolios for each other to "swap" interest rate streams. The swap's value depends on the variability of interest rates within the cost or revenue streams traded. If interest rate volatility is upward, cost streams are less valuable and revenue streams are more valuable; the reverse is true for volatility downward.

Insurance markets are like derivative asset markets in that insurance policies (contracts) are valued based on the assets they protect. An insurance premium is paid by the policyholder, which is the cost of risk reduction against unseen future costs, such as a car accident or a fire in one's home. A combination of policyholder statistics and actuarial tables that include demographic statistics and probabilities of claims based on the policyholder's characteristics determines the premium value. Two problems of asymmetric information exist when providing insurance, called adverse selection and moral hazard. Adverse selection is a screening problem. A risk the insurance company faces is not having 100% of the necessary information to separate good from bad risks. Moral hazard is an incentive problem. Once the insuree is provided insurance, the insurance company takes a further risk because it does not have 100% of the information about the insuree's incentives toward risking the assets insured once insured. This issue of asymmetric information comes up later in our course, and is considered by most economists to be the genesis of any profits available on financial markets. Banking is one of those markets, the subject of Chapters 6 and 7.

Key terms

1 Actuary: a job which defines the riskiness in providing insurance to a firm and helps price insurance premiums.
2 Adverse selection: a screening problem in a transaction.
3 American option: an option contract in which the option writer (the party which paid the premium) can execute the contract at any time before the expiration date.
4 Asymmetric information: a condition in which one side of a transaction has more information than the other side.

5   Call option: an option contract in which the side buying the underlying asset pays the other side the option premium and retains the right to execute the contract.
6   European option: an option contract in which the option writer (the party which paid the premium) can execute the contract on the expiration date.
7   Execution date: the date at which a futures or forward contract matures.
8   Expiration date: the date at which an options contract matures.
9   Moral hazard: an incentive problem in a transaction.
10 Option premium: the amount paid by the writer of an option contract to the side which remains obliged to fulfill the contract terms.
11 Price discrimination: the ability to charge two different prices for the same good or asset at the same time, sometimes in two different markets.
12 Put option: an option contract in which the side selling the underlying asset pays the other side the option premium and retains the right to execute the contract.
13 Screening process: the process by which one side of a transaction attempts to reduce the adverse selection problem.
14 Strike price: the price of the underlying asset inside an options contract.
15 Swap: a derivatives contract where the two sides trade interest-bearing securities, usually fixed interest rate securities for those that pay or cost-variable interest rate flows.

Questions and problems

1   Explain the differences between a futures and an options contract.
2   Provide a numerical example of making an economic profit from the use of a futures contract.
3   Provide a numerical example of making an economic profit from the use of an options contract.
4   Explain how a derivative asset can act as "insurance" for losses from the spot price of a financial asset or commodity changing.
5   Explain the economic meaning of the option premium.
6   Should the option premium rise or fall with the time to expiration for an option? Explain.
7   Should the option premium rise or fall with larger volatility in the underlying asset's spot price? Explain.
8   Explain why two banks would engage in a swap.
9   Explain why an insurance market exists.
10 Explain why a driving record helps reduce the asymmetric information problems in providing insurance.
11 Define and provide examples of adverse selection and moral hazard in insurance.

Websites and suggested reading

Websites

These are major American exchanges for derivatives:
American Stock Exchange (AMEX): http://www.amex.com/
Chicago Mercantile Exchange (MERC): http://www.cme.com/
New York Mercantile Exchange: http://www.nymex.com/index.aspx

Suggested readings

Akerlof, George (1970) "The market for lemons: quality uncertainty and the market mechanism", *Quarterly Journal of Economics*, 84 (3), 488–500.

An encyclopedic text on derivative markets, albeit with a lot of mathematics, is MacDonald, Robert (2003) *Derivative Markets* (Prentice Hall).

6 Financial intermediaries

Introduction

Banking is a precarious business. Under certain conditions, banks could lend out more than they should, and shift the risk of their own lending practices onto the depositors which use banks to ironically reduce risk. Imagine a situation where a depository institution (commercial banks, savings banks, savings and loan associations, and credit unions) lent out all its depositor's funds. If any of these loans defaulted, some depositors would lose money. Banks make money from depositors remaining confident that the bank understands its own risk, is diversified against major shocks affecting its ability to provide liquidity, and has a borrower pool that supports the bank's strategic goals concerning profit.

In the United Kingdom, a bank called Northern Rock was the center of much controversy when a bank run took place in September 2007. Bank depositors lined up to withdraw their money from the failing bank, and Northern Rock became the first bank in many years, for its size, to have such a problem. Northern Rock was not exposed to subprime mortgage risk from the United States, but had an overexposure to financial leverage in providing mortgages in the UK. As central banks began to tighten credit and force banks to borrow from interbank markets, due to a lack of good information about the riskiness of the banking industry, Northern Rock found its source of low-cost funds suddenly demanded by larger banks that had also exposed themselves to higher risks and were willing to pay a slightly higher interest rate to reduce the threat of insolvency. Northern Rock happened to be caught in the middle, and their depositors became further exposed.[1]

Countrywide Mortgage is a large lending brokerage; Countrywide was the United States' largest mortgage lender in 2007. It engaged in lending to subprime, alt-a, and other high-risk mortgage markets. As the American housing market began to turn downward in 2007, adjustable-rate mortgages began to rise in cost for borrowers. Many of the loans had so-called "teaser" rates, low fixed rates for a short number of years that began to rise with market rates after an introductory period. Many of these loans follow the LIBOR rate, which increased simultaneously with the housing price downturn. The rising number of home foreclosures combined with natural market pressure on the number of houses for sale to rise, causing even lower expectations of these markets and more housing units to come up for sale.

Countrywide, as had many other financial institutions in the United States and Europe, converted housing markets into derivative markets where mortgages (and the houses that collateralized them) drove a secondary market for bundled loans. Banks and financial institutions further speculated on a housing boom without having to find new real estate. However, as the forces of foreclosures and market cycles began simultaneously, so did the illiquidity of these mortgage-based securities. As these securities became illiquid, financial institutions stopped buying bundled mortgages from banks. The links between investment and commercial banks came to the forefront of economic news and potential economic problems.

Financial intermediaries are businesses like any other. This chapter focuses on the basics of these firms, starting with depository-based banking and then on to financial institutions such as investment banks. The differences between thrifts and commercial banks as depository institutions are also discussed, with a focus on credit unions, the possible future of all banking. A discussion of banking risk, in pursuit of net interest margin, concludes the chapter. This chapter provides a qualitative analysis of financial institutions while Chapter 7 is more theoretical. We begin with banks as businesses.

Businesses that inventory money

Financial intermediaries are categorized two ways. The first is a depository institution, where customer deposits are taken and used by the institution to make revenue, generally from lending deposits. Depository institutions are borrowers and fiduciaries of the depositors, liable for the liquidity of depositor funds. If the bank fails to provide the depositor with liquidity, legal issues are the least of the bank's troubles. Bank runs and possibly panics happen due to such inabilities. Further, depository institutions share the risk of deposits with the customer. The depositor has money in the bank, and the bank lends money. The depositor risks the money being lost due to the bank's inability to function correctly and the bank is liable. Non-depository institutions do not share that risk with their customers. These institutions are true financial intermediaries, charging a fee for their services as the customer takes all the financial risks. The customer still provides funding to these institutions, but the "deposits" are either not liquid outside a specific event taking place or have large liquidity costs.

Both depository and non-depository institutions use financial leverage to generate profit. The use of customer funds, in any form, allows the financial institution to invest in markets with expected higher rates of return in such a way as to gain from a spread on the initial costs. This spread is the focus of all financial institutions, and is called different names in different markets. However, each institution described below has the goal of achieving the largest spread. Let's begin with the quintessential depository institution, the commercial bank.

Depository institutions

Commercial banking

Banks promise security for depositors and sometimes an explicit rate of return. Without an explicit rate of return, the promise of security provides an implicit rate of return. Commercial banking has its roots in business banking, providing liquidity and business services for firms first and foremost. Commercial banks have expanded beyond business customers to household deposits to be lucrative sources of both funding and new business for banking products. The credit card industry, for example, grew as a result of a larger proportion of households taking advantage of offers made by banks to establish personal lines of credit. These lines of credit evolved into the credit card industry we know today. However, banks are ultimately focused on drawing in funding and sell other banking services and deposits to business and household customers. These include interest-bearing accounts, such as certificates of deposit, and other investment vehicles that are considered low risk and provide low-cost funding for banks.

Savings banks and savings and loan associations

The thrift industry, composed of depository institutions that focus on household deposits and lending to households, has generally been split into two submarkets. The first is savings banks and savings and loan associations (S&Ls). A savings bank looks a lot like a commercial bank in structure. The large difference is that time deposits (interest-bearing accounts of all types), rather than demand deposits (checking accounts of all types), are the funding basis of savings banks and S&Ls. Further, a savings bank directs its lending efforts toward households rather than business lending. The emphasis in thrifts is placed on time deposits; savings banks face a smaller spread based on cost of funding versus the commercial bank. Through the 1990s, savings banks struggled against the expansion of commercial banking into household markets, and as a result diversified their deposit offerings and access to liquidity to look more like a commercial bank. Because savings banks emphasize time deposits, they can better forecast the customer's liquidity needs, and use that timing to gain slightly larger spreads.

Savings and loan associations are similar to savings banks with one large difference. Instead of being available to the public, S&Ls are funded by members. The members are the S&L's customers and their borrowers. S&L members are provided a rate of return on interest-bearing accounts higher than that of competing savings or commercial banks, and the rate on borrowing is lower than competing institutions. S&Ls survive on member loyalty; members look within the S&L for the majority of their banking needs and may stay with a lower net rate of return because of customer service or connections to the institution. The member pool of funds can also be invested elsewhere, and many S&Ls are run similarly to non-profit organizations and credit unions.[2]

Credit unions

Credit unions have become very popular in the last 25 years, and have expanded beyond their original focus on employee banking within a single firm. In representing these employees, a credit union would simply pay for itself and not profit from the employees' needs. Credit unions are considered non-profit organizations for this reason, generally a service-providing subsidiary of a firm or industry. Many of a credit union's functions are the same as those of a commercial bank. The credit union accepts household and business deposits, and provides full liquidity services, as well as interest-bearing accounts, and products that directly compete with other depository institutions. Credit unions also provide investment services for their members.

There is much furor in the United States over the regulatory environment in which credit unions operate. Commercial banks look at credit unions as major competitive threats, especially in regional markets where credit unions thrive. Credit unions must provide the same basic cost and revenue advantages for its members as an S&L or savings bank in competition with the commercial bank. One of the cornerstone arguments commercial banks have against the credit union remaining outside the regulatory walls is the non-profit status of these firms.[3]

Depository institutions all have one thing in common: they hold deposits. Investment banks and other financial institutions do not hold deposits, but manage client assets in other forms.

Case study 6.1 Polish credit unions

To provide some perspective on how credit unions work internationally, Poland's credit union industry is an intriguing case study. Two components make it somewhat unique in Europe. First, as a former Communist country, its market economy is still developing and only since 1992 has there been any financial market activity that would allow credit union or commercial banking growth generally. Second, the movement is very strong and an appeal to the religious aspects of Polish life was a driving force in the industry's growth. In 1992, Poland received a grant from the US Agency for International Development (USAID) to begin the construction of a post-Communism banking system. The World Council on Credit Unions (WOCCU) provided assistance for these new firms as well as in structuring of Poland's credit unions.

The number of credit union members in Poland grew from only 14,000 in 1992 to over one million in 2004 served by over one hundred credit unions (World Council on Credit Unions, 2004). A national association of cooperative savings and credit unions was established to monitor and regulate this industry in Poland. There is also a mutual insurance society that protects deposits in the event of a financial downturn as well as classic insurance products otherwise. There are investment-banking functions that parallel bank deposit functions of these credit unions. For many of Poland's citizens, credit unions became a way to be introduced to banking in a market setting. Because a credit union is a mutual banking system, credit union members share and pool risk. The Polish government took the lead from Western markets and stood out of the way as these institutions grew. These firms are fully integrated with each other, using the same software to track funds and provide customer service; this characteristic makes job and deposit mobility from one credit union to another very easy within Poland.

As discussed in Chapter 6, the requirements to become a credit union member in the United States are less stringent; it has become easier to be a member in the United States. In Poland, one must belong to an "association" before becoming a credit union member. There are two major categories. As a reflection of Catholicism's dominance in Poland, a member of a "Catholic Family Association" can join a credit union. If someone is not of the Catholic faith, they can join a credit union if they are members of an association that focuses on financial literacy and knowledge. In either case, credit unions in Poland attempt to help impoverished citizens by providing services and access to financial markets otherwise not available from the commercial banking industry. There is even a publishing firm that disseminates literature to credit union members about finance and banking.

While credit unions in the United States are non-profit organizations for tax purposes, they act in many ways as for-profit businesses. Markets demand that characteristic of credit unions. In a country such as Poland, where the economy reset itself in 1992, the nascent efforts of both international philanthropy and a well-designed system based on providing financial services, education and tools to many households otherwise barred from using them is a model for financial institutions worldwide, especially in developing countries. Table 6.1 shows statistics published by WOCCU about the Polish Credit Union market:

Table 6.1 Polish credit union industry summary as of 2007

Credit unions: 67
Members: 1,668,555
Penetration rate: 6.07% (% of credit union members of population)
Savings (US$): 2,738,952,522
Loans (US$): 2,102,003,618
Reserves (US$): 186,758,452
Assets (US$): 2,983,529,442

Source: WOCCU (http://www.woccu.org/memberserv/intlcusystem/icus_country?region=EU&c=PL).

Non-depository institutions

Investment banking

The word "bank" is used here because a client of the investment bank has "deposits" in the form of assets managed by the firm, but the assets lack the same liquidity as commercial bank deposits. In modern investment banks, liquidity is provided by investment banks in conjunction with a depository institution. Investment banks are also known as brokerages, as they act as a "broker" for the purchase of financial investments. Some investment brokerages include: JP Morgan Chase, Goldman Sachs, Deutsche Bank, Credit Suisse First Boston, and Barclay's Capital. Investment banking has two large sectors. The first is financial advising, classic brokerage. The client relationship here is in asset allocation, investment strategy and asset management. The second is underwriting, or funding of publicly traded companies and other commercial financing activities of the investment bank.

At no time is the investment bank at risk for the client's principal, apart from any illegal practices. The firm's financial advisors act as agents of their clients in an attempt to maximize client wealth. Each transaction, regardless of the client buying or selling, is charged a fee or commission. The investment bank also finds revenue in the spread between their cost of funds and the rate of return they can leverage on the open market. Investment banks are in many ways just like a commercial bank in the way they seek profits. Suppose an investor provides $10,000 in funding to the investment bank. The investment bank will assign a financial advisor to this client, and the $10,000 will be allocated according to the perceived risk attitude of the client with regard to their wants and needs concerning income for consumption. The investment bank uses the funds for its own strategy, always with an eye on the client's liquidity demand and rate of return. Commissions are in many ways the cost of either illiquidity or liquidity for the investment bank as transferred to the client. This is why commissions are paid on both purchases and sales of financial assets through investment banks.

Insurance companies

In Chapter 5, insurance was discussed in brief concerning its connection to derivative markets. Thinking about the operations of an insurance firm, insurance is very much like banking. Insurance is also split into major subindustries, casualty and life insurance. Casualty insurance is a prepaid asset for the insured which covers against an unknown event that incurs cost. Classic examples are fire insurance in a home, auto insurance for drivers, health insurance, and other types of insurance where an event takes place that causes the insured, or someone else who is injured by the insured's actions, financial harm.

The insurance company charges an insurance premium, the cost of the prepaid asset, to the insured client. These costs are paid by the client on a regular basis to fund the insurance company. An insurance policy is the structure of the fiduciary relationship between the insurance firm and client. The policy describes the terms under which the insurance company would have to pay out money toward an insurance claim. In the case of auto insurance, there are many categories of potential cost for an accident. Some include medical costs to both the insured and other injured parties, the value of damaged vehicles or other property, and other expenses incurred in an accident. Further, insurance companies structure policies to include deductibles. The deductible is an initial payment of money toward the cost of a claim, the amount asked for a down-payment of sorts after an accident. The deductible helps share the cost and risk of an accident with the client, and this reduces the insurance firm's risk. The higher the deductibles the insured party is willing to pay, the lower the insurance premium. The insurance company uses financial leverage to profit from the collected premiums net of payout costs, investing net premiums in the financial markets and funding itself further through revenue derived from investments. This is true for any type of insurance.

Life insurance, however, is much more like investment banking than casualty insurance. Life insurance is insurance against your death. Upon your death, a beneficiary receives a payment based on the amount of insurance purchased. Suppose you were 30 years old and wanted $250,000 in life insurance. One type of life insurance you could buy is term insurance. Term insurance is much like casualty insurance where the casual act that delivers an unforeseen cost is the loss of your life. Generally, the premiums associated with term life insurance are a function of the client's age and relative health. The lower the client's age and better the client's health, the lower the insurance premiums. This reflects a lower probability of death and thus payout for the firm. Actuarial science is a branch of mathematical finance and probability theory that focuses on forecasting payouts for insurance firms and tries to increase the certainty based on information provided by the client. Term life refers to the fact that these policies expire after a certain number of years, which means to keep the life insurance for a longer period, one would have one's health reassessed upon expiration.

Whole or universal life insurance is much more like a savings account where a death benefit exists parallel to the account's value. The premiums are much larger, but are also a function of age and relative health. The idea with whole life is that the policy lasts for the life of the client, regardless of how long the client lives. To entice investors to diversify and purchase such insurance, part of the universal policy is a death benefit and the other is a low-risk, generally guaranteed rate of return investment. Much like investment banking and depository institutions, life insurance provides funding for the insurance firm to invest in other assets and attempt to financially leverage in such a way as to outpace their costs. The insurance firm seeks a spread in the financial markets above both their guaranteed rate of return and death benefits paid on average to policy holders. Insurance ultimately seeks to use client premiums in such a way as to generate revenue to more than cover claim values.

Pension plans

A pension plan has both investment banking and insurance elements within its structure. When a worker retires, the immediate problem is income generation. Pensions provide income to retired workers from worker contributions over time. By saving while working, an asset accumulates in the worker's name. The pension plan is ultimately an investment account where the taxation of gains and principal may be shifted to the time when withdrawals take place. Social Security in the United States is a form of pension plan, and was constructed as a fully funded system.[4] Private pension plans are meant to be fully funded, where money invested by the worker is kept in the worker's name and funds no other workers' pensions. Private plans circumvent that problem by using financial leverage and allowing the worker to make some investment choices, and thus take some of the risks. Since some of the funding is at risk, there is not a guaranteed rate of return on pension funding in every case. When guaranteed funding lags behind the market's rate of return or if the population begins to retire early and has a higher life expectancy, pension plans lose their margins.[5]

Fringe banking

Another category of financial intermediary is fringe banking. Examples of these firms are check-cashing services and pawn brokerages. A fringe bank is named as such because it acts like a lender but remains on the fringe of any regulatory environments and does not collect deposits. In the case of a check-cashing service (or payday lender), the client provides evidence of future income as the collateral for a short-term, personal loan. The check-cashing service loans the money before the worker is paid, and then charges interest on that loan. The interest rates are not conventional market rates, as the risks are very high to the firm and there is no explicit regulatory environment beyond usury laws governing these financial transactions. Check-cashing services place a lien on worker wages, and as protection will not generally lend out more than one paycheck at a time. Further, these firms cash checks for those who do not have a bank, again acting like a bank but outside a true regulatory environment. They take a relatively large fee for such services.

   The pawn brokerage uses goods instead of future income as collateral for lending, but is similar in structure to the check-cashing firm. A client who needs cash can "pawn" a good for a loan, where the pawnbroker holds or inventories goods and lends money to clients using the good's value as the loan's basis. The pawnbroker charges a large interest rate, again because the regulatory environment allows a larger rate and there is inherently a larger probability of default on such transactions. If the loan defaults, the pawnbroker simply puts the goods up for sale in a store front that acts as a clearinghouse for items used as collateral. The "pricing" of the goods initially is very important. For example, pawnbrokers may mistake a cubic zirconium stone for a diamond. If this happens, much more will be lent than the jewelry is worth. Further, the price of gold as a commodity can easily affect the pawn shop's margins; a drop in the interbank rate in the United States drops the prime rate in bank lending in such a way as to provide a policy-driven margin for the pawnbroker, which normally has a line of credit based on the prime rate. The lending rate remains high while the cost of funds fall.

   In summary, these firms all act as intermediate steps in financial transactions, whether there is a deposit or not. Banks and thrifts are depository institutions, and all look very similar to each other. Non-depository institutions vary greatly in the services they provide, but all seek the same outcome: profit on financial leverage. The accounting structure of a bank provides insight into its pursuit of profit and potential risks taken to gain financial leverage.

Things to remember

Financial intermediaries are split into two categories.

- Depository institutions which hold deposits as liabilities and convert them into loans as assets
- Non-depository institutions which act as true financial intermediaries to facilitate transactions from one party to another without holding a liability in any one party's name.

The bank's balance sheet

A depository institution, such as a bank, is like any other business. It has assets, liabilities, and some amount of equity held by its ownership regardless of corporate structure. In Chapter 7, this process will be made analogous to a business that produces a physical good, such as bolts or cars or hamburgers, and is examined in a microeconomic framework. To understand the microeconomics of a bank discussed in Chapter 7, it is important to understand a bank's accounting structure.

Assets

The bank's assets begin with cash and cash equivalents called reserves. The bank's reserves are split into two large categories, where there may or may not be a requirement to hold cash. Cash held by the bank for expected depositor demand is in the form of vault cash or bank reserves. Bank reserves can take the form of either a checking account held at other banks or at the central bank in the bank's name. The key is the immediate liquidity of these accounts to satiate depositor demand. In a fractional reserve system, the central bank decides on a certain percentage of bank deposits be held in these forms, at a minimum. The bank may hold what we will call extra reserves in Chapter 7 as a function of internal bank policy, adaptation to new risk environments and changing rates of return on cash equivalents that bear interest.

The major use of reserves is loanable funds. We will split the use of reserves for lending into three major categories. First is governmental lending. This is the purchase of government debt which acts both as a diversification strategy on the part of the bank and as a way of financially communicating with the central bank when open market operations are used for monetary policy purposes. In countries that do not have viable government debt markets for their domestic sovereign lending, these banks purchase other nations' debt, such as that of the United States, United Kingdom and Euro Area. Second is interbank lending. In the United States, these are known as federal funds loans. These are loans provided by banks to other banks, generally for reserve requirement satiation. There may also be federal fund loans provided to help a bank that is failing and needs to reorganize its assets to support itself. Banks also hold private loans in the form of either commercial or household lending. These loans are the backbone of everyday business at the bank and where the majority of bank risk comes into play. Chapter 7 expands on this section of the bank's balance sheet at length.

Other assets include the physical assets of the bank, such as buildings, land, desks, chairs, computers, etc. While it is more important to understand that the bank inventories and sells money, and thus has money as its asset base, it generally must operate with some amount of physical capital. It is also important to note that these physical goods act as a buffer against the bank's riskiness in lending and its ability to pay back its depositor and other creditors. Banking regulation in most of the advanced nations of the world requires banks to hold a certain amount of their assets as physical capital.

Liabilities and owners'/shareholders' equity

The bank's liabilities are mainly the customers' deposits, both demand and time. There are also wages payable, accounts payable and notes payable much like any other firm. However, it is the deposits that provide the genesis of lending on the asset side of the balance sheet. Reserve requirements are based on the level of these deposits. Banks, for this reason, focus their marketing efforts first on the attraction of deposits and then on the attraction of borrowers. There is also an account for notes payable, the long-term debt of the bank that acts as further liabilities.

Regardless of business structure, the bank will have some amount of paid-in capital which provides initial funding. In the corporate structure, the paid-in capital would generally be outstanding stock. Also, retained earnings are in this category, where the retained earnings provide dividends for the firm's owners from the accumulated profits of the bank. Smaller banks may use their equity as the initial source of lending, regardless of the market, and attempt to establish themselves in their market. The net income of the bank flows into this account.

Net interest margin

The bank's income statement looks similar to any other firm. Revenue is generated from fees and interest payments of borrowers, and expenses are generated by wages and salaries, utilities, interest payments, and other business expenses of the bank. However, most bankers will tell you that they do not watch any specific costs unless an anomaly has taken place. The world of banking boils down to a concept called net interest margin or NIM. NIM is the spread between the revenue derived from each dollar lent by the bank and the cost of each dollar lent on average. For banks that have mainly demand deposits, the interest cost of those accounts is low, but the maintenance costs, the day-to-day maintenance of customer demands for liquidity, may be high. For time deposits, maintenance is episodic while interest payments are higher. The expenses are spread over all these transactions.

Banks are classic firms in their use of both economies of scale and economies of scope. Economies of scale is the idea that as more of a good is produced, the average cost of the good falls toward a minimum point. There is a specific amount of production at which the average cost is minimized; the firm achieves economies of scale until this minimum point is reached. Economies of scope is spreading the cost of production over many related products in such a way as to reduce the firm's costs overall. There is some number of products at which the firm minimizes the average cost of adding an additional product line. Bank management attempts to reduce costs using technology, low-cost customer service representatives ("tellers"), and products that complement each other well to serve customer needs. It is the asset allocation managers of banks who have a dynamic job and one that involves most of the bank's risk. Banking costs are more predictable and manageable than revenues. The revenues of the bank are constantly shifting with market forces and changes in lending risk.

Banking risks

The ways in which the bank faces risks is similar on the surface to that of individual investors; there are four risks the bank, or any depository institution, faces when it lends money.

Default or credit risk

The risk of providing credit is that the loan will not be paid back. This is the primary risk of the bank. Because the bank uses lending as its main revenue generator, larger credit risk can reduce net interest margin very quickly. Banks focus a lot of energy and time, which ultimately means cost, on the reduction of credit risk. Economists have investigated credit risk as one of many examples of risk in transactions involving a systematic lack of information. For example, banks struggle with assessing the riskiness of potential borrowers to separate the good from the bad ones, those that will pay back the loans and those that will default. Unfortunately, banks also struggle to assess the riskiness of those deemed good borrowers once the loan is furnished. Just like the provision of insurance from Chapter 5, the bank faces asymmetric information risk in lending. Adverse selection takes place because no matter what borrower is selected, risk is inherent in the choice. Moral hazard exists because even if the bank lends money to someone their screening process deemed a "good" borrower, as soon as the loan is furnished there is a "hazard" or risk that the borrower will not act morally concerning the loan (pay it back).

From the lending perspective, the bank attempts to minimize adverse selection, though it can never eliminate it, by asking for information about the borrower. Credit scores, documentation of income and assets, the marital status of the borrower, their work and residence history, and many other data can help the bank assess a borrower's relative riskiness. Credit scores, as discussed earlier in this text, provide a way to gauge the riskiness of the borrower from their credit history and give data on paying credit back. The borrower can help the bank by a process called "signaling". A larger down-payment, adding another party to the loan that is responsible if the borrower does not pay (a co-signer), and allowing other assets to act as collateral, all signal to the bank that the borrower wants the loan with every intention to pay it back. Because the borrower has an incentive to provide information that is either false or disguises a borrower as a good risk, the bank is unlikely to gather 100% of the correct information about the borrower to perfectly assess their ability to pay back the loan as systematic risk in their screening process.

The moral hazard problem is related but not the same as the adverse selection problem. Once the borrower passes the screening process, the bank must then decide how much money to risk on the good borrower, knowing there is a probability that, once provided the loan, the incentives to pay the loan back may change. Because banks face this risk, they generally reduce the amount they are lending to reduce their loan portfolio's risk exposure. This process is called credit rationing. Another way banks ration credit is to reject loan applications randomly or use specific information and reject borrowers. This contraction of credit availability naturally increases the interest rate on loans.

A natural answer as to how the bank can react to these risks is to arbitrarily increase interest rates and reflect the risk directly in a higher cost for borrowers. The flaw in that logic is twofold. First, if a bank arbitrarily increased rates, they may lose good borrowers to competitors which deem the borrower worthy of credit at a lower rate and thus lose revenues. Banks use similar methods to assess credit-worthiness in an attempt to reduce price competition in lending. Further, if a bank increased rates, the good borrowers may either delay using credit or reduce consumption. As a result, only bad borrowers would remain at the market interest rate. Finally, if this rate was relatively high, and the borrowers are likely to default, the higher cost of debt would probably speed up the default process rather than compensating the bank. Economic theory suggests that credit rationing, the bank's manipulation of the loanable funds supply, reduces both the moral hazard and adverse selection problems depending on what step in the process credit is rationed.

Liquidity risk

This is the risk of the bank not having depositor money available upon the depositor's demand or by contractual agreement to provide liquidity. Reserve requirements in a fractional banking system are meant to avoid this risk, or at least minimize it. However, activity in the interbank loan markets involves the reduction of this risk. Banks are probably worried more about the depositor funds becoming unavailable versus the interest cost of interbank loans.

Interest rate risk

This is the risk of the bank's assets and liabilities not matching concerning their maturities. In Chapter 2, we discussed the expectation theory of interest rates; long-term interest rates, say on a ten-year bond, will naturally be higher than short-term rates due to the lack of certainty involved in the longer-term rate of return. The yield curve reflects the expectations theory, which depicts the yield on an investment on the vertical axis and time on the horizontal. Figure 6.1 shows the typical yield curve, where t = time.

If the bank correctly allocates assets, funding will have short-term, low rates and revenues will have long-term, relatively higher rates. The bank is at risk of the yield curve flattening and reducing the spread between revenues and cost. Interest rate swaps, as discussed in Chapter 5, are used to maintain this spread, and thus reduce this risk. A similar risk, called trading risk, is the risk inherent in the investments beyond the loans of the firm, which are made to combat the interest rate risk. If the bank does a poor job of managing the return on its other assets, it exposes itself to both of these risks simultaneously. Banks allocate assets to maximize profits. In Chapter 7, we see a model of banking, and of financial intermediation in general, that shows an optimal asset allocation for a bank.

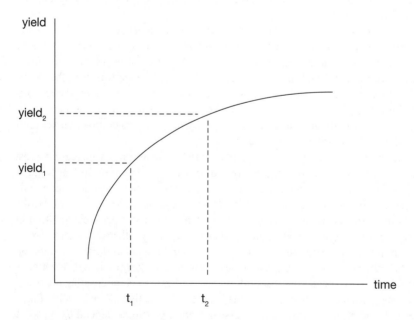

Figure 6.1 The yield curve.

Case study 6.2 Northern Rock becomes National Rock

Exposure to risk is something depositors do not want from their bank. In the United Kingdom, a bank called Northern Rock became the poster child for banks gone wrong and a harbinger of events to come in 2008 when it became insolvent in late summer 2007 (Shin 2009). The bank was ultimately nationalized by the Bank of England in February 2008 after seeking and receiving support for depositor liquidity as its loan portfolio began to fail in September of 2007. As the lender of last resort in the United Kingdom, the Bank of England provided loans to Northern Rock both to stabilize depositor fears in Northern Rock's solvency and also to provide a signal to the world economy that the Bank of England was reacting to these issues quickly and in the consumers' best interest. Northern Rock became an example of a bank that gained access to lending through wholesale credit markets rather than classic interbank lending, where rates are lower and supervision is higher; the exposure to higher costs and sinking revenues from bad loans put Northern Rock at risk of failure and depositors at risk of losing their money.

However, the choice to nationalize the bank is another matter. As in other developed economies, the order of operations for a failing bank is to first provide depositors with safety by looking for another institution to assume the deposits of the bank by another firm acquiring the failing bank's assets. Offers came from both current investment banks and other funds in England, including Lloyds. Many firms would put bids in and Goldman Sachs was to draw up a financing plan as the ultimate transaction underwriter. In February 2008, the UK government announced that no bids provided sufficient value for taxpayers or stockholders, and nationalized Northern Rock. The initial effect of this choice was to first remove Northern Rock stock from being tradable on the London Stock Exchange. It also meant government officials would go through the firm and "cleanse it" of further damaging loans, and sell off pieces of the bank's assets until taxpayers were compensated or the assets were gone. Through the summer of 2008, the reconstruction of Northern Rock made it a better company in terms of riskiness. Some of the assets were simply removed from Northern Rock's books as a function of being unsalable. Others were split up between multiple companies as a way of diversifying the risk exposure.

The United States, at the time of this writing, continues to debate the nationalization of major banks, as a reaction to massive losses in stockholder portfolios would not guarantee these stockholders any value. Large bailout packages have the US Treasury purchasing preferred stock of certain firms and bank failures have a quasi-nationalization feel. It is likely the update of this case would include American banks that were briefly but completely nationalized in the public interest (*The Economist* 14 March 2009).

Summary

Financial institutions, both depository and non-depository, use money as their inventory and good produced. These firms include such companies as commercial banks, savings banks, savings and loan associations, credit unions, investment banks, finance companies, insurance firms, pension plans, and fringe banks. The bank's balance sheet is like any other firm, made up of assets, liabilities and owner's equity. The assets of the bank are dominated by loans, credit provided by the bank to firms and consumers. Bank liabilities are dominated by customer deposits, a large part of the bank's funding. The income of the bank is driven by the bank's ability to earn net interest margin, the spread between the average revenue from lending and the average cost of loanable funds. There are three key risks to that net interest margin, including liquidity risk, credit or default risk, and interest rate risk. Credit risk is the largest risk facing the bank concerning its choice to lend money. This is due to problems of asymmetric information, where the bank has less information than the borrower concerning the ability of the borrower to pay back a loan. These problems are known as adverse selection and moral hazard. Both problems can be reduced by signaling by the borrower and by the credit rationing of the bank.

Key terms

1   Alt-a loans: a type of subprime loan, where conforming loan conditions are not in place, but the loan is made.
2   Bank panic: mass depositor withdrawals at many banks simultaneously.
3   Bank reserves: a bank's deposits at the central bank or at other financial institutions in cash or cash equivalents, which act as part of loanable funds.
4   Bank run: mass depositor withdrawals at one bank.
5   Commercial banking: a depository institution that focuses on business lending and deposits as its main business.
6   Credit or default risk: the risk of a borrower not repaying a loan.
7   Credit rationing: the act of restricting loans to a credit market based on augmented asymmetric information problems, such as adverse selection and moral hazard, where the market is presumed not to be pricing those risks correctly.
8   Credit unions: non-profit, depository institutions specializing in providing services to a specific subset of a population.
9   Deductible: the co-payment in an insurance claim.
10   Demand deposits: checking account deposits, where the owner can demand their money at any time.
11   Depository institutions: banks that specialize in holding customer deposits.
12   Economies of scale: a condition where increasing the amount produced reduces average production costs.
13   Economies of scope: a condition where increasing the range of products produced reduces average production costs.
14   Extra reserves: reserves available, but not lent by banks.
15   Fiduciary: the representative of an agent in a transaction.
16   Fractional banking system: when reserve requirements exist in an economy, banks can only lend a fraction of their reserves.
17   Fringe banking: banking functions that live outside banking regulations, such as pawn brokerages and check-cashing establishments.
18   Insurance premium: the amount paid to own insurance.
19   Lien: something held as collateral, usually the house or car purchased when receiving a loan, against a loan.
20   Liquidity risk: the risk of an inability to convert an asset into cash.
21   Mortgage-based securities: financial assets representing mortgage loans, much like derivatives where the underlying asset is a real property loan.

22 Net Interest Margin (NIM): the difference between the average rate of return on lending and the average cost of funds for a bank.
23 Non-depository institutions: financial institutions that do not hold deposits, such as investment banks.
24 Paid-in capital: the amount initially invested in a firm as equity.
25 Pension plans: funds that hold what workers pay in for retirement and invest in an attempt to profit from financial leverage.
26 Required reserves: the percentage of deposits central banks require of depository institutions to not lend.
27 Retained earnings: the amount of earnings of a firm not paid in dividends, available for investments.
28 Savings and Loan Associations (S&Ls): a financial intermediary specializing in holding member deposits and lending to members.
29 Savings banks: a depository institution that specializes in holding savings deposits for customers and lending to consumers rather than businesses.
30 Subprime loans: loans which have more risk than the average borrower.
31 Term life insurance: insurance against the possibility that the policy holder will die, much like car or home insurance as it acts as a prepaid asset.
32 Thrift banking: any depository institution that is not a commercial bank.
33 Time deposits: deposits that are like bonds, where a specific time elapses before the funds become liquid again. Examples include CDs and savings accounts.
34 Whole life insurance: life insurance where a financial asset exists parallel to a term life insurance policy.
35 Yield curve: a graphical representation of the term structure of interest rates, linking short-term and long-term yields or returns on similar assets.

Questions and problems

1 Explain the primary difference between a commercial bank and a thrift as depository institutions.
2 Explain how a bank uses financial leverage for profit.
3 Explain how an investment bank is like a commercial bank that lends.
4 Explain how insurance works like a bank.
5 Why are deposits not the assets of the bank? Explain.
6 What risk is the yield curve measuring of the four risks given for banks? Explain.

Websites and suggested readings

Websites

See the FDIC website for data and readings on banking in the United States: www.fdic.gov. Also see the American Bankers Association: www.aba.com/abaef/consumers.htm.

Suggested readings

Costa, Dora (1998) "The evolution of retirement: an American economic history, 1880–1990", *National Bureau of Economic Research Series on Long-Term Factors in Economic Development*, Cambridge, MA.

The Economist (2007) "The English Patient", 8 November 2007.

Moody, J. Carroll (1971) *The Credit Union Movement: Origins and Development, 1850–1970*, Lincoln, NE: University of Nebraska Press.

Stiglitz, Joseph E., and Andrew Weiss (1981) "Credit rationing with imperfect information", *American Economic Review*, 71 (3), 393–410.

7 The microeconomics of banking

Introduction

Like any other business, financial intermediaries have sales, administration, building costs, electricity bills, accounts payable, and office supplies expenses. What makes these businesses different from most others is that the product sold is money. This is true for commercial banks, insurance companies, and investment banks alike. These firms sell services also, but these services are tied to the storing and investing of money in order to make revenue. Financial intermediaries take profits from financial leverage, or in the form of commission as a percent of investor revenue made on a transaction, or both. It is important to view the financial intermediary, especially banks, like any other firm.

This chapter's focus is on the microeconomics of banking decisions, which entails some review of basic price theory from microeconomics. Maximizing profit is assumed to be behind all decisions made by the bank to either approve or reject loan applications, choosing to hire a customer service representative, buying government debt securities, or taking in new deposits. Regulations concerning banking and financial markets are discussed briefly, especially international differences between regulatory environments. We assume here that the profit maximization decisions made by banks are done with the appropriate regulatory environment in mind and acting as constraints on activities. Demand and supply functions are discussed as in any other business. The interaction of the marginal utility and marginal cost for the consumer takes place alongside the interaction of marginal revenue and marginal cost for the financial intermediary. The pursuit of net interest margin lies at the heart of the bank's profit function.

This chapter begins with an overview of demand and supply for deposits to fund the loanable funds market described in Chapter 2. The profit functions and optimality for a bank are also shown. A bank's profit is assumed to be derived from three major borrower pools: households and firms (private loans), government, and interbank borrowers. The regulatory environment of banking and financial intermediaries is discussed and compared internationally. Banking regulation, including the current and likely future of mortgage lending regulation, is also discussed. International regulatory environments, such as the Basel 2 Accords which began in 2008, provide a contrast to the American banking environment. A discussion of some recent banking crises, including the most recent one that began in 2007, concludes the chapter. The possible connection to monetary policy in the bank's decision-making acts as a bridge between this chapter and the introduction to central banks in Chapter 8. The events of 2008 may reshape banking regulation worldwide.

Price theory and banking

This first section is a reminder of basic microeconomics within the context of banking and other financial services. The bank is viewed like any other firm, deciding on its optimal inputs and prices such that the quantity of services provided maximizes profits. Second, the bank uses a variety of market signals to make its internal decisions, and also uses some internal policies to constrain itself against too much risk exposure in lending. To simplify the analysis, assume that the bank has three general uses of deposits as loanable funds. These are private loans, government loans and interbank loans. We begin with a review of simple concepts from microeconomics in terms of deposits, which are the key funding source for loans. Figure 7.1 shows the simple market equilibrium for the use of deposits, where R_{DEP} is the cost of deposits in terms of a nominal rate of interest the bank must pay. Q_{DEP} is the quantity of deposits held by the bank and owned by depositors.

The demand side

Like any business, the demand for inputs is derived from the demand for the firm's final product. In this way, the demand for deposits is derived from the demand for loans by borrowers. Loan demand is a function of household, firm and government spending. It is also a function of interest rates and the availability and types of substitute financing. Households and firms will demand bank services to hold their deposits versus other choices. However, we will instead view this as the demand for deposits by the bank as a necessary input to the loan process. This demand by the bank is a function of what depositors are willing to provide the bank, which means the household supplies funding to the bank, which then supplies funding back to households, firms and the government.

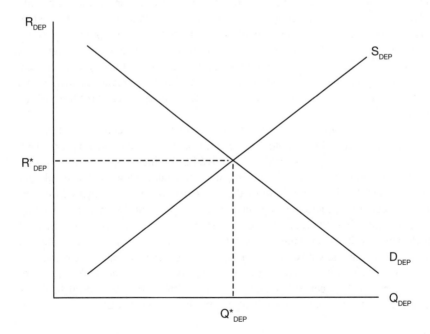

Figure 7.1 Equilibrium in the market for bank deposits.

As we discuss in Chapter 9, there is a connection between loan demand and money demand or liquidity. When households and firms borrow money, they are simply demanding liquidity. In Chapter 2, one of the interest rate definitions was the opportunity cost of holding money; another was the cost of borrowing. These are connected in the loanable funds market. Lenders charge interest to pay for this cost, reflecting a market process and mechanism for money. Utility maximization, as discussed in Chapter 9, drives the decision to borrow.

From a microeconomic standpoint, we should think of the demand curve the bank faces for loanable funds as being downward sloping, but relatively flat (price elastic). Two related reasons exist for this hypothesis. Banks have some price-setting power individually which means they can restrict loans and force the "price" of loans to change. Credit rationing by banks would then allow the interest rate to rise. If the banks were more willing to lend, rates would fall. Also, from the consumer's perspective, there are many substitutes for an individual bank's loans. However, the banks are not delivering a perfectly substitutable product. A lower interest rate at one bank will not cause the entire market to shift toward that bank. The law of demand ultimately binds these reasons together. Marginal revenue, derived directly from the downward-sloping demand curve, is also downward sloping due to diminishing marginal returns. As more loans are made by the bank, the risks are larger, which means the returns on the margin fall. Figure 7.2 depicts both of these functions.

The supply side

The supply of loanable funds is from banks through households, firms, and governments that are net savers. We assume that the bank will hold the deposits of those that act as net savers and thus make the ultimate choice to supply loanable funds. Households and firms supply bank deposits, which fund its demand for deposits, a function of their estimated demand for

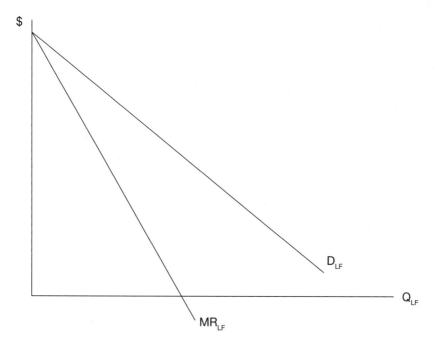

Figure 7.2 Demand and marginal revenue for the typical bank.

loanable funds. Like any other firm, banks face variable and fixed costs. The bank's pursuit is to maximize profit, and thus it is more illuminating to look at average costs than total cost. The relationship between average and marginal costs is that average costs fall more slowly than marginal costs, and also ascend more slowly. Average and marginal costs are equal where average cost is minimized; it is after this point that the numbers of loans provided by the bank begin to lose economies of scale. These costs stem from the administration of deposits and loans. Figure 7.3 depicts the relationship between average and marginal costs for a typical bank.

Profit maximization is based on the equality of marginal revenue and marginal cost. Banks take deposits from consumers and decide from these funds, as well as paid-in capital, the amount to lend to private borrowers. From the determination of optimal funding for private lending, the bank is constrained in what it can lend to the governmental and interbank markets. This decision process is based on the assumption that the marginal rate of return on private lending exceeds the marginal return in the other markets. For a bank, the number of deposits committed to private loans depends on the cost of deposits to the bank and opportunity costs of lending elsewhere; the revenue derived from lending is simply the expected rate of return on each additional dollar lent. This allocation issue leads to multiple challenges for the bank loan managers. First, how the marginal cost is determined is a large question. The bank must decide on how it views other opportunities and its cost of deposits. By focusing on non-interest-bearing funds, the bank may reduce costs but also struggle to raise deposits. Decisions the bank makes concerning its marketing, structure and customers partially determine its costs. The remaining costs depend on input markets otherwise. Second, the expected rate of return is an issue for banks to determine and depends on many factors. The risks discussed in Chapter 3 encompass all the risks that calculate expectations. These expectations change every day and not necessarily through market signals.

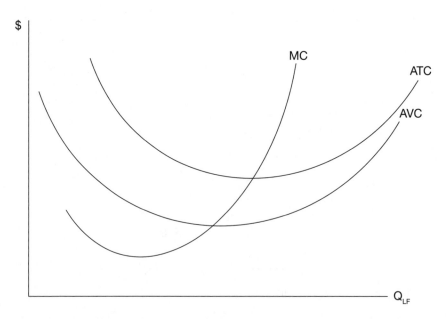

Figure 7.3 Average and marginal costs for the typical bank.

The profit-maximizing bank

The equality of marginal revenue and marginal cost determines the quantity of loans the bank lends to private customers. To derive its marginal revenue, the bank must determine a demand curve for its loans. For marginal cost, the bank must determine a total cost curve. The question of the banking market's structure is discussed in more detail later; however, if the bank exists in a perfectly competitive environment, the marginal costs and loanable funds supply curve will be the same. For now, let's assume the bank is in a monopolistically competitive environment, such that the bank can adjust its interest rates on both loans and deposits, but in very small ways. Revenues for the bank consist of the quantity of loans (Q_L) in terms of the local currency (we will use the US dollar here) multiplied by the average rate of return on the bank's current loan portfolio to private consumers (R_L^ε). This is the number of dollars collected on the average loan. The amount of dollars lent on the interbank market (Q_{IB}) is multiplied by R_{IB} for revenue. Revenue is also derived from holding government debt securities, if a market for the domestic government's debt exists, equal to $R_{GD} \times Q_{GD}$. We will assume that the bank is a price-taker in the interbank and government loan markets and that the bank receives a risk-free return from these markets. The private loan rate, R_L^ε, is an expectation and unknown. It is in this rate that the dynamics of bank decisions take place. For investment banking and insurance, a similar revenue structure exists for the use of client funds.

The bank's costs are summarized by the average interest rate paid on deposits (R_{DEP}) multiplied by the number of deposits held by the bank (Q_{DEP}). The bank is assumed to face a cost function that is based on administrating both deposits and loans,

$$TC = TC(Q_L, Q_{DEP}, Q_{IB}, Q_{GD}) \tag{7.1}$$

an increasing function in all these activities. These costs include utilities, wages, desks, computers, et cetera, at the headquarters bank and its branches. The key is that this total cost function is differentiated by the type of activity; there are specific costs associated with deposits and loans. The average and marginal costs are easy to find from Equation 7.1. The average cost is simply the total cost function divided by the quantity of loans.

$$AC_L = TC_L/Q_L \tag{7.2}$$

The marginal cost is the incremental change in total cost from an increase in the amount of dollars lent.

$$MC_L = \Delta TC_L/\Delta Q_L \tag{7.3}$$

Equation 7.3 shows that for each additional dollar of lending (ΔQ_L), the bank faces an additional cost specific to that additional dollar amount (ΔTC_L). A similar marginal cost exists for deposits, interbank lending and the purchase of government debt by the bank. In sum, these marginal costs equal the bank's marginal cost as a whole.

$$MC = MC_L + MC_{DEP} + MC_{IB} + MC_{GD} \tag{7.4}$$

The marginal revenue of the bank is simply the change in total revenue as a result of an increase in the amount of bank lending or deposits held. Much like the marginal cost function in Equation 7.4, the marginal revenue for the bank is the sum of segment-specific marginal revenue functions.

$$MR_L = \Delta TR_L / \Delta Q_L \tag{7.5}$$

$$MR = MR_L + MR_{DEP} + MR_{IB} + MR_{GD} = R_L + MR_{DEP} + R_{IB} + R_{GD} \tag{7.6}$$

The bank's profit function

The bank's profit function is total revenue less total cost from the above. Equation 7.7 is that function.

$$\pi_{Bank} = TR(Q_L, Q_{DEP}, Q_{IB}, Q_{GD}) - TC(Q_L, Q_{DEP}, Q_{IB}, Q_{GD}) \tag{7.7}$$

When seeking the optimal quantity of each type of loan to hold, as well as the optimal deposits to hold, the bank also faces the constraint that its loanable funds are only available from deposits. Regulations on banking begin here, as most central banks use fractional banking, requiring their depository institutions to hold a certain amount of deposits from lending in any form. This reserve ratio or requirement is represented by RR below, where RR is a number between 0 and 1.

$$Q_L + Q_{IB} + Q_{GD} = (1 - RR) \times Q_{DEP} \tag{7.8}$$

The sum of all loans is equal to the deposits available beyond required reserves for lending equal the available deposits; this can be used to replace some of the terms in Equation 7.7. By recognizing that the net position of the bank on the interbank market is a function of the decisions on private and governmental lending, replace Q_{IB} in Equation 7.7 with $Q_{IB} = (1 - RR) \times Q_{DEP} - (Q_L + Q_{GD})$. This leads to the following profit function, used for inference concerning the bank's decision making.

$$\pi = (R_L^\varepsilon - R_{IB}) \times Q_L + (R_{GD} - R_{IB}) \times Q_{GD} + (R_{IB}(1 - RR) - R_{DEP}) \times Q_{DEP} - TC(\bullet) \tag{7.9}$$

Equation 7.9, while more complex, provides more insight into the aggregate struggle the bank manager faces. Notice in each term of Equation 7.9, the net return on that particular loan is the difference between the loan's interest rate on the loan and the interbank rate. These differences are called yield spreads. As each yield spread increases, the bank can make more profit by shifting deposits toward that particular market. For example, as R_L^ε rises, the marginal revenue derived from lending to consumers and firms rises, providing banks with an incentive to increase their risk exposure to these private markets. If the interbank rate falls, the same dynamic would take place; there would be disincentive for banks to lend to other banks as that specific rate of return was decreasing relative to R_L^ε.

These loan rates are opportunity costs of each other. If the bank lends to its government, it cannot lend that same money to other banks or private borrowers. The firm optimizes its aggregate loan amount where marginal revenue equals marginal cost for each individual market. Table 7.1 shows these equalities for each loan market the bank has available.

It is difficult to assume that the marginal cost for each of the loan markets is the same. Private loans are more complex, due to the inherent risks, and thus $MC_L > MC_{GD} = MC_{IB}$. Figure 7.4 shows the firm's choice of loanable funds, based on the availability of deposits, given the demand, marginal revenue and costs curves of Figures 7.2 and 7.3.

Table 7.1 Marginal revenue and marginal cost functions for each loan market

Loan market	MR	MC
Private loans	R_L	$R_{IB} + MC_L$
Government loans	R_{GD}	$R_{IB} + MC_{GD}$
Interbank loans	$R_{IB}(1-RR)$	$R_{DEP} + MC_{IB}$

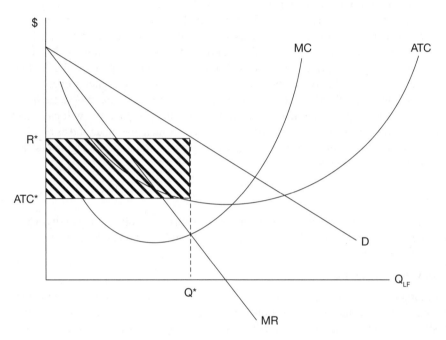

Figure 7.4 The typical bank's equilibrium choice of loanable funds.

The optimal quantity of loans

The optimal quantity of loans made by a bank is based on a complex set of decisions concerning asset allocation. Assuming a bank is a price-taker in both the interbank and governmental loan markets, equilibrium is determined where the market rate of return is equal to the average cost of funds. To simplify the model here, assume that the marginal cost of administrating an interbank or governmental loan is the same and constant. With that, the bank will now assess its private loan market's expected rate of return versus the given rates of return in the other markets, whichever is largest.

Suppose the expected nominal rate of return on private lending was 5 percent, where the rate of return on interbank lending was 4 percent and the government loan market average rate of return, also riskless, was 3.9 percent The bank would use the 4 percent rate in the interbank market to augment the marginal cost determining the private loan's overall marginal cost. If the expected rate of return exceeds the known cost of funds, including the opportunity costs from other markets, the bank will continue to make private loans.

As loans are made, two changes take place. First, the reduction in demand for interbank and governmental debt reduces that debt's price and increases the average rate of return. This leads to a larger MC_L. Second, the bank's provision of more loans reduces the rate of return on loanable funds due to the law of diminishing marginal returns. As the bank lends out more money, the expected rate of return decreases as the demands of good borrowers are satiated, leaving more bad borrowers. As good borrowers are provided loans, the expected rate of return on loans made to the remainder of the market decreases. Both of these reactions in the loanable funds market drive the MR_L and the MC_L closer together until they are equal. When equal, the bank cannot derive any more profit from the private loan markets, and then looks to other alternatives, which have naturally higher relative rates of return. The remaining funds are allocated across the interbank and governmental debt markets in a similar way until profits are maximized or no more loanable funds remain. It is possible for the bank to either satiate the market demand or to run out of funds because of its choice to maximize profit.

The reason that banks may not satisfy the market's demand for lending is due to its information asymmetry with private borrowers. The interbank and governmental securities markets are considered perfectly competitive and supply will equal demand every time. However, as a matter of either bank policy or profit maximizing, a bank may not lend its entire loanable funds supply. What does it do with its remaining funds? We will call these funds "extra reserves", as they are extra beyond those used for loanable funds and as required reserves in a fractional system. These funds act as a way of signaling to regulators that depositors, not profits, come first.

Things to remember

Like any other business, banks are trying to maximize profits by lending at a quantity where the marginal revenue (MR) is equal to the marginal cost (MC) of another dollar lent.

Regulatory environments

Financial market regulation is similar worldwide. There are three tenets of any regulatory environment. First is consumer protection. In financial markets, this means protecting the depositor or client against the intermediary's risk-taking practices. It also means consumer protection against predatory pricing of deposit rates, services and products. Second is protection against monopolization. This may mean limits on branch banking, integration of investment and commercial banking, or merger and acquisition activity. Limiting branch banking is connected to consumer protection; the perceived outcome of banking market monopolization is predatory pricing. Third is the prevention of bank or financial institution failures. This is different from consumer protection in that it transcends the bank to include stockholder and financial market protection more generally. Deposit insurance, reserve requirements, central banks acting as lenders of last resort, capital requirements at banks, and many other legal regulations protect the bank against itself. The issues over any regulatory environment are to increase competition and lower prices for consumers. Bank failures in the United States and Japan, other historic financial crises worldwide, and the introduction of the euro have forced some regulatory environments to change. In 2008, there was discussion concerning changing requirements on lending in the wake of the US subprime crisis, and extending that regulation to cover all financial market transactions in lending. One agreement that was recently changed is the Basel Accords.

The Basel I and II Accords

Capital requirements force banks to distribute their assets in ways that reduces risk-taking and provide physical assets in some percentage of the total as a buffer against the failure of other assets to appreciate in value. In 1988, the Basel I accords began as an international agreement that a certain percentage of assets must be held as physical capital. The United States, the major nations of Europe, Japan, and Canada were those involved. Banks with foreign loans were to hold eight percent of their risk-weighted assets as physical capital. This agreement changed the way banks allocated assets and also the volume of loanable funds available for borrowers worldwide. The weighting of risk is simple, and rises from zero to ten to 20 to 50 to 100 percent risk; these weights provide an indicator of how risky a bank's portfolio is at any time.

The Basel II accords are based on Basel I and also expand them. It is a general agreement on risk-taking by banks; there are three "pillars" upon which the new accord is constructed. The first is minimum capital requirements and is similar in structure to the original Basel accords. The major changes include new ways to measure credit risk, equally weighting assets to calculate the necessary minimum amount of capital. This first pillar also sets minimum capital holdings against securities, such as securitized mortgages. The imputed risk in securitized mortgage assets, such as collateralized debt obligations, led to their own requirements in capital. Operational risk is also explicitly defined in the Basel II accords, and is set against credit risk to further weight assets for the capital requirements. Operational risk is the risk of rate of return losses due to problematic internal practices at banks. The more this operational risk exists, the larger the risk weighting on the bank's non-capital assets. Finally, trading-book risk is defined and also assigned a weight, where trading-book risk is the risk of exposure to derivative assets used by the bank to hedge against other positions. In summary, the first pillar expands the risk definition and weighting of Basel I and asks for more diversified weighting of asset risk by banks and financial institutions.

The second pillar is about supervisory review, and provides four principles for risk and management supervision at banks. The first is about strategic asset management versus the riskiness of bank portfolios and a bank's capital value. It is essential for banks to foresee changes in risk and have a strategic reaction to risk. The second is about the operation of review and monitoring of capital adequacy. This is concerned with setting metrics and processes to assess banks' asset allocation. The third is about holding banks to a capital requirement above the minimum and implementing strategies to capital levels above that minimum mark. This third principle is about banks constructing internal policies to monitor the minimum capital held by the bank and to set that minimum above the Basel II floor. This puts further distance between the bank's risks and its asset base. Finally, the fourth principle is about the triggering of responses to asset risk changing and the bank's reaction. Policies and metrics should be in place to indicate when and how the bank should react to new risks as a result of changing rates of return. Regulators should have rapid reactions to a lack of restoration of capital if used to support bad debt losses.

The third pillar is concerned with market discipline in lending. The two main aspects of this pillar are disclosure requirements and risk exposure assessment. Disclosure requirements are discussed briefly below, but banks generally should ask for disclosure such that adverse selection and moral hazard problems are minimized. Banks are asked to disclose to regulators the risk exposure of their lending portfolio, the capital level against the risk-weighted asset base and finally the assessment risk overall in the bank.

These three pillars govern banking regulations philosophically in the major countries of the world. There are many historical banking crises since 1980 to choose from to showcase problems with financial market regulation and the possible consequences; only four are discussed here in brief. The bank and thrift problems in the United States during the 1980s had their roots in the 1960s and were a mix of bad regulation, risk-taking and lack of oversight. The Japanese crisis of the 1990s and beyond has similarities to the American experience of the 1980s. Real estate speculation and a lack of oversight propelled the Japanese crisis. The tequila crisis of 1994 in Latin America and the Asian flu of 1997 are similar to each other. Speculation on currencies in the midst of bad monetary policy and banking regulation caused bank panics in the countries involved. Finally, there is a discussion of current banking problems in the wake of the subprime mortgage issues. The parallels to all the above banking and financial crises are ominous.

Case study 7.1   Fast to lend, slow to lend: late 2008 as a wild reversal in lending

During the first decade of the new millennium, banks were a case study of innovation. New types of loans were invented on a regular basis. As an industry, banks were lending money and then bundling these loans, constructing mutual funds of loans that were for houses, cars, education, and other purchases, as new securities to sell to financial markets. The beauty of this arrangement was that lending institutions did not have to hold their own lending risks. Once the loan was made, banks could then convert the loans to cash and lend again by simply selling that debt in bundled forms to hungry investors. Investors were willing to take risks, especially on bundled mortgages, because home values that acted as underlying assets in these bundles had risen rapidly.

After a brief downturn in the wake of the terrorist attacks on 11 September 2001, banks found a large amount of wealth in consumer hands and a culture of using financial leverage to consume and financial innovations providing more choice for lenders and borrowers alike. Loans such as alt-a, subprime, reverse amortization, interest-only loans, and other types were assembled and lent (Mills and Kiff 2007). Risky loans have existed for centuries and these new loans had three simple ideas behind them.

The first was to engage a new market in the use of financial leverage, where some borrowers who would never participate in borrowing for a home could now buy a home with a minimum amount of down-payment (sometimes as low as three percent, a so-called "zero per cent down" loan), did not have to provide a large amount of income stability proof, or could choose not to pay any principal and simply pay only the interest on the loan. All these mechanisms reduced the borrower's risk while the secondary markets for mortgages used investors worldwide to both spread and move the risks. The original lending facility making decisions on borrower risk did not face that risk over the life of the loan.

In September 2007, after a year of instability in real estate markets, the market began to finally falter. Wider equity markets were slower to react to possible recession, especially one caused by real estate prices contracting. Another phenomenon was that homeowners were using fast-rising net worth in their homes to consume. The process of using homes as banks based on unrealized gains in wealth exposed homeowners to home values rapidly falling. Throughout the 1990s, and most of this decade, home prices showed no signs of retreat. One of two outcomes awaited the homeowner who ate the equity built during the last two decades. The first was a need to refinance the total debt package and potentially sell the home if the interest payments from the combined loans became too large. The second was to foreclose on the property, in the worse case, if the home lost so much value that the home's sale would not pay off the accumulated debt.

Unfortunately, home price contraction was so rapid that foreclosure activity increased rapidly, forcing home prices down even more quickly. Many banks were unable to sell new loans to secondary markets and had to hold their own debts. Financial markets worldwide began to sell off assets, and securities markets followed real estate markets as the general, worldwide exposure to risky lending became more obvious. By August 2008, banks in the United States slowed down their lending to allow the markets to stabilize and also awaited the first in a series of "bailout" payments initiated by the Federal Reserve and the US Congress. Other countries have followed suit with emergency funding for financial markets, bailout plans, and central bank action.

Once this funding was received, banks did not begin lending en masse again immediately. This became a large mystery and debate in banking as of 2009. The loanable funds at banks in the United States increased rapidly, almost one trillion dollars of potential loans sitting in bank vaults. Figure 7.5 shows the evolution of these balances from 1970 onward.

For banks at the beginning of 2009, their largest problems centered on knowing where to lend money at low risk given the relatively low interest rates worldwide. As central banks everywhere began to follow the American lead on lowering interest rates, lending rates fell as monetary expansions took place and banks watched a reduction in their net interest margins. As a result, there were no incentives to lend. The reversal is a stark reminder about the banking model of doing business, though the market will slowly provide incentives.

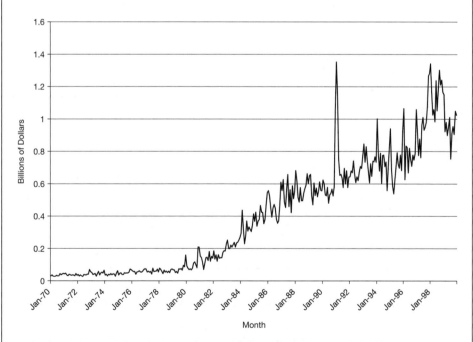

Figure 7.5a Excess reserves at US banks (available funds not lent), 2008$, 1970–1999.
Source: Federal Reserve Board.

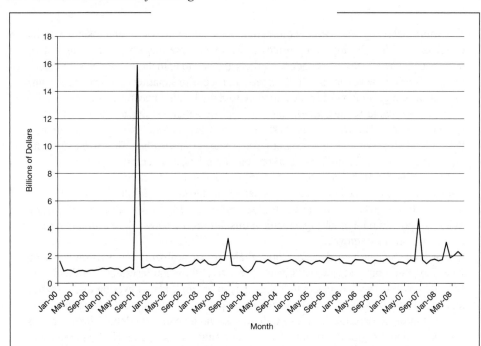

Figure 7.5b Excess reserves at US banks (available funds not lent), 2008$ Jan 2000–July
2008.

Source: Federal Reserve Board.

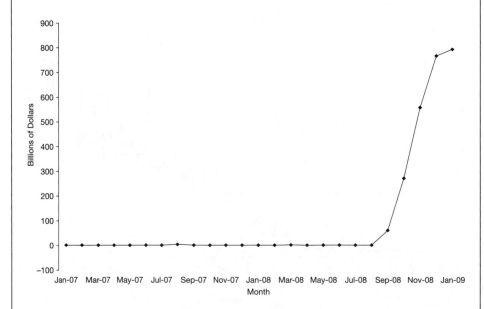

Figure 7.5c Excess reserves at US banks (available funds not lent), 2008$ Jan 2007–Jan 2009.
Source: Federal Reserve Board.

Things to remember

The Basel II accords are meant to be the worldwide agreement on banking regulation. Though it is unlikely the Basel II accords will remain as currently written, the three pillars are likely to remain, as they reflect common sense.

* Setting minimum capital requirements
* A mandate for supervisory review
* A market discipline in lending.

Case study 7.2 Whatever happened to the Basel II Accords? Basel III in the wake of financial crisis

In 2008, a new multilateral agreement about banking regulations and practice was supposed to go into effect. As discussed in Chapter 7, the Basel II accords expanded the Basel I accords from 1998 and did so in such a way that made risk front and center in policing lending and balance sheet management of banks worldwide. The financial crisis of 2007 and beyond reduced the new accords' strength as the fruition of banking risk was the culprit in many minds for financial market disarray. Newspapers published stories that banking risk had exposed balance sheets of banks, financial institutions and other companies alike to bad debt that may lead to widespread, worldwide bankruptcies. Capital requirements for banks under Basel II were to be larger for banks with risky loan portfolios, forcing lenders to convert more available loanable funds to "capital" or funds that could not be lent to cover against those risks. Banks riskiness rose so quickly that normal auditing procedures could not assess that risk in real time, even if they were continuous, real-time audits (which is the future of banking in any developed nation after the 2008 banking crises); banks had leveraged themselves in such a way that their capital requirements could not keep up with the escalating amount of downgraded debt.

In January of 2009, the Bank of International Settlements (BIS) began to publish potential enhancements to the Basel II accords for all three pillars. The BIS is the portion of the World Bank charged with clearing of or administrating balance of payments imbalances for countries with deposits at the World Bank. In brief, the enhancements are as follows, from the Bank of International Settlements (2009), and subject to change.

Potential changes to Pillar 1

Banks that hold toxic mortgage-backed securities or bundles will have even higher capital requirements than holding single mortgages, especially if the risk in those assets is externally rated concerning riskiness.

Potential changes to Pillar 2

This enhancement addresses flaws in risk management practices revealed by the financial crisis, which in many cases were symptoms of more fundamental short-comings in governance structures at financial institutions. To strengthen supervisory guidance, countries need (ibid.):

- firm-wide governance and risk management;
- the capturing of off-balance-sheet risk exposures and securitization activities;
- incentives to manage risk and returns over the long-term.

The supplemental Pillar 2 guidance also incorporates key recommendations from the following Basel Committee initiatives (ibid.):

- Principles for sound liquidity risk management and supervision (September 2008);
- Supervisory guidance for assessing banks' financial instrument fair value practices (issued for comment on 28 November 2008); and
- Principles for sound stress testing practices and supervision (issued for comment on 6 January 2009).

Potential changes to Pillar 3

The Basel Committee developed proposed revisions to the existing Pillar 3 requirements, focusing on the following six areas, specifically how securitization of loans is handled and valued (ibid.):

- securitization exposures in its trading book;
- sponsorship of off-balance sheet lending;
- the Internal Assessment Approach (IAA) for securitizations and other liquidity facilities;
- re-securitization risk exposures;
- valuation with regard to securitization exposures; and
- pipeline and warehousing risks with regard to securitization exposures.

These disclosures complement the other pillars and help market participants to better understand a bank's overall risk profile. Whether these proposed enhancements will be accepted, work in practice, or be followed by financial institutions of the world remains unseen. What is obvious is that coordinating risk regulation in the world's major financial centers should reduce future risk-taking and exposure in the wake of the financial crisis sparked by risky lending and banking practices.

The FDIC and FSLIC crises of the 1980s

The US banking crises of the 1980s began in the late 1960s and were exacerbated by a poor and slow set of regulatory reactions, bad macroeconomic policies and risk-taking by financial institutions. The two insurance corporations, the Federal Deposit Insurance Corporation (FDIC) and the Federal Savings and Loan Insurance Corporation (FSLIC), were also in charge of regulating their specific industries under their depository institution umbrellas. For a flat fee per $100 deposited at the bank, these governmental entities monitored banking activity in the United States, specifically reserve and capital requirements, and provided deposit insurance. The deposit insurance covers banks against both liquidity and credit risks.

Both were created by the Glass-Steagall Act. The Glass-Steagall Act also restricted the direct interaction of commercial and investment banking, which was repealed in 1999 along with other portions of the Act. The FSLIC was created as part of the National Housing Act in 1934 in the hopes of expanding deposits in savings banks and savings and loan associations to fuel home ownership loans and ultimately home ownership itself.

Before the late 1960s, these insurance companies provided security to depository institutions and their customers, and these institutions' growth was driven by this security. It was in the late 1960s that potential banking crises began to show their face. A regulatory event took place in 1967 that reduced the ease by which thrifts in specific could attract funds for lending. Regulation Q, the regulation that places a maximum on the rate at which depository institutions can pay for deposits of all types, was reduced to approximately 5 percent. Beginning in 1967, the United States experienced inflation that increased nominal rates of interest above the Regulation Q ceiling and forced depositors to reassess the rate of return on bank deposits. Many of the spreads between the Reg Q cap and the appropriate Treasury Bill rate were as much as 2.5 percent in favor of the Treasury Bill.

Because both government debt securities and other low-risk investment vehicles, such as mutual funds, paid more in nominal terms than did deposits due to Regulation Q, a process called disintermediation began. Disintermediation takes place when bank depositors reduce their level of deposits due to changing rates of return at the bank. One misconception is that depositors leave the financial markets altogether. This is not necessarily true. This asset reallocation increased financial market asset demand outside banks to take advantage of rising nominal rates of return and threatened the depository institution's ability to fund new loans. Short-term interest rates remained very volatile through the beginning of 1970s; in 1973, Reg Q was suspended on deposits greater than $1000 for a short time (from July 1973 to November 1973). As short-term interest rates fell due to inflation affecting mainly long-term deposits and rates, disintermediation slowed down and deposit growth resumed.

The United States experienced multiple, short-lived bouts of disintermediation in the 1970s. The bouts were due to volatile US inflation, which became more tied to international energy prices in the 1970s. By 1979, another round of disintermediation began as energy prices, specifically oil prices, rose rapidly. The growth of money market mutual and Treasury Bill funds throughout the 1970s increased the ease of deposit withdrawal. The Monetary Control Act of 1980 began a phase-out of Regulation Q, to be completed in 1986, as part of a larger financial reform package. Nineteen seventy-nine was a devastating year for the American economy, and began a three-year recession in most of the world.

Interest rates rose rapidly in the United States through the end of 1982, with conventional mortgage rates peaking at approximately 22 percent. Because of disintermediation in bank deposits, and simultaneous contractions in loanable fund demand, banks faced income statement and balance sheet crises simultaneously. The inability to easily increase deposits, due both to rising costs of federal fund loans and competition from other financial assets, forced many banks to fail. Many blame the failure of thrifts in specific, as they relied exclusively on interest-bearing deposits. Interest rate risk became the ultimate issue for savings and loan associations, manifesting itself ultimately as a maturity mismatch. This is a yield curve inversion which also inverts the bank's profitability. Other thrifts also suffered from corruption, greed, and some risky behavior. The FSLIC could not control the problem, nor find other institutions to assume the failing banks' deposits. Once the federal regulators had tried to infuse liquidity into the thrift industry in an attempt to save failing companies, it became more apparent that the FSLIC was going to have to pay out on lost deposits from failed banks, and that it was going to become bankrupt itself. The Financial Institutions Reform, Recovery, and Enforcement Act (FIRREA) of 1989 sealed the fate of the FSLIC, and moved its insurance functions to the FDIC.

The FDIC and commercial banks also suffered in the 1980s, not from regulatory failure and mismanagement, but from the risky behavior allowed and brokered in many ways by federal agencies. Two specific types of risk-taking took place at commercial banks, which were ironically protected by Regulation Q's stipulation that checking or demand deposits were paid zero nominal interest. The first type of risk-taking was in providing sovereign loans, specifically loans to emerging markets in the late 1970s to boost their economies. These countries, which included Mexico, Brazil, Argentina, Chile, Costa Rica, and Venezuela, began to borrow heavily during the 1970s. Much of this was based on rising commodities prices which ignited these economies' growth. As the oil price increased, especially after 1979, banks saw these nations as new, profitable markets. The price of oil began to fall beginning in late 1982, and it was Mexico's inability to pay its interest on sovereign debt that began a default cycle that would be later named the "world debt crisis of 1982".[1]

Many of the loans provided were based on the LIBOR. As interest rates rapidly increased, the borrowing cost of these debts rose in tandem. As costs rose, energy prices fell, reducing the much-needed revenues for these countries to help service their debt. Further, since the debts were denominated in dollars, the rising value of the dollar due to the high demand for American debt, specifically US Treasury securities, forced the value of these debts to rise even more rapidly. Bond-rating agencies examined these signals and began to downgrade sovereign loan ratings on the secondary market. This forced a contraction of primary market transactions to refinance the debt or to provide more debt. Mexico's government, in August of 1982, announced they could no longer meet their interest payments and other nations took that as a signal that it was time to suspend their own payments until a renegotiation could take place. Sovereign loans rely on the borrowing governments to raise taxes, print money or sell assets to pay off these debts in the worst case. Banks worldwide that were overexposed to these loans began to fail. But this was not the only risk-taking.

Many banks in the United States (and some banks elsewhere) also exposed themselves to real estate speculation for new oil reserves during the late 1970s and early 1980s. Borrowing companies were constituted to prospect for oil in a similar fashion to a gold rush from the mid-1800s. These firms began to employ expensive engineering and geological firms to help with this process, all based on the price of oil providing large enough revenues to cover costs if firms found oil first and in large quantities. These loans were also structured as variable rate loans based on the LIBOR. As rates rose rapidly in the early 1980s, coupled with oil prices steadily falling again, the profitability of these debts also fell. The southern portion of the United States was hit hardest, specifically Texas, Louisiana, and Oklahoma. Continental Illinois, the eighth largest bank in the United States at the time, failed as a result of its exposure to such loans in these states.[2]

In sum, both the FDIC and FSLIC problems were based on oil prices rising rapidly, but the reactions of commercial banking versus thrifts were much different. Through the 1970s, the banking industry was very volatile, and landed at the bottom hard in the 1980s as the lack of regulatory foresight led to mass withdrawals of funding from thrifts and eventual maturity mismatches in thrift balance sheets. For commercial banks, risky foreign lending brokered by the US government increased credit risk at banks. Two questions remain from these crises. Was the regulatory change large enough? Would this episode be repeated? The Japanese banking crisis of the 1990s showed that little was learned from this episode.

Things to remember

The FDIC and FSLIC crises had similar outcomes, but different reasons for their genesis.

*   The FSLIC crisis and ultimate bankruptcy was caused by problems with regulators not reacting in step with market realities
*   The FDIC crises and ultimate restructuring was caused by risky lending by banking.

The Japanese banking crisis of the 1990s

The Japanese banking industry suffered in the 1990s from regulatory problems and real estate speculation in much the same way their American counterparts did in the 1980s. Japan's banks split banking duties up into short- versus long-term financing for firms, providing liquidity for trusts and pensions, financing small businesses, and also financing primary products industries. This structure came from the aftermath of World War II to provide distinct banks for distinct markets rather than have oligopolistic banks dominate the financial landscape. The Japanese Postal System also acted as a savings bank; by 1998, 45 percent of savings deposits were held with the Japanese Post Office (Craig 1998).

Banking regulations in Japan are a shared responsibility of the Bank of Japan, the Japanese equivalent of the Federal Reserve, and the Ministry of Finance. There is also a deposit insurance corporation, similar to the FDIC. Unlike the United States, where Congress votes on new regulation regardless of the branch of government that proposes legislation, the Japanese Ministry of Finance can change regulations as it sees fit. At one time, the Bank of Japan was under the Ministry of Finance; in 1998, the Bank of Japan became an independent body (ibid.). Most banks are examined annually, and the two agencies shared that work. The Deposit Insurance Corporation was established in 1971 but only acted in 1991 concerning a bank merger to help an ailing bank for the first time.

Three categories of problems are cited as reasons why the Japanese banking crisis took place. First, real estate loans in the 1980s to Japanese borrowers buying their own homes or second and third homes elsewhere led to a speculative bubble in real estate. This included American markets in Hawaii, Los Angeles, and other major cities around the world. Betting that housing and commercial space prices would rise into the foreseeable future, and certainly into the future of the loan, banks lent money rapidly to take advantage of rising real estate prices. The Japanese economy, which soared through the 1980s, fueled this growth. Second, long-standing relationships between government and industry caused problems between industry and the banks that left banks barely profitable in the first place. Risk was under-priced as a result of the governmental relationship with banks such that banks were left less profitable than they could have been under a more market-based setting. There are also relationships between industry and the banks, where major corporate firms own large portions of the major Japanese banks. This relationship reduced incentives to price loans based on riskiness. The banks in many ways were part of both a bank holding company, where many financial firms lived under the same corporate umbrella, and a savings and loan association. The firms within the bank holding company were both the borrowers and the stockholders of the bank. The relationship was formed to achieve group goals, not individual bank success. The bank was merely the conduit to the group goal, which generated the holding company's ultimate wealth and the economy's full employment.

Once loans began to fail, these relationships left banks without any diversified positions to make up losses; banks began to fail. Further, risky loans were made to emerging market economies in southeast Asia that suffered from credit risk when the Asian currency crisis took place in 1997. This "Asian flu" spread to Japan due to these loans. The Ministry of Finance and the Bank of Japan assigned the amount of new lending each bank could make in each new quarter of the year. This assigned the maximum loan amount possible, and constrained the market directly. By using the savings of Japanese workers and providing low-cost loans to industry, the Ministry of Finance pushed the cost of capital down such that they provided a low-cost way for firms to expand. This strategy both fueled and hindered sustained growth of the Japanese economy through the 1980s after World War II and into the 1990s. The real estate market in Japan and elsewhere contracted in the early 1990s. Japanese banks were left illiquid because their real estate loans were failing. The second punch that began a second and prolonged round of banking problems in Japan was the Asian currency crisis of 1997.[3]

The Tequila Crisis of 1995

The practice of assessing the risk of private debt in many countries is not the same as in major industrialized nations. In many Latin American countries, private debt was assessed monthly, where interest rates payable on those debts were adjusted according to a re-pricing of that debt. Because private debt in many less-developed or emerging nations is priced in terms of foreign currency, it exposes the borrower to fluctuations in the exchange rate as well as asset-specific risks.

When a pegged exchange rate (fixed to the specific value of another currency) is used, pressure can quickly build behind the domestic currency. In the case of Mexico, expected inflation pressure began to build in the early 1990s, and the American recession of that same period drove a larger trade deficit. With pressure on the Mexican peso to revalue, along with heightened riskiness in the Mexican economy, private debt in Mexico began to see a sharp rise in cost. As speculators began to bet against the peso, the peg between the peso and dollar had to be removed. Once it was removed, the peso's value dropped rapidly, causing the expected inflation to become actual inflation. The flight to dollars by the Mexican economy as a cover against the risk in the peso exacerbated that movement.

The collapse of credit in Mexico that ensued threatened banks, businesses and consumers alike. Because Brazil and Argentina had similar international relationships and debt markets to Mexico, speculators saw a spreading of the crisis to these countries, and the crisis spread. Mishkin (1999) suggests that one large lesson to be learned from this crisis is that the credit market's institutional relationships in emerging countries may be different than in developed countries and the same policies used in developed countries (bailout plans of banks by the government lending cash or taking over banks) may not work in emerging markets. The current financial crisis in the United States and beyond will test that idea.

The subprime crisis of 2007 and beyond

While the title of this problem concerns a certain type of loan provided for housing, history will reflect on this US financial crisis as one of regulatory problems, risky lending and con-sumerism in a confluence to cause financial failures. The regulatory problem lies in the allowance of lending where a lack of documentation led to small amounts of information asked by lenders and a different market for the borrowers. The subprime lending market is one where the borrower either does not meet the minimum standard to receive a conventional loan or does not have evidence or documentation enough to support receiving such a loan. These were higher-risk loans collateralized by two sources. The first was the prediction of higher housing prices, the asset being purchased with a mortgage. If housing prices continued their unprecedented climb upward, the loan's value was supported even if the borrower was unable to pay the adjustable-rate mortgage provided to compensate for credit risk. Loan default meant the bank made a profit from selling the underlying asset, the rising-price home. As a result, higher home prices fueled the subprime markets.

Second, there was a long practice of both private and governmental agencies supporting credit risks taken by banks through purchasing mortgages on the secondary market. The banks would originate the loans and American firms such as the Federal National Mortgage Association ("Fannie Mae"), the Federal National Mortgage Corporation ("Freddie Mac"), the Government National Mortgage Association ("Ginnie Mae"), and many "private-label" companies would purchase a quantity of "bundled" loans from banks and securitize them in a type of mutual fund called collateralized bank obligations or CBOs (see Figure 7.6). Shares could be purchased in the CBOs, acting like a derivatives market. Much like a viral infection, the risky loans spread quickly among many different financial market participants that were also betting on the housing market rising in value. The demand for these securitized mortgages somewhat reduced the bank's credit risk and passed it on to many institutional and individual investors.

The problem was risky lending itself. The trend in housing prices, even if the secondary market for mortgages was either small or non-existent, would have fueled more riskiness. In home lending, a statistic of note to assess risk is the loan-to-value (LTV) ratio. This ratio is a primary indicator of credit risk. As the ratio rises in value, the loan is larger versus its value, and can rise for two reasons. First, it can rise because home equity loans are added to the primary mortgage, or second mortgages are provided to an initial home purchase. Also, the LTV can fall due to the home's value falling or a combination. When subprime mortgages were originated, many had relatively low down-payments, implying the LTV begins very high. If the home's value begins to fall, the LTV rises, which indicates increased pressure for the home to sell. If the homeowner foresees the LTV rising toward one, there will be incentives to get out from under this rapidly insolvent asset. Beginning in summer 2006, slowing down a little in fall 2006, and beginning again rapidly in 2007, the number of existing housing units for sale increased rapidly in the United States. This was a reflection of both LTV ratios rising and adjustable-rate mortgages adjusting upward. However, the initial riskiness taken by both banks and borrowers exacerbated the market's downward movement, as a large subgroup of homes was exposed to risk simultaneously.

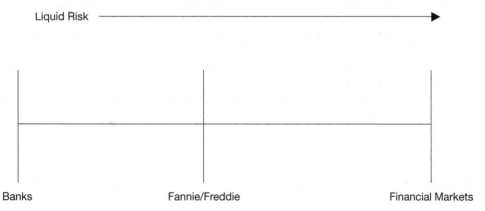

Figure 7.6 The old way: selling bank loans to the open market.

The borrowers and banks are both to blame for these problems. Consumerism in the United States is a widely debated issue. On the one hand, consumerism fuels jobs, income and tax receipts at all levels of the economy. We will learn later that the stimulation of consumption incentives is a key focus for monetary policy. However, the use of a home as a source of funding provided consumers with both an enhanced availability of credit and more risk. As home values went up, a wealth effect took place in the United States, and consumption rose with housing prices acting as collateral. While consumerism also made many people homeowners, it also made many people who should not have been homeowners such. One could argue that the borrower (consumer) was willing to take risks because of a perception that never-ending consumption could come from investing in a home that would rise forever in value and use it as a credit card. See Figure 7.7.

In summary, the subprime crisis is still unresolved at the time of writing this text. More details are discussed in terms of regulatory reactions to these changes and how monetary policy is trying to solve the crisis when we discuss central banking in Chapter 8. Recognizing that central banks can manipulate the profit-maximization incentives of a bank is a major step in understanding the way policy transmits itself to the macroeconomy. In all these crises, central banks have either tried to salvage the situation or have exacerbated the problems.

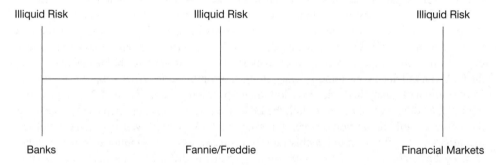

Figure 7.7 The financial crisis of 2007 and beyond.

Things to remember

The financial crisis of 2007 and beyond was caused by the confluence of three main events:

- housing prices experiencing a speculative bubble fueled by banks lending in a risky manner and the financial markets funding speculation;
- financial markets and the macroeconomy in the United States experiencing a natural cyclic downturn; and
- world commodity prices rising rapidly and further contracting consumer demand beyond the natural cycle and the reduction in housing prices.

Summary

The microeconomics of the banking industry are the same as the microeconomics of any firm. Banks produce money from money, but also use inputs such as labor and capital. Lending takes three forms in the model of this chapter. The bank either lends to private concerns, firms and households, to other banks in an interbank market, or they buy government debt securities. The bank's allocation of assets depends on matching marginal revenue and marginal cost for each type of loan. Because the marginal revenues and costs are all linked to each other; as one market changes so do the other markets. The bank maximizes profit by allocating assets until all three of these markets are delivering a quantity of loanable funds where marginal revenue equals marginal cost. Because the banks have an incentive to take some risks, banking and financial market regulations are meant to protect the consumer from this risk-taking. The Basel II accords have to set worldwide standards on risk-taking, accountability, capital requirements, and many other issues in banking.

The United States has the prototypical regulatory structure, where the Federal Reserve acts as the main regulator; the FDIC acts as insurer of deposits and regulator simultaneously. The FDIC remains as a demand deposit insurer (there are some private insurers), but almost failed in the 1980s. Its sister entity, the FSLIC, did fail. The Japanese banking crisis, elements of which remain to this day, was also a function of regulatory failure, but also of the relationships between banks, the government and businesses. In many ways, Japanese banks were not regulated enough. Finally, at least at the time of this writing, the United States is experiencing another financial crisis, this one spread throughout banking and other financial markets. The currency crises of the 1990s put further strains on banking, as has the subprime crisis of the new millennium's first decade. The likelihood of regulatory reform that will spread to investment banking and potentially derivative markets is high, and Basel II may not be too far away. Chapter 8 discusses how central and commercial banking are linked to each other through regulation and policy.

Key terms

1 Disintermediation: the act of withdrawing funds from a financial intermediary.
2 Federal Deposit Insurance Corporation (FDIC): the governmental insurance agency in the United States which guarantees a certain level of bank deposits and acts as a regulatory arm of the government for the banking industry.
3 Loan-to-value (LTV) ratio: the percentage of a loan to the value of the asset purchased with that loan.

Questions and problems

1 Explain how the market for bank deposits, shown in Figure 7.1, differs from the market for loanable funds, discussed in Chapter 2.
2 Are the deposits held by a bank their assets or liabilities? Explain.
3 Explain the role of the rate of return on government debt in the bank's profit maximization decision.
4 Explain what would happen to the number of loans made by the bank if the interbank rate (R_{IB}) fell from its current level.
5 Discuss two differences between the thrift and commercial banking crises of the 1980s.
6 Discuss two similarities between the crises of the 1980s and the current financial environment in 2008.
7 Discuss two differences between the crises of the 1980s and the current financial environment in 2008.
8 Discuss two similarities between the US crises of the 1980s and the Japanese banking crisis of the 1990s.

 9   Discuss two differences between the Japanese banking crisis of the 1990s and the current financial environment in 2008.
10   Explain a maturity mismatch for a bank.
11   Disintermediation is specific to banking. Why? What caused this problem as a precursor to the banking problems of the 1980s in the United States? Explain.
12   Do you believe that banking reform works? Explain.

Websites and suggested readings

Websites

Information about the Basel II Accords can be found at: www.federalreserve.gov/generalinfo/basel2/default.htm.
Article from FRB, San Francisco on "Safe and Sound Banking", October 2006: http://www.frbsf.org/publications/economics/letter/2006/el2006-26.pdf.

Suggested readings

For advanced students, see Frexias and Rochet (2007) *Microeconomics of Banking*, 2nd ed. Cambridge, MA: MIT Press.
Santomero, Anthony (1984) "Modeling the banking firm: a survey", *Journal of Money, Credit and Banking*, 16 (4), Part 2: Bank Market Studies, 576–602.

8 Connections between commercial and central banking

Introduction

In western Africa, there are many countries which were European colonies before the Second World War. After the war, many of these countries gained independence either peacefully or by revolution. As with any new country, there is a need for a new central bank. For the 15 countries in the Economic Community of West African States (ECOWAS) there are three currency unions. In what is now the West African Monetary Zone (WAMZ), the search for the correct form of central bank has been a tumultuous one, and one that has settled on the formation of a common currency that is now tied directly to the euro. These countries use the European Central Bank (ECB) as their monetary authority. Western African nations consist of many different types of economies, most of them simple and primary products based. The largest economy in this area, Nigeria, is not part of this currency union, remaining tied to the pound sterling. These nations lack a strong financial center and use larger economies as financial anchors.

What does this mean for banking within these countries? From Chapter 7's discussion of how a bank operates, private banks need to substitute loans with low-risk securities and need a depositor base to fund new loans. If a nation does not produce its own currency or waits for a signal from another country's central bank to do so, monetary policy could become somewhat impotent. For a central bank to operate correctly, private banks must react to interest rate signals and incentives to follow central bank policy. This is a challenge for the WAMZ nations.

Case study 8.1 The beginnings of an African continental currency: the Eco to the Afro

On 1 December 2009, the Economic Community of West African States, or *ECOWAS*, plans to formally introduce a new, unified currency. The currency, called the *Eco*, includes countries from both the CFA Franc Zone and the pound sterling's West African Monetary Zone. The eco would combine the two currencies into one based on the euro. This is a major step forward for these countries, where a history exists of civil and regional war, price instability, and diverse economies that may have a difficult time participating in a single currency area (Ojo 2004).

One of the important issues in monetary union is macroeconomic "convergence", conditions that make the macroeconomic situation in each country similar. In Chapter 13, we speak of optimal currency areas briefly, but this case is really about the function of central banks. Many of these countries are heavy fiscal spenders and use their

---

monetary authority's printing press to pay for it. Because this type of coupled activity leads directly to inflation, a currency area is strained by member countries that have large fiscal spending and cannot pay for it through the collection of taxes alone. The amalgamated central bank will engage in providing some financing and bonds, but countries, as in the euro area, are asked to control their fiscal spending within a certain percentage of their gross domestic product. The countries in the proposed Eco area are Benin, Burkina Faso, Cape Verde, Côte d'Ivoire, The Gambia, Ghana, Guinea, Guinea Bissau, Liberia, Mali, Niger, Nigeria, Senegal, Sierra Leone, and Togo (Benessay-Quere 2005).

Data for these countries are somewhat sketchy and even the larger countries have had sporadic reporting to entities such as the World Bank. There is some talk, and the Eco's introduction is meant to be a major step forward, about an African currency. The West African Monetary Institute (WAMI) was charged with supervision of the amalgamation process and specifically analyzing the convergence of these countries toward each other's macroeconomic situations. Table 8.1 provides the criteria.

Adhering to specific goals of monetary policy is difficult to accomplish in an environment where multiple decisions-makers exist that can easily force the central bank to pursue indirect goals, such as maintain the confidence of foreign investors or stabilize interest rates as fiscal deficits rise. Economies that act as one reduce the risk of a single central banking; this is especially true in the ECOWAS, where the Eco will be fixed to the euro and thus maintenance of that exchange rate is the number one goal. Will Africa as a continent have a common currency by 2020? It is very unlikely the Afro will appear if convergence criteria remain determining factors in that decision. Masson and Pattillo (2005) give a comprehensive overview of the history and possibilities of currency union in Africa.

Table 8.1 Criteria for convergence in ECOWAS

	Percent or value	*Max or Min*
Primary criteria		
Inflation (consumer prices)	5%	Max
Fiscal budget balance (excluding grants)	–4%	Min
Foreign exchange reserves (months of imports)	3 months	Min
Monetization of debt (% of tax receipts of preceding year)	10%	Max
Secondary criteria		
Tax receipts (% of GDP)	20%	Min
Public investment (% of expenditure)	20%	Min
Public salaries (% of expenditure)	35%	Max
Real interest rate (treasury bonds) (%)	0%	Min
Change in the real exchange rate (year on year)	stable	

Source: Benassy-Quere (2005).

Central banks manipulate their balance sheets to initiate and propagate changes in the money supply. As the amount of excess reserves is manipulated by central bank policy, private banking reacts by adjusting their portfolios. Central banks generally also regulate their domestic financial markets. In some countries, the central bank does relatively little regulation (the European Central Bank), and in other countries regulation is extensive (the US Federal Reserve).

This chapter has four sections. The first introduces central banking as a concept and discusses international differences in organizing central banking systems. The connection to private banking is obvious from this organization. The second section turns toward the Federal Reserve System in the United States, a system that is most copied throughout the world by other central banks in structure. The Federal Reserve provides an example of how central banks are meant to function and why the original arrangement may need some changes. Next, the regulatory functions of central banks are discussed briefly, especially their international differences. In short, central banks are asked by their governments to regulate financial markets because private banking and investment banking are linked economically. Finally, the theoretical ideas of how a central bank is supposed to work and how the private banking sector is meant to be involved are also discussed. These tools and goals of monetary policy are the links between banking and the macroeconomy. A brief discussion of policy constraints, and the choice of discretion versus rules in monetary policy formation, end this chapter and propel us toward a discussion of money demand and monetary policy in Chapter 9.

Central banking: an introduction

Throughout this text, with good reason, central banking has been mentioned as a unifying force in the banking system. Central banks are quasi-governmental entities in most countries, providing currency to the economy, administering monetary policy, and regulating domestic financial markets. Central banks are meant to act in the public interest, functioning as servants of the people to reduce risks through their actions. In some cases, central banks help to set and maintain exchange rates, especially if there is a political agreement to fix the domestic currency's value to another specific currency or a basket of foreign currencies. They act as the lender of last resort in most countries, a place that private banking and other financial entities can come in a time of crisis for a low-cost loan meant to resurrect a failing institution. Later in this chapter, two instances of central banking bailing out non-bank entities show that central banks may use the discount window to maintain financial stability when any financial institution, such as a bank, hedge fund or insurance firm, is on the brink of collapse and that failure threatens the vitality of the domestic financial system.

Central banks face challenges initiating monetary policy, tracking and following macro-economic variations that result to the goals of policy, and the macroeconomic effects sought by policy makers. The bridge between them consists of instruments and targets.

Monetary tools

In macroeconomic principles courses, three tools of monetary policy are normally discussed, and two others are alluded to or ignored because they are somewhat obscure and difficult to find examples for easily. The first is the main way central and private banks communicate with each other financially. This communication is called an open market operation (OMO). These OMOs are the buying and selling of bonds on the "open market", where that market is concentrated on private banks shifting the composition of their assets to accommodate new monetary policy. Next is changing the discount rate (ΔDR), or changing the interbank interest rate target (ΔIB). The discount rate is the rate of interest at which central banks lend to private banks through a "discount window". This window is where a central bank acts as the lender of last resort for banks and other financial institutions on the brink of collapse. In practice, central banks do very little day-to-day lending through this mechanism. Instead, they allow the private banks to engage in lending to clear reserve requirements. In this market, changes in the interbank rate determine the cost of banks not holding enough reserves.

It is important to recognize that most central banks either explicitly set these rates or have a target rate in mind when changing either policy rate. Many countries have limited to no interbank lending, so the discount and interbank rates are essentially the same. Finally, the reserve ratio itself may be changed (ΔRR), manipulating the amount of loanable funds the bank has by changing the quantity of deposits available for lending. This monetary tool is used rarely, as a change in a reserve ratio creates a market signal of financial crisis if the ratio is increased and may signal too large a level of confidence in banking if decreased. The reserve ratio ultimately signals systemic riskiness in banking in one direction or the other.[1]

The final two tools are known as selective credit controls and moral suasion. Selective credit controls are limits set on specific financial markets that set the availability of credit in the macroeconomy. Examples include limits on margin lending, regulatory limits on deposit rates such as Federal Reserve Regulation Q, and branch banking regulations such as Federal Reserve Regulation D. Moral suasion is the use of audits, larger fees and penalties on risky banks to provide incentives for private banks to self-police their lending practices.

Two common themes permeate any choice of monetary tool by the central bank. First, the central bank affects interest rates no matter how the policy travels through the macroeconomy toward its potential goals. Second, each tool is related to one another through the interbank rate. The interbank rate has become one of the most important macroeconomic statistics of our time, and is a large shift in the industrialized world from monetary aggregate measures dominating central banking in practice. The next section discusses the five monetary tools in detail, specifically their effects on interest rates.

Open market operations (OMOs)

This is the most-employed tool of modern central banks, a daily adjustment mechanism by monetary policy-makers. Larger economies' central banks trade their domestic government's short-term debt with private banks to make this work. Smaller economies may use larger economies' government debt as a proxy for their own if domestic government debt is not internationally salable. If the smaller country has fixed exchange rates with a specific larger economy, the use of the larger country's debt is a likely alternative to domestic debt. What the central bank is trying to achieve is a fine tuning of excess reserves held by the bank in either loanable or non-loanable form to private markets. Central banks provide market incentives for their private banks to either purchase or sell these debt securities; a common misconception is that the central bank orders its private banks to make these exchanges. The reason this tool is known as an open market transaction is that the central bank is acting as a market participant where private banks are their preferred customer and vendor.

When the central bank buys government debt from the private banks, it is offering to do so at a higher price than the current market value. This is the bank's incentive to make the sale; if the bank can sell the securities at a price greater than the market, a profit incentive drives their actions. In Chapter 2, bond prices were explained as moving inversely with their effective rates. In the case where the central bank is trying to buy bonds from private banks, offering a higher price makes the effective rate of interest on the bonds lower, further providing incentives to sell the bonds to the central bank and reinvest the proceeds in relatively higher rate of return securities. When central banks sell government debt to private banks, the incentive is to offer the bonds at lower than market prices, providing the private bank purchasing the securities with a higher effective rate of return on the now less-expensive bonds.

Open market operations affect interest rates other than the short-term government debt market. When private banks trade assets (government debt) for others (loanable funds to be turned into loans), the trade is based on the profit-maximizing principles shown in Chapter 7. Central banks assume this connection to be true, and are indirectly manipulating the supply of loanable funds through these open market operations. When the central bank buys securities from banks, the supply of loanable funds should rise as banks receive cash for their securities, which augments their excess reserves. The market for loanable funds knows this to be true by watching the market for government debt, and adjusts their expectations on loan rates accordingly. As the supply of loanable funds rises, interest rates fall, and attract the borrowers necessary to clear the surplus of funds in the market. This is due to the lower interest rates providing incentives to borrowers on the margin to augment their debt holdings due to a lower cost of debt. Because other securities markets compete with bank loans and other lending instruments, other interest rates follow the open market operation.

To summarize, open market operations that buy securities from private banks lower interest rates; when central banks sell securities, interest rates rise.

Changing discount and interbank rates

While open market operations change interest rates in a continuous way, central banks employ changes in discount rates for discrete jumps from one interest rate level to another. For example, in July 2007, the European Central Bank increased their discount rate (DR) by 25 basis points (one-quarter percent). The rate did not slide between its former and new levels, it jumped to the new level. This immediately increased the interbank rate in the euro area by 25 basis points, as the interbank market is directly tied to the discount rate. In the United States, the Federal Reserve reduced its discount rate 17 times between September 2001 and June 2004, only to turn around and increase the discount rate 14 times after that when a policy change took place. The Federal Funds Rate (FFR) target remained 100 basis points (one percent) less than the discount rate throughout this timeframe. On 17 August 2007, the spread became 50 basis points, and on 16 March 2008 the spread was dropped to 25 basis points. The actual interbank rate is market-driven and manipulated, if needed, by OMOs. Other economies have different names for the interbank rate and its target, but retain a similar rate structure to the ECB and Federal Reserve.

Both rates represent costs for similar funds. The DR is the rate charged by the central bank for loans provided as a lender of last resort. Most central banks, unless an interbank market does not exist in a specific country, are not in business to provide daily lending to private banks for a shortage of required reserves. Only in times of crisis will most central banks lend to a private bank; a specific bank's imminent failure increases the default risk in interbank lending, and other banks that have surplus funds may not lend to a troubled bank because of augmented risk. For daily purposes, central banks point borrowers to the interbank market for two reasons. First, the interbank market is just that: a market for excess reserves. The assumption is that there is as much supply as there is demand, naturally clearing the market and keeping the central bank from being involved. Second, interbank rates that exceed their associated discount rate serve as a penalty of sorts for using too many reserves for lending. In the United States, the DR has been both above and below the FFR target rate by policy edict.

As the interbank rate target falls, the central bank tries to provide system-wide incentives for firms and households to spend more by reducing the cost of consumption today; other interest rates are expected to fall. When OMOs are not enough to stimulate the macroeconomy, central banks generally turn toward a rate change. When policy rates rise, the central bank tries to increase interest rates across the economy. This quantum change to interest rates upward is meant to slow the macroeconomy by increasing the cost of capital for firms and consumption by households.

To summarize, when the interbank rate target falls, other interest rates are projected to fall; as the interbank rate target rises, other interest rates rise. Figure 8.1 shows the FFR and the US discount rate since 1970.

Changing the reserve ratio

In fractional reserve banking systems, private banks are required to hold a certain amount of their deposits as non-loanable funds. As discussed in Chapter 7, these funds are required to maintain a certain amount of the depositor's funds for depositor demand. Banks are at risk of depositor withdrawal *en masse* when they are unable to provide their customers with liquidity on request. Required reserves are meant to be held as cash or cash equivalents, the most liquid assets held by the bank. Once the reserve ratio is set, most banks attempt to loan the maximum amount of excess reserves. Some banks exceed this amount and leverage themselves in the interbank market as described above; other banks hold more than the required reserves by internal policy for use as loanable funds in the interbank market or as additional buffers against episodic, unanticipated surges in depositor demand for funds. The bank is assumed to take the reserve ratio as a constraint in the optimization of profit from loanable funds and make decisions accordingly.

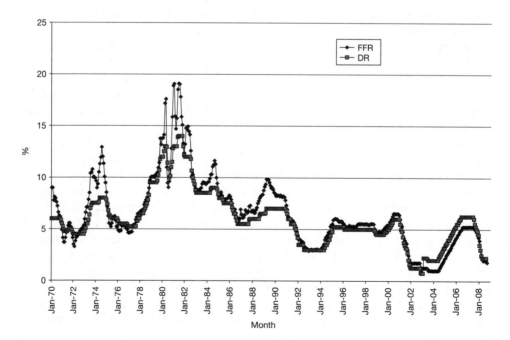

Figure 8.1 Comparison of federal funds and discount rates in the United States, 1970–2008.
Source: Federal Reserve Board.

Changing the reserve ratio is thus a rare move and a systemic signal of changes in the central bank's perception of banking industry risk. To lower the reserve ratio is to provide more loanable funds availability to all banks simultaneously. As a result, a lower reserve ratio leads to lower interest rates. When the reserve ratio is increased, the signal is that banking is more risky and every private bank is being asked to hold more cash and cash equivalents in reserve versus lending. Depending on the magnitude of this change, the financial markets may react very poorly to such a move. As the reserve ratio rises, other interest rates rise. Generally, these changes are small and rare due to the general signal the changes send.

Selective credit controls and moral suasion

The final policy tools are less explicit in their effects on interest rates across the economy. Selective credit controls are specific limits and mandates central banks place on banks and other financial institutions that change the availability of loanable funds. Two examples are margin loan limits and limits on the rates banks can pay for deposits. Margin loan limits are limits placed on what percentage of an investor's portfolio can act as collateral for loans to purchase financial securities. These margin loans are generally provided by investment banks rather than commercial banks or thrifts, and do not affect the level of deposits in the banking system directly. However, because the margin loan market is providing loans, the level of deposits at banks may be affected indirectly, which then affects the amount of loans available overall and interest rates. For example, suppose the current level of the margin loan limit is 50 percent of an investor's portfolio. What this means is that if the current market value of an investor's portfolio is ¥10,000,000, the Japanese investment bank which holds this portfolio can only lend the investor ¥5,000,000 at a maximum. If this margin loan limit is set at 60 percent instead, the investment bank can now lend the investor up to ¥6,000,000. This increases the availability of credit in financial markets, and lowers rates of interest on such loans. As a result, borrowers increase their financial leverage to take advantage of lower-cost funds to purchase financial investments, which increases the cash holdings of those who sell securities to the investor/borrower. Bank deposits are augmented. This change theoretically increases loanable funds at banks, reducing interest rates otherwise.[2]

Most central banks limit the rates their private banks can pay for interest-bearing deposits. Such a limit, Regulation Q in the United States as discussed briefly in Chapter 7, is meant to protect banks against markets forcing their costs to rise too rapidly. This assumes that households and firms will always have some portion of their asset portfolio in interest-bearing accounts at banks and thrifts as a matter of liquidity and security. This controls the amount of funds that flow toward the bank, and the amount of loanable funds.

Moral suasion regulates banks by threat or practice of audits, fees and other costs of regulation that provide incentives for banks to self-police their lending practices. A bank's lending "morality" is a function of the higher costs. For example, suppose the Bank of England felt that British banks were too risky in their lending but did not want to explicitly change interest rates to reflect those new risks. One way to reduce risk is to audit certain banks, threaten audits, or financially penalize banks based on certain metrics, such as too large a debt to asset ratio. While not an interest rate signal, the end result of moral suasion should be a change in the availability of loanable funds as private banks react to the central bank's new practices concerning the loanable funds' "morality". The interest rate then changes due to these threats. Many central banks audit specific banks that borrow excessively from either the discount window or interbank markets, an indication of higher risks in the specific bank's lending portfolio. Some central banks also charge fees for audits or for violations of specific banking metrics as regulation. More audits and fees act like monetary contraction. Moral suasion can also be expansionary; if central banks decide to audit less often or to reduce fees for excessive borrowing, monetary expansion may result.

Summary on monetary policy tools

All five monetary tools are assumed to affect interest rates by affecting the supply of loanable funds. It is not necessarily the case that these funds originate from commercial banks or thrifts, though the bulk of these funds do in practice. Monetary policy tools that are contractionary act to increase rates of interest by reducing the amount of loanable funds available: selling government debt to private banks, increasing either the interbank rate target or the reserve ratio. Monetary policy tools that are expansionary act to reduce interest rates by increasing the supply of loanable funds: buying government debt from banks, or reducing the interbank rate target or reserve ratio. Selective credit controls and moral suasion act either as expansionary or contractionary depending on their effects on the costs of funds. Table 8.2 provides a quick summary of the interest rate effects of the three main tools.

Table 8.2 Comparison and summary of main monetary tools

ΔOMO	ΔFFR target/ΔDR	ΔRR	*Effect*
Sell treasuries	FFR/DR rises	RR rises	Rates rise
Buy treasures	FFR/DR cut	RR cut	Rates fall

Bridging between monetary tools and goals

Central banks use so-called monetary instruments and targets to assess the movement of monetary policy from the change initiated by the tools discussed above and the goals of policy discussed in the next section. Figure 8.2 shows this movement in simple terms.

It is important to understand that every central bank tracks its policies through a mix of specific macroeconomic indicators. Monetary theory has now settled on two major indicators. Policy should affect inflation, output or a mix of the two, and changes in the market quantity of monetary aggregates, such as M_1 and M_2, provide evidence that the changes are taking place. Monetary aggregates may move for reasons other than policy-initiated changes, and

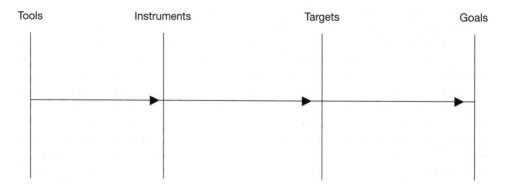

Figure 8.2 Policy transmission continuum.

also, because money demand may be causal to income and interest rates rather than be driven by them, monetary policy-makers have shifted to tracking interest rates instead of monetary aggregates as instruments of monetary policy. Short-term government debt and actual interbank rates serve as instruments in most countries. Targets include unemployment and inflation rates, real long-term interest rates, and real GDP growth. These targets depend on a specific central bank's philosophy, as some central banks have single goals of inflation control, such as the European Central Bank, while others try to balance between stimulating output growth and controlling prices.

Transparency is also a major issue, and both monetary theory and practice have suggested that central banks become more efficient when their policy changes are both anticipated by the macroeconomy and transparent in how the central bank reacts and expects the policy to move through the macroeconomy. Both policy history and theory agree that monetary goals must categorically be concerned with larger macroeconomic variables, but are also constrained by financial market changes and issues.[3]

Monetary policy goals: direct and indirect

Central banks face many challenges concerning monetary policy, especially in achieving goals set forth by most governments and monetary theory. Since Keynes' *General Theory of Employment, Interest and Money*, monetary policy has been at the forefront of macro-economic research because of its perceived ability to act quickly when needed to affect the economy and its apparently explicit links to major economic variables. As discussed above, these links have been challenged, empirically tested, refuted, and then born again. One consistent link between policy and practice has been the unanimity around the possible goals of monetary policy. Macroeconomists now suggest four monetary goals. First is price stability. Control of inflation has become the world monetary focus of the twenty-first century. The last century was rife with hyperinflation episodes, most of which took place in either war-torn or developing economies. Many theorists lay the blame at the feet of poor, myopic monetary policies. Further, stabilizing inflation has obvious, positive economic outcomes. The preservation of household purchasing power alone is a driving force behind focusing on inflation as a policy goal.

Second is the stimulation of real income growth. Much of the debate in monetary theory does not center on policy's link to inflation, which is regarded as intuitive, but rather to real economic activity. Assuming the macroeconomy is not at full employment and has the ability to augment productivity, monetary policy may be able to stimulate firms to increase their investment in capital goods and for households to purchase more durable and non-durable goods. Some believe that monetary policy may also act like a technology shock, where the supply side of the economy is affected by policy. When policy is initiated to create economic booms in business cycles, more real income for the macroeconomy is the policy goal. Third, a related goal is the reduction of unemployment or increase of employment. Assuming that the stimulation of real GDP comes from more spending as a result of monetary policy, this slightly different view suggests that policy can stimulate job growth. Instead of stimulating the firm's purchase of new plant and equipment, policy stimulates the firm's purchase of labor hours. Both these goals have an ability to create more real income for the economy, but use different inputs to do so.

Finally, but not necessarily less important, is the maintenance of an appropriate exchange rate. In countries that choose to fix their domestic currency's value to another, exchange rate defense or maintenance against changes in the balance of payments (BOP) is the only goal of policy. In countries that have floating or market exchange rates, this goal is not a prime concern, but may be policy's focus from time to time. Generally, larger economies choose to have floating exchange rates. Canada, as an example, uses the Canadian dollar/US dollar exchange rate in its policy decisions directly because of its dependence upon trade with the United States concerning its real GDP levels.[4] However, the Canadian dollar floats against major currencies including the American dollar. The following section details each of these goals and how policy tries to achieve them, followed by three indirect goals that act as policy constraints on the central bank's direct pursuit of these four direct goals.

Price stability

Inflation can be ruinous for a macroeconomy when it is not the by-product of demand-side growth. When aggregate spending outpaces aggregate output, inflation occurs as a reflection of scarcity. Since goods, services and debts are all priced in terms of the domestic currency, the supply of that currency changes prices directly. For example, when monetary policy is expansionary, there will immediately be inflationary pressure in the macroeconomy for two reasons. Monetary expansion is meant to stimulate more spending, met by production levels rising as firms have an ability to charge higher prices as demand exceeds supply. Without inflation to cover the rising costs of production (due to the scarcity of inputs), firms lack profit incentives to produce more goods. For that reason, inflation can be a by-product of demand-side growth. In contrast to fiscal policy, a monetary expansion creates more currency, which means each currency unit that existed before the policy change is now worth less. This translates into higher prices in terms of that currency. When the macroeconomy is fully employed, money and prices still have a positive relationship, which in its limit is a percentage match, one-for-one with the creation of money. Real output growth does not result from a monetary expansion once the economy reaches full capacity.

Central banks seek to control inflation because rising prices threaten the purchasing power of income and wealth. A simple example is nominal versus real wages. Suppose you work at a video store and are paid ten dollars per hour. If general prices increase, that ten dollar wage does not purchase as much as it did before inflation. Without some adjustment to nominal wages, the real wage after inflation is less than ten dollars. Another example is portfolio investment. Suppose your portfolio gained ten percent last year, but inflation was three percent. The real return on your financial investment was only seven percent. Inflation, for this reason, acts like a tax; when monetary policy is expansionary, government spending is funded partially through seigniorage, the revenue raised by printing money which has also been referred to as an "inflation tax".[5]

Since income taxes are levied on nominal and not real income, inflation causes more taxes to be taken from workers. This phenomenon, known as "bracket creep", comes with progressive taxes and inflation. This is also true for financial markets. Suppose an investor sold stock and made a 20 percent profit from the original cost. Suppose further that inflation was 20 percent from the time of purchase to the time of sale. When the investor reports the gain for tax purposes, the investor will be taxed on the nominal profit. The real profit is zero, but taxes are levied on nominal profit. Of course, the investor could have sold this stock along the way and purchased financial investments that would have grown faster than inflation had the price increases been anticipated.

When inflation is unanticipated, uncertainty over real income and rates of return can affect financial and goods markets. In 2001, the Argentinean economy began reacting to inflationary forces that were otherwise suppressed because of poor monetary policy and a lack of reaction in all markets. By December 2001, the economy was on the brink of collapse and inflation was poised to repeat a performance the Argentineans had seen on three previous occasions in 30 years; in 1995, inflation soared and financial markets teetered on the brink of collapse as the result of the "Tequila Crisis".[6] If inflation is anticipated, all parts of the macro-economy can make adjustments that naturally reduce inflation pressure. The uncertainty involved once inflation is upon the economy can be quite devastating. Social chaos and revolution generally coincide with hyperinflation episodes, when inflation runs at more than 50 percent per year.

In summary, price stability is the focus of monetary policy in industrialized nations throughout the world. Because inflation has adverse effects on real outcomes, it is difficult both politically and economically to choose other policy goals. However, in times where inflation is not a problem and stagnation may be coming from a lack of incentives in capital or labor markets, monetary policy may be able to provide some stimulus to real GDP or employment growth.

Stimulate real GDP or employment growth

While there are subtle differences between these monetary goals, they are similar enough to combine here. When a central bank expands the money supply, it provides incentives for firms to purchase capital (increase real investment) and to hire more labor hours. Ultimately, the central bank would like to stimulate both. The classic channel of monetary policy affecting real investment at firms stimulates more labor hours hired because capital and labor are complements rather than substitutes in production. Robert Solow, a Nobel Laureate in economics, built a model based on the supposition that every economy gravitates toward an optimal capital-labor ratio, not just a specific capital stock or employment level alone, and policy could be used to move the economy from one capital-labor ratio to another that coincides with a higher level of total output.

Real GDP growth from monetary policy assumes that the economy has room to grow. This interest rate channel suggests that when monetary policy is expansionary, and interest rates fall because the central bank buys government debt from private banks or reduces the inter-bank rate or reserve ratio, firms have an incentive to increase their purchase of real investment goods. This purchase stimulates more real GDP through a multiplier effect on household consumption; an augmentation of real investment implies a larger productive capacity as well. This way of looking at monetary theory assumes that monetary policy has the ability to reduce the real rate of interest which acts as a component in the firm's cost of capital, the economic cost of the firm purchasing a piece of machinery, for example.[7]

A parallel story takes place in the labor markets, and is based on the idea of sticky prices. Sticky price theory suggests that when markets are not in equilibrium, there may be monopoly forces at work to keep prices at levels that do not allow markets to clear. Further, because the average firm has an incentive to know the goods market better than the average consumer, prices are more mobile than wages when a policy shock takes place. There is little debate that monetary policy builds pressure on general prices to change; if general prices move faster than nominal wages, higher prices erode the real wage. A lower real wage provides firms with incentives to hire more labor hours at a relatively lower real price, increasing the demand for labor. As the demand for labor increases, the firm can afford to pay a slightly higher nominal wage to lure those unemployed into taking a job, so long as the new real wage remains lower than the pre-policy real wage. An increase in employment results from these movements.

In summary, expansionary monetary policy is the way a central bank pursues this combination goal. The reason why these goals are sometimes separate is because some economists believe central banks struggle to affect labor markets versus capital markets, and the effects on investment are much more intuitive with respect to theory. However, as we will see in Chapter 10, the tradeoff between inflation and unemployment underscores an inherent conflict between policy goals and the practical importance of monetary policy's ability to affect labor markets.

Maintaining an appropriate exchange rate

In economies where exchange rates are fixed, this is the only goal of policy in theory. When an economy chooses fixed exchange rates, the use of monetary policy for domestic purposes is considered to be abandoned. The anchor economy, the economy with which an exchange rate agreement has been made, does not want the current rate manipulated or pressured to change one direction or the other. Central banks are sometimes asked to use monetary policy to control for exchange rate pressure from economic activity. The United States has recently fought China politically to relieve pressure on the Chinese currency strengthening due to massive Chinese trade surpluses with the United States, especially in this decade.

Ultimately, the debate concerning how central banks should act in the midst of fixed exchange rates is definitional. What is an appropriate exchange rate? When fixed, the agreed-upon rate is usually the best candidate, but most currency agreements come with some room for maneuver. If the exchange rate floats, theory suggests that monetary policy should not be used to manipulate this rate, as this is the choice to allow market forces to determine its value. Exchange rates are always open to some fine tuning; even floating exchange rates may be deemed relatively too high or too low and market forces not acting quickly enough to counter the economic pressure, pushing the rate in a certain direction. Over 60% of the world's economies are pegged to either the dollar or the euro in 2009.

Case study 8.2 Do discount rates matter?

The discount rate is the interest rate at which central banks lend to their domestic banks. The interbank rate is the domestic rate at which banks lend to each other; the LIBOR acts as the international rate for these loans. In developing countries, an interbank market may not exist, and international banks may not be willing to lend money to a bank where the political and economic stability is in question. The central bank in such nations plays a vital role in acting as a facilitator of banking and to protect it against bank runs and a lack of funding. In a market where banks struggle to lend to each other, what interest rate should the central bank charge its local banks? The LIBOR, as described in an earlier case, is an international rate at which banks can borrow worldwide and not rely on a broken, domestic interbank market or an unreliable central bank for lending. It also allows banks to borrow in other currencies than their domestic currency.

The role of the discount rate is important where an interbank market does not explicitly reside. In many cases, especially for emerging economies, the central bank will act as the interbank market for domestic banks. So instead of targeting an interbank rate to shape the functionality of banks lending to each other, they are truly setting the cost of funds for banks. The spread between the LIBOR and these discount rates provides a measure of the flow of funds for banks.

In a recent article by Rai et al. (2007), the movements of official discount rates in Germany, France, the United Kingdom and Japan have larger effects on short-term interest rates than on long-term interest rates. All these economies have sophisticated financial markets and thus react quickly to new information, generally known as announcement effects. These announcement effects are more likely to change short-term rates than long. The short-term is defined here as three- or six-month rates. Financial deregulation in these countries is seen as making the announcement effects more rapid (ibid., p. 910). The flow of information through the markets depends on the market's competitive structure; as more competition takes place, the effects of policy begin before they are announced. This study suggests that the UK's short-term rates become much more closely tied to its official discount rate than in the other countries because deregulation began sooner than in other nations. As a result, the announcement itself of a discount rate, and thus a monetary policy, change was reduced; the effects began to happen before the announcement. So, discount rates seem to matter as long as the central bank is credible in its policies.

Indirect goals that constrain direct goal pursuit

Central banks have constraints in pursuing the goals above that act as indirect goals. Because central banks act as regulators of financial markets in their country, times exist where direct goals must be abandoned for the domestic economy's stability. In some cases, a country is dependent on foreign financial capital and must walk away from pursuing real GDP growth to continue and attract foreign investors with relatively high interest rates. Domestic financial markets themselves may suffer from interest rates that have drifted too high or have fallen too fast. The stabilization of interest rates, rather than the stabilization of prices, may create more pressure for central bank action. Though stabilizing prices and interest rates are related, they may also conflict with each other in cases where rates are relatively too high. For example, suppose the Royal Bank of South Africa recognized interest rates were rising rapidly, and wanted to reduce rates. Inflation is initiated when reducing upward interest rate pressure, constraining the pursuit of price stability as a goal of policy.

The prevention of financial crises is the main constraint on central banks pursuing the direct goals above. If the central bank must provide funding as the lender of last resort, the money supply expands and the goal of price stability is abandoned. Unfortunately, there are many cases in which preventing financial crises means bailing out risky banks and other financial intermediaries because of already runaway inflation, creating hyperinflation pressures. Foreign investors provide alternative financing to a country, and must remain confident in the domestic currency's value and financial market stability. Suppose there was a threat of massive inflation in an economy. It would be consistent with the pursuit of price stability to increase interest rates and reduce inflation pressure, naturally restoring the confidence of foreign investors. However, if the goal of monetary policy is to stimulate real GDP growth, raising interest rates to keep foreign capital flowing in may reduce incentives toward output growth. If interest rates fall too low, net interest margins at banks become smaller and smaller, and there is a call to augment interest rates simply to restore banking profits and reduce the risk of bank failure. If a central bank chooses to increase interest rates under such a scenario, it may abandon goals of employment and output growth.

Notice that these constraints do not infringe the pursuit of price stability as a goal unless interest rates are seen as relatively too high. The constraints above are difficult to overcome as domestic financial markets pull at central banks constantly for action.

Things to remember

There are three indirect goals of monetary policy or constraints on the achievement of direct goals.

- the stability of interest rates;
- raising or maintaining the confidence of foreign investors; and
- acting as the lender of last resort.

Monetary discretion vs. rules

Monetary discretion, where a central bank has the ability to set goals at will and change as economic realities make it necessary, versus a monetary rule is a continued debate.[8] A monetary rule sets policy actions based on certain macroeconomic criteria. For example, if the ECB rule is two percent inflation per annum, the stated goal of monetary policy is price stability and targets the annualized inflation rate at two percent. If expected inflation data are actually greater than two percent, the economy is going to act as if the central bank will reduce the money supply. There is a potential inflation bias when monetary discretion is allowed. Most monetary rules have price stability goals; the money supply is more credibly tied to general price levels than to employment or economic growth. Some monetary rules are exchange-rate based; when an economy chooses a fixed exchange rate, regardless of its form, the central bank of that economy essentially sets a monetary rule. However, monetary discretion exists in economies either where inflation is seen as a tolerable vice associated with economic growth or where the pace of nominal economic growth is expected to be faster than price growth.

Another issue concerns central bank independence. If a monetary rule exists, is the central bank a truly independent body? A rule must be enforced to be effective. If the economy's government intends to enforce monetary rules, penalties may be necessary; one suggestion is to tie the compensation of central bankers to the economy's performance. Others are the dismissal of monetary policy-makers if the rule is violated. An index of central bank independence is accepted as a way of measuring the level of autonomy that exists. The index measures the way central bankers are appointed, the level of government involvement, whether price stability is stated in its charter as the prime goal of the central bank, and whether the government has limits on its ability to borrow or derive seigniorage revenue from the central bank. Weights to each are assigned for cross-country comparisons, and an index is born. Many researchers have then used such an index to compare economic performance and the independence measure as a way of finding inflation bias. For example, the European Central Bank is likely to have a smaller level of independence than the Federal Reserve because there is a strict monetary rule for the ECB.

Summary

The connections between central and commercial banks are both explicit and implicit. Explicitly, the central bank acts as partial or complete regulator of banking and financial markets within an economy, a funding source for the banks, clearinghouse for check clearing and all bank transactions, and the protector of deposits for households and firms. Implicitly, the central bank acts on the financial market's behalf to make the industry more efficient, to provide signals about new banking risks, and audit banks as independent third parties. Theory suggests both explicit and implicit policy relationships, more of which is discussed in Chapter 9.

Monetary goals and tools are connected to one another. Monetary goals include price stability, augmentation of either employment or economic growth (or both), or the maintenance of an appropriate exchange rate depending on the exchange rate regime and importance of trade to the economy in question. Some constraints on achieving or focusing on these goals also exist. These include the prevention of banking and financial failures, augmenting foreign investor confidence and stabilizing interest rates and financial markets rather than prices. There are inherent conflicts because of these constraints in pursuing specific policy goals. Monetary tools are similar worldwide: open market operations, changing discount rates, changing interbank rates or interbank target rates, and changing reserve requirements are the main policy tools. Certain selective credit arrangements exist that tie central banks to other markets. Moral suasion is a way that central banks can use their audit function to shape risk-taking at banks.

Central bank independence is a crucial question concerning accountability and pre-dictability of policy. It is argued that independent central banks gain from the freedom of changing as the economic winds blow, while they may have an inflation bias. Non-independent central banks may be tied to government decision-making explicitly or may face a monetary rule which constrains their behavior. Monetary instruments and targets assist central banks in tracking policy and its movements through the macroeconomy. Chapter 9 brings in the other side of the money market, money demand.

Key terms

1 Basis points: a representation of interest rates where one per cent equals 100 basis points.
2 Discount rate: the rate at which a central bank lends to private banks in its economy.
3 Federal funds rate: the interbank lending rate in the United States.
4 Floating exchange rate: a market-driven exchange rate.
5 Hyperinflation: a condition where inflation is greater than 50 percent on an annual basis.
6 Interbank rate: the rate of interest at which banks lend to banks.
7 Interest rate channel: the transmission mechanism of monetary policy that suggests policy affects lending rates, which affects the opportunity cost of real investment to affect real income.
8 Monetary policy goal: the aim of monetary policy.
9 Monetary policy instruments: the initial effect of monetary policy on the macro economy.
10 Monetary policy targets: the secondary or indirect effect of monetary policy on the macroeconomy.
11 Monetary policy tools: the policy change taken by a central bank to initiate monetary policy.
12 Moral suasion: a monetary policy tool that threatens an increase in auditing if augmented riskiness is perceived by the central bank.
13 Open market operations (OMO): the buying and selling of government debt securities by a central bank to manipulate the effective government debt interest rate in the open market.

14   Price stability: the goal of stable and controlled inflation by a central bank.
15   Reserve ratio: the reserve requirement of a fractional banking system, the actual percentage to be held by banks against their deposits.
16   Seigniorage: the profits of a government from printing currency.
17   Selective credit arrangements: specific credit arrangements controlled by central banks: for example, the percentage limit on margin lending.
18   Sticky prices: a condition where aggregate prices move slowly in response to aggregate demand shocks, such as monetary policy.
19   Stimulation of real income growth: a monetary goal focused on augmenting real gross domestic product in an economy.
20   West African Monetary Zone: the currency area in western Africa consisting of Gambia, Ghana, Guinea, Nigeria and Sierra Leone.

Questions and problems

1   Explain the effects of open market operations (OMOs) on the macroeconomy.
2   Explain why buying government debt from private banks allows the central bank to manipulate interest rates.
3   Explain why selling government debt from private banks allows the central bank to manipulate interest rates.
4   Explain the profit incentive of banks to engage in OMOs with central banks using the logic of Chapter 8's model of banking.
5   Explain why changing the discount rate allows the central bank to manipulate interest rates.
6   Explain why changing the interbank rate or its target rate allows the central bank to manipulate interest rates.
7   Explain how changing the reserve ratio in a fractional banking system allows the central bank to manipulate interest rates.
8   Explain the goals of monetary policy and their constraints.
9   Why are the indirect goals known as "constraints"? Explain.

Websites

The Fed in brief: http://www.frbsf.org/publications/federalreserve/fedinbrief/index.html.
Describing the Federal Open Market Committee and its operations: http://www. philadelphiafed.org/education/fomc.html.

9 The domestic market for money

Introduction

One of the drawbacks to printing money is that it represents potential consumption. There is a thirst for money that has permeated all parts of our society, where confusion takes place between the pursuit of money and the pursuit of wealth. Popular music and culture uses currency symbols to represent power over other people and money is seen by many to be a panacea for problems. There is little doubt that possessing money solves many of life's trifles, but it still represents what could be rather than what is. It is difficult to convince children, especially teenagers, that money is simply a representation of consumption and not consumption itself.

In Chapter 1, the definition of money was something possessing the following characteristics simultaneously: medium of exchange, standard of value, standard of deferred payment, and store of value. All of these are important, but many economists have focused on the medium of exchange characteristic most of all. The interplay between the store of value and medium of exchange characteristics has caused an expansion of what specific assets are considered money. Three measures of money exist. M_1 is medium of exchange types of money, cash and its equivalents. M_2 adds interest-bearing forms of liquid accounts held by individuals to M_1; M_3 adds institutional accounts. M_3 has fallen out of favor with some central banks, especially the Federal Reserve; on 23 March 2006, the Federal Reserve announced the official end of data tracking the M_3 quantity of money. Why? While the official reasoning was vague; most likely it was due to a lack of volatility in M_3 money. M_2 is now considered that measure.

Money faces a market for its distribution that follows economic incentives like any other good or service. Its production is partially centralized; if the only measure of money was currency, the central bank would be the monopoly provider. Since money is also a store of value, banks help round out the quantity of money supplied at a given interest rate due to their profit incentives in either storing or lending money. This chapter links the supply side of the money market to its demand side.

The first section of Chapter 9 breaks down the demand for money, the motives for holding cash in a non-interest bearing form. These motives are associated primarily with the work of John Maynard Keynes, an economist who began a revolution in monetary theory. Second, a money demand function is hypothesized, where money demand is linked to consumption and savings directly. How the financial and goods markets interact has much to do with how people demand money. Income is used to both consume and save, which stimulates money demand for both these acts. Next, the money supply curve is derived and equilibrium in the money market is shown. This equilibrium brings together banks and the economy's circular flow; central banks change the entire money supply and assume banks will act through profit-maximizing incentives to help achieve monetary goals. There are multiple ways in which monetary policy affects the macroeconomy; these transmission channels are linked to the interest rate channel discussed in Chapter 8. In Chapter 10, the connection between inflation and unemployment is used to suggest that central banks ultimately form policy to affect one or both of these macroeconomic variables. We begin with money demand.

Money demand: why cash circulates

Money supplied by the central bank circulates because households, firms and governments all consume and need money to purchase goods and services in monetary economies. The medium of exchange function is the primary driver of money demand. To hold and not use cash in an interest-bearing form is to save; there are, of course, many different ways to save and interest paid on a cash equivalent is one of them. To purchase another form of financial investment, the saver must liquidate (turn into cash) another financial asset or use idle cash. Economists posit three "motives" for demanding money, all linked to either consumption or saving.

Transactions motive

This motive is the foundational reason for money demand. This is for current purchases of goods and services, where the motivation is to make transactions. For example, suppose you need to buy groceries. To pay for these groceries, you need some form of cash or a cash equivalent. Grocers offer multiple payment methods: cash, ATM cards, debit cards, checks, and credit cards usually, where a credit card is not money. When you pay the credit card bill, you will then have a transactions motive for money; the liability initiated by the credit card's use does not change your motivation for money demand, it just changes the timing. Holding cash or a cash equivalent is part of this motive more than any other.

Precautionary motive

This motive is similar to the transactions motive, with one small difference. A positive amount of money demand for precautionary purposes is for unforeseen transactions. In this case, the consumer is not sure whether a transaction will take place. For example, we know people who hold cash for reasons other than immediate consumption. You probably have relatives who lived through hard times at some point in their lives. Having cash around was maybe a rare occurrence. The idea that "cash is king" is partially driven by a precaution against bad times. In large economies, domestic legal tender is for all debts public and private. For that reason, people hold cash for transactions they intend to make and those they have not yet encountered.

A classic example of the precautionary motive is if you are traveling and do not have the ability to use another form of payment to pay for a good or service. In most countries, vendors are not required to provide multiple payment options for customer payments. Cash is the singular way that if goods or services are offered by a vendor, the vendor must accept as payment. If you are traveling in remote areas, cash provides a lot less stress. For this reason, you may withdraw more cash than you intend to spend, losing the interest you could earn on the extra cash while traveling but avoiding the cost of having no cash. This precautionary motive reduces additional liquidity costs of transactions.

Case study 9.1 Cashless society – using bankcards and gift cards as currency

Computer technology has expanded the possibilities in how banking records are kept, transactions are made and recorded, and the ability to use no cash when making purchases of all types. Is it possible that society will be completely cashless and all transactions will be electronic? Two camps have come up around this idea. The first suggests that there is a psychological rate of return in holding cash. Having cash advertises potential consumption to others, and the social acceptance of someone holding cash and making this fact apparent to all else is of major intrinsic value. For this reason, cash will always be held. The second reason cash may always be held is the inability to make an electronic transaction in certain locations. The infrastructure needs to reach remote locations with the necessary technology to provide a way for all parties involved to feel safe in making the transaction. Some conspiracy theorists are suggesting that people will be implanted with microchips, walk by a scanner which reads the chip, and cash will be obsolete as a medium of exchange; the chip will transfer funds to merchants (with a lot of other information potentially). While we are some time from having implants like this, the idea of a cashless society suggests that efficiency gains from technology will push holding cash to its natural limit of zero and speed commerce along at a faster pace.

A study by Gerders (2008) provides some trends and ideas as to where money demand in non-cash liquidity is going. The authors performed a survey of depository institutions concerning the use of automatic teller machines (ATMs) and checks. The number of checks paid in the United States has been declining, while the number of electronic payments has been increasing; the volume of electronic payments exceeded the number of check payments in 2003; the number of debit card payments exceed the number of check payments in the United States in 2007 (Gerdes 2008). The study implied that the dollar value of checks exceeds the dollar value of electronic transfers; businesses are still using a paper trail for transactions. To substantiate that idea, the study stated that credit unions had the smallest shares of checks and greater shares of debit card and ATM use versus commercial banks and savings institutions (ibid.). Regional variation shown in the Federal Reserve Board study has implications for larger country networks, such as the euro area and other currency unions in the future, as to how cash is demanded and used.

The European Central Bank (ECB) reports that many countries in Europe are rarely using checks in transactions when cash is not used (Garcia-Swartz et al. 2006). Much like the American example, there exist regional aspects of reducing the use of checks. Eastern Europe and Germany use a very low amount of checks, while southern Europe (including Italy and Greece) use a relatively large amount of checks in transactions. The United Kingdom shows relatively low use of checks versus other countries in western Europe, except for Spain, which uses very few checks. One reason for this regionalism may be due to either infrastructure (where the infrastructure is very good in Germany) or an inability to easily process check-clearing (as in eastern Europe). In France and the United Kingdom, the mix of use of cashless instruments is more balanced, suggesting that the culture and infrastructure have not yet intersected enough to move more consumers away from checks. The data in Garcia-Swartz et al. (2006) suggest that we are becoming more cashless and even more checkless every day. However, it is unlikely society will ever become completely cashless.

Speculative/savings motive

Keynes, in extending classic economic theory, added this motive due to the times in which he lived. The worldwide depression following the American stock market crash of 1929 changed the way households and firms viewed banks as institutions. The failure of many banks and the loss of depositor wealth made banks seem like as wild a wager as their financial companion, the stock market. Keynes suggested that people were sometimes motivated to remove their money from interest-bearing accounts at the bank because they no longer wanted to take the risk of losing the money in other assets or holding the cash at home versus an uncertain future in the bank deposit. When a household withdraws funds from its account, the household speculates on the bank no longer being a going concern and is willing to give up the bank's interest payments for peace of mind.

In a similar way, a household which perceives the bank is not competitive in their interest payments versus the expected rate of return on other assets available has an incentive to withdraw cash to pursue other opportunities. When the household withdraws this money, the household speculates that the rate of return on another asset purchased, or utility derived from the consumption made with the liquidated funds, exceeds the rate of return on or utility derived from owning the bank account. The motive to save in ways outside the bank changed this motive from a speculative motive to a savings motive. Holding a diversified portfolio of assets, which may include the aforementioned bank account, implies that the household will liquidate accounts, interest-bearing in specific, to not only consume but also to save. The household speculates that the interest rate paid by the bank is too low.

These motives all center on a common theme. The theme is that they help explain why the money demand curve is downward sloping, based on both consumption and savings motives. Further, these motives help explain the mechanics by which monetary policy motivates households to change money demand. It is now time to build a money demand function and equate demanding a quantity of money to demanding a quantity of goods. This idea helps later explain why a foreign money market also exists. First, let's assume that cash and cash equivalents held by agents in the macroeconomy are in either interest- or non-interest-bearing accounts. Money demand is specifically for non-interest-bearing forms of money only, where interest-bearing forms are considered an alternative. For this reason, the short-term interest rate on money is the opportunity cost of both holding cash outside a bank account that pays interest and of consumption itself.

Things to remember

There are three motives for money demand, or holding cash in a non-interest bearing form.

- transactions motive, or the holding of money for everyday transactions;
- precautionary motive, or the holding of money for unknown, episodic transactions; and
- speculative/savings motive, or holding money to purchase assets as savings vehicles rather than money held in an interest-bearing account.

Money demand and utility-maximizing consumers

Because money demand is juxtaposed to goods demand, it has many similar characteristics. For example, there is a price for money. While this price is not explicit, it is the opportunity cost of holding money instead. This is important because economists analyze money as if it is a "good"; economic analysis is neater when simple demand and supply curves exist. Monetary economists have taken their lead from microeconomics in building a theory of how money enters the economic choices of households, firms and the government.

In 1956, an economist at Columbia University named Phillip Cagan published a way to analyze money demand that has been used extensively since.[1] He built a simple formula based on the motives suggested above. Money demand is a function of an interest rate (or an amalgam of rates that represented the opportunity cost of holding money) and income at the macroeconomic level. This money demand function suggested that representative agents, the average "household", possessed a similar demand for money. The macroeconomic level of money demand was simply the sum of the quantity demanded over all representative agents at a specific rate. However, each agent derived utility, the satisfaction of consuming a good or service, from demanding money. Utility from money demand had the same characteristics as utility derived from consumption in microeconomics.

A representative agent derives utility from money through the potential consumption of goods and services that money represents. Financial theory, as we saw in earlier chapters, suggests that money is nothing more than yet another asset inside the household's portfolio, just like stocks, bonds and real estate. The difference is that money only appreciates in value by the interest it earns by the choice not to consume. Therefore, if the household wishes to gain more satisfaction from consumption, it must also gain satisfaction from demanding and consuming money, parting with the utility derived from earning interest on the money instead. The interest rate, regardless of its representation, is then the "price" in the domestic market for money. As interest rates fall, the utility gained from both more goods and money consumption rises. Additional income provides more utility from consumption regardless of the price; income shifts the money demand curve. If you are given a rise at your job and now have a larger salary, economic theory suggests that you will consume more normal goods and services than you previously did. In a monetary economy, the only way this is possible is to simultaneously demand more money. Cagan's model put a functional form to money demand that made the analysis of money more quantitative. An example of this "Cagan-style" money demand function is shown in Equation 9.1.

$$M^D = \beta_0 + \beta_R R^\varepsilon + \beta_Y Y \tag{9.1}$$

All variables are in natural logarithms here, which allows for a simple linear function to come from the more complex theory. This money demand function equates nominal money demand (M_D) to a linear combination of a constant, β_0, on expected nominal interest rate (R^ε) and nominal income Y. This equation's coefficients on interest rates and income are the focus of analyzing money demand. How responsive the nominal amount of money demand is to changes in interest rates and income is represented by the elasticities, β_r and β_y respectively. Another, similar way of viewing money demand algebraically is to divide both sides of Equation 9.1 in its levels by the aggregate price index. This leads to Equation 9.2, the real balances equation.

$$\frac{M^D}{P} = \beta_1 + \beta_r r + \beta_y y \tag{9.2}$$

Equation 9.2, again in logarithmic form, shows that the real balances, $\frac{M^D}{P}$, represent the goods and services money can buy. Real balances are affected by changes in the nominal interest rate versus inflation, real interest rates, and changes in real income. Assuming β_r is less than zero seems reasonable; an increase in real interest rates leads to a β_r percentage decrease in real balances because of the law of demand. For real income, we assume that β_y is positive. The relationship between inflation and money is a long-debated question. This question is one that has dichotomized macroeconomic policy and theory, and we begin with the classic view of money, in contrast to the Cagan model.

The Quantity Theory: money as a medium of exchange

Inflation, as a monetary phenomenon, seems simple enough. If the central bank infuses too much money, versus its demand, the value of money falls like any other good. Of course, if money has less value, the same number of currency units now buys fewer goods and services in real terms, and inflation comes from a surplus in the money market. With too much money comes too much demand, and inflation is generated from shortages in goods markets that parallel the money market surplus. One way to view monetary policy in practice to control inflation is to supply only a certain amount of money needed to satiate demand.

The Quantity Theory of Money, based loosely on an idea of classical and neo-classical economists, such as Irving Fisher (1911), suggests that a mathematical identity exists between the amount of money in circulation and the total value of final goods and services in an economy. In the Cambridge version of this model, real GDP is replaced by a number of transactions to represent units of goods and services. This identity is shown in Equation 9.3.

$$M \equiv k \cdot P \cdot T \Rightarrow M \cdot V \equiv P \cdot y \qquad (9.3)$$

If a central bank knew the money supply (M), the current aggregate price level (P), and the quantity of all money-based, market transactions made in the macroeconomy (T), then k is a number found to make the identity hold. It is the value and calculation of this "Cambridge k" that has dichotomized monetary economics since Keynes's *General Theory*. The inverse of k is equal to V, and V symbolizes the velocity of money. Velocity is the number of times each currency unit in circulation is used in a given period, usually a year. In a sense, velocity is a measure of money demand, how money is used to make nominal transactions, equal to PT. If we think of transactions as a quantity of goods and services or real gross domestic product, y, we have the modern version of the Quantity Theory, the latter portion of Equation 9.3.

The constancy of money's velocity is one of the Quantity Theory's foundations. Initially, this idea may be of little consequence; prices and output may change such that they equal the money supply change and a constant velocity. However, pundits of this theory suggest that there are no real effects and that the percentage change in the money supply is mirrored by an equal percentage change in prices. The only way there are no real effects from monetary policy is if two assumptions hold: (1) the economy is at full employment; and (2) velocity is constant. Suppose velocity of money is not constant. This allows real GDP to change along with the money supply, especially if the inflation rate does not match the percentage change in the money supply. For many years, the evidence from the Great Depression and the postwar decade suggested that Keynes was right and that the Quantity Theory had failed in its initial assumptions.

Milton Friedman revived these assumptions in his 1963 study with Anna Schwartz, *A Monetary History of the United States*, which empirically tested the Quantity Theory over a long period. Their results suggested that while short-term differences from the initial assumptions existed episodically over the long history of a unified currency in the United States, the Quantity Theory held with a constant velocity. Friedman further used this evidence to suggest that the tradeoff between inflation and unemployment espoused by Keynes and made operational by Phillips (see Chapter 11 for more) may not exist except for episodic changes. If this was true, Friedman suggested that monetary policy must be predictable and be set such that the inflation rate was optimized for the economy. Friedman and Schwartz went so far to suggest that inflation is always a monetary phenomenon.[2]

The lesson to be learned from the Quantity Theory is a challenge that exists on the supply side of the money market. The money supply, by definition, has an effect on nominal income proportional to the way money is demanded. In a sense, velocity is a multiplier for monetary policy, which is why velocity is generally seen as a proxy for money demand. If velocity is constant, the effects on nominal income are very predictable. By the mid-1970s, the arguments about monetary policy had shifted to how policy was anticipated by markets rather than the constancy of velocity, which was readily accepted. The stagflation of the late 1970s, however, shifted monetary theory and policy again. This evidence changed the way monetary policy was monitored and conducted worldwide.

With this new evidence, monetary economists were once again questioning the Quantity Theory and its initial assumptions; Monetarism, the idea that the use of monetary policy to stimulate the economy had no real effects, became archaic and shunned. Monetary theorists now focus on how to optimize the way policy affected the Phillips tradeoff between inflation and unemployment as discussed in Chapter 10.

Case study 9.2 Chile and libertarian economics: Friedman vs. Keynes vs. military rule

John Maynard Keynes was one of the first economists to articulate, outside a highly socialist viewpoint, the power of government policy to intervene in markets and support recessions as well as restrain inflation. Keynes's influence on economic sciences is analogous to Einstein's on physics. Because of Keynes, central banks and legislatures across the globe consider both fiscal and monetary policies to solve problems of recession and provide balance to markets that simply do not know their way. A lack of full information makes markets resist smooth transitions from one cycle to another; policy can guide them back to sanity.

Milton Friedman disagreed with that idea partially. He agreed that fiscal policy had limited power in that by acting as a consumer, the government could force more inflation onto an economy, especially if that consumption was funded by monetary expansion. This "inflation tax" idea was one of Friedman's main ideas concerning any type of monetary expansion (Friedman 1971). His belief was that markets worked well if left relatively untouched by government, and, if the government had to get involved, it should be to stimulate businesses, not to stimulate further consumption and thus inflation. Supply-side economics is something that Milton Friedman did not invent but he was always credited with being its flag bearer. Libertarian philosophy, one based on personal liberty and a reduced hand of government, is also something Friedman agreed with but was more associated with than was due. Governments should provide tax incentives for businesses, reduce corporate and personal income taxes, and then simply get out of the way for businesses. Ultimately, Keynes felt that policy should and could act to stimulate the demand side of the macroeconomy while Friedman supported policies that focused on businesses creating products and jobs on the supply side.

Whether government intervention and control was better than letting capitalism reign less fettered by government has been tested by Chile since 1970. In the 1970s, the Chilean economy endured currency crises, political turnover and a dysfunctional economy. The one constant in post-war Chile has been copper exports, which have been primarily owned by, expropriated from and then re-owned through foreign direct investment (FDI) by multinational corporations. Inflation rose episodically since 1970 in Chile, sometimes as hyperinflation. Between the years of 1973 and 1977, Chilean inflation averaged over 100 percent per year, and wages rose in nominal terms at a slower rate. These problems meant that Chilean workers suffered greatly during that decade. The recession and worldwide stagflation of the late 1970s and early 1980s represented a relative low point for the Chilean economy. After years of military rule where individual choice was restricted and policies were heavily socialist bordering on totalitarian, Chilean politics and economics looked toward libertarian policies and ideology to swing the country the other way. One way to see how this unfolded is in the privatization of Chilean social security, their government pension system.

In social security systems, as in other pensions, there are two ways to fund the payments to recipients. One is a fully funded system, where the contributor invests in a specific account and that account is for that person or entity only. The system is "fully funded" in that the investments of the individual are specific to that person and there is no reliance on other contributors to help pay for recipient benefits. The second system is known as a pay-as-you-go system; the young pay for the old because the amount of contributions from the older generation does not cover the current payments. Many social security systems have this problem because the amount of payouts over time has grown at a pace quicker than the growth of contributions.

Chile's system was broken before the 1990s. From a social equity standpoint, it was important that those in the old system were covered in the new system. A recent article in the *Christian Science Monitor* (2005) provides information about these changes. The first change covers workers who retired before 1980 and guarantees minimum pensions for poor workers. The main change was the obligatory monthly payroll deduction of 12.3 percent. Ten per cent goes into the worker's own account, administered by one of six private pension funds, while 2.3 percent covers administrative fees. Unlike in the US, the payroll tax is funded entirely by the employee. At retirement – age 60 for women, 65 for men – they take out what they put in, plus the accumulated gains. This is really the key connection to the new and old systems. The payment is mandatory and part of the tax code, acting as forced savings. At 12.3 percent, the contribution is relatively small; the contribution level is smaller than that in the United States. The difference is that this is paid completely by the employee rather than shared with the employer, as in the United States.

Individual choice, one of the cornerstones of libertarian economic and social ideals, is the final step away from the old system to the new. A voluntary, tax-deductible savings plan administered by banks is allowed for those that want to contribute more. This provides an incentive to save. One can withdraw before retirement, or add it to a pension. One issue is that Chile still constrains the choice of investing the funds. However, this difference has helped support Chile's growth throughout the 1990s and 2000s thus far (Fortin 2008).

The market for money

By combining the ideas of Chapter 8 and the motives for money demand, we can now formulate a market for money as economists do for any other good. Figure 9.1 shows the typical money market, where the quantity of money in circulation is on the horizontal axis and the real interest rate on interest-bearing forms of money is on the vertical axis.

Notice that the demand and supply curves are typical of any good. Demand is downward-sloping because the interest rate represents the opportunity cost of holding money; as the interest rate falls, that opportunity cost falls, and incentives exist to hold more cash that does not bear interest. For the supply curve, if we think of banks as the "suppliers" of money, the upward slope represents an incentive mechanism also. As interest rates rise, the bank has a large incentive to increase the quantity of money available because bank revenues are rising. That is only going to happen if demand shifts along this curve.

We will assume that the money supply curve shifts only as a function of monetary policy. Financial innovation, whether it is a technological innovation that makes bank delivery of cash easier or a new type of asset that represents money, can also shift the supply curve. We will assume for now that the money supply curve is solely shifted by central banking. Another point of controversy is the upward slope of the curve. If the central bank is the monopoly source of money, and there is no way for a private bank to hoard cash and release money into circulation based on incentives from money demand changing, a vertical money supply curve

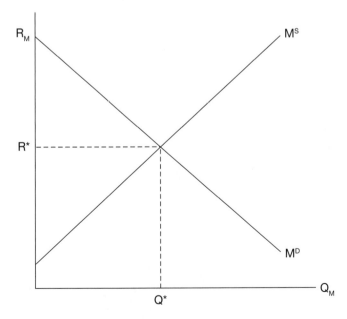

Figure 9.1 The market for money.

makes sense. However, it is both more realistic and connected to basic economics to have an upward-sloping curve.

Shifting the money demand curve, as discussed previously, is due mainly to a change in income. As income rises, because money is considered a "normal" good, more money is demanded at all rates of interest. This is because households or firms need money to purchase normal goods and services in a monetary economy. Two other reasons why money demand may shift is a change in consumer confidence and a change in the population. A rising population will demand more goods and services, and thus more money. A less-confident consumer base, for example when economic times are uncertain for the worse, leads to a shift of the money demand function toward the origin.

When thinking about how money is to be used, the speculative motive is critical. In the *General Theory of Employment, Money and Interest*, John Maynard Keynes suggested that the speculative motive was the key connection between monetary policy and manipulating money demand because of risk; as in any financial market, portfolio reallocations affected consumption of both final and capital goods. As a result, interest rates were artificially too high to push the economy to full employment. This result was in stark contrast to the Quantity Theory, where money demand is a simple outcome of consumption only. Money is not seen as an asset in the Quantity Theory, only a medium of exchange.

Policy examples

To show how policy works, some graphic examples help. First, we see what happens when the money supply increases. Suppose there are open market operations that augment the money supply. The central bank's purchase of government debt securities from its banks increases available funds and reduces the effective rate on the securities. This provides an incentive for banks to offer more loans and, as rates fall, incentives exist for consumers and firms to borrow. Figure 9.2 shows the shift.

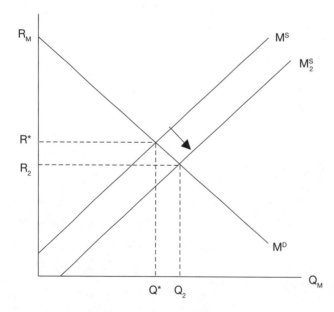

Figure 9.2 Policy shock in the Money Market.

Now, in classical economic theory, the movement from one equilibrium to another would be smooth from the first intersection point to the next and with a vertical M^S curve. However, in the Keynesian tradition, the new equilibrium will also end up at that second intersection, where R_2 and Q_M^2 represent the intersection, but the movement will not be a straightforward change from one to the other. There is an information problem that exists between the banks and their borrowers. This problem leads to a slower, more circuitous movement of the interest rate toward equilibrium. Figures 9.3 and 9.4 show these movements. A monetary contraction has the same problem in raising interet rates. The information problem that exists causes rates to go up slowly and then, in fact, fall a little toward equilibrium.

The next two chapters explore more about monetary policy and its effects on the macroeconomy. This primer should serve to begin your thinking about why there may be more than one interpretation of reactions to a monetary shock. Finally, Figure 9.5 shows the effects of income rising on money demand. We will investigate this later as an increase in speculative demand following a fiscal deficit funded by new government debt securities being issued.

Monetary transmission mechanisms and policy

A key research area in monetary theory is how monetary policy propagates through the economy to affect unemployment, output and prices. Economists have categorized five different transmission mechanisms or "channels" for a change in the money supply. They include the interest rate channel, cost channel, exchange rate channel, equity channel, and credit channel, where the credit channel has both a narrow and broad version.[3]

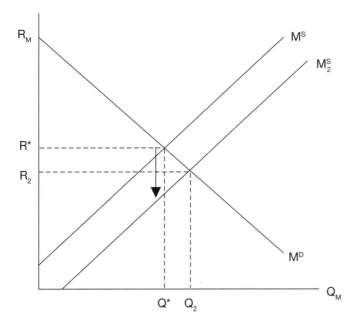

Figure 9.3 The initial effect of monetary policy.

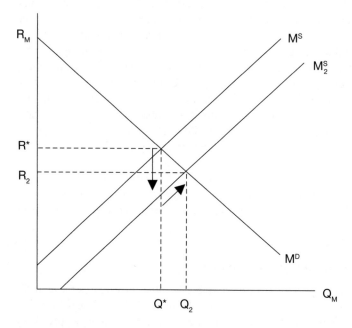

Figure 9.4 The liquidity effect of monetary policy.

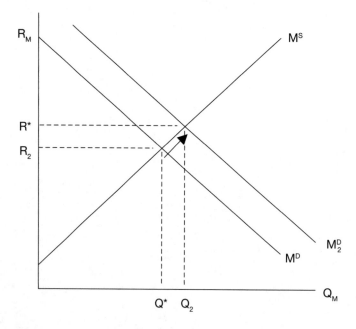

Figure 9.5 A money demand shock.

Interest rate channel

This is the textbook version of monetary policy, where the debate centers on real (Keynesian) versus nominal (Monetarist) adjustments based on goods or asset market imperfections or both. The Keynesian revolution was based on the possibility that monetary policy had real effects. This is the basic Keynesian transmission mechanism, where monetary policy affects banking decisions such that predictable policy outcomes flow. For example, a monetary contraction should lead bankers to face higher costs in lending, thus they naturally contract available loanable funds, transmitting higher costs of borrowing or consuming now. Chapter 11 uses this channel for basic analysis, and Chapter 12 extends this to include the exchange rate channel.

Broad credit channel

When firms or consumers carry adjustable-rate debt, new monetary policy can force a change based on the borrower's balance sheet. For example, a monetary contraction should lead firms to pay more for adjustable-rate debt, and possibly reduce their asset values through higher capitalization rates. The adjustment to consuming less provides the economic effect of policy. Larger firms and banks are likely to have the power to use different parts of their balance sheet as a buffer against unforeseen monetary policies. The broadness of these firms and banks provides shelter against changes in interest rates if needed, where a change in consumption and investment by these firms propels policy. Bernanke and Gertler (1995) is seen as a seminal paper about the broad credit channel.

Narrow credit channel

This channel of monetary policy suggests that smaller firms do not have as many options as large firms in finding financing for projects. Small banks suffer from a similar fate, as their small size does not allow a large amount of diversification and protection against new policy environments. Smaller banks tend to loan to small firms as a result, and if a country, region or industry is dominated by smaller firms, the narrowness of credit options, on both the buyer and seller side, leads to relatively large policy changes as a result. The key idea here is, in the wake of monetary policy, smaller firms and banks dictate the volatility in financial markets. Kashyap and Stein (1994) is seen as a key paper for work on the narrow channel.

Cost channel

This cost channel is a relatively new channel of policy being studied, focusing on the way firms adjust prices due to interest rate changes because their costs are tied directly to the interest rate. This change is passed on directly to customers through higher prices, and acts much like a supply shock on the economy, the antithesis of the Keynesian framework; monetary policy may be an aggregate supply shock instead of demand. Ravenna and Walsh (2005) is a recent example of this literature.

Exchange rate channel

This channel is the cornerstone of the New Open Economy Macroeconomics (NOEM) models, starting with Obstfeld and Rogoff (1995). However, this channel also has ties to the

Mundell–Fleming (1961, 1962) model literature concerning differential effects of monetary policy within a region. In short, if monetary policy is contractionary, the exchange rate should initially rise (the policy-making country's currency should appreciate versus other currencies not engaging in monetary contraction). After the initial increase, market forces begin to work that may nullify monetary policy effects on domestic variables except under specific conditions. One of the main reasons to form a currency union is to avoid this channel disturbing the macroeconomy. Chapter 12 looks at this channel in depth.

Equity price channel

Asset prices may adjust quickly as a result of unforeseen monetary policy. This includes stocks, houses, business, et cetera. Two issues are involved with this channel. First, as interest rates rise, consumers who own assets experience a negative wealth effect on consumption. This propels policy toward its foreseen outcome and is in line with standard theory. Second, asset prices are driven down by higher interest rates, reducing the profits to be made by business using equity financing to expand or to build new homes. As interest rates rise, residential and business investment in real capital falls because of an expected lack of demand. This is also related to the standard theory because investment demand falls as interest rates rise. However, this is not because of banks changing their lending practices; these changing are happening in equity rather than debt markets.

Summary

This chapter provides a background on money demand and the domestic money market, where the market is viewed in a similar way to the market for any good or service. Intuitively, this connection makes sense because a consumer, firm or government needs money to purchase goods and services in a monetary economy. There are three motives for demanding money. They are the transactions, precautionary and speculative/savings motives. Each is tied to either consumption or saving of income. Money demand is posited as a downward-sloping function of interest rates and is shifted by changes in income.

The Quantity Theory of Money is the classical economist's attempt to link money supply and money demand due to the use of money as a medium of exchange. The initial assumptions of this model are that velocity of money and real GDP are constants, because of long-run stability assumed by the classic model, and thus monetary policy has no effects on real GDP. The Keynesian model of the money market relaxed the assumption of constant velocity and fully flexible prices, which implies that a change in the money supply has real effects. Graphical examples are provided to show how monetary policy could affect this market. Finally, a brief discussion of monetary transmission channels discusses the ways economists view the propagation of monetary policy through the macroeconomy, where each channel is similar to the interest rate channel proposed by Keynes himself.

Key terms

1   Monetarism: a school of thought that suggests money supply is the main way in which inflation is determined.
2   Precautionary motive: the motive of money demand to hold cash in a non-interest-bearing form for emergency purposes.

3 Savings motive: the motive of money demand to hold cash in a non-interest-bearing form to purchase financial assets.
4 Speculative motive: the motive of money demand to hold cash in a non-interest-bearing form outside of a bank because the risk of the bank failing has risen.
5 Transmission channel: the ways in which monetary policy transmits its effects on the macroeconomy; these include the interest rate channel, credit channels, cost channel, exchange rate channel, and equity price channel.
6 Transactions motive: the motive of money demand to hold cash in a non-interest-bearing form for everyday transactions.

Questions and problems

1 State and explain the three motives of money demand.
2 Explain why the quantity of transactions balances held by consumers and firms domestically would rise as the domestic money supply was increased by the central bank.
3 Explain why the quantity of precautionary balances held by consumers and firms domestically would rise as the domestic money supply was increased by the central bank.
4 Explain why the quantity of speculative/savings balances held by consumers and firms domestically would rise as the domestic money supply was increased by the central bank.
5 Discuss the utility idea in terms of holding money in the context of money acting like a good or service.
6 Explain why β_r would become more negative as the central bank became more inclusive in their measure of money supply (using M_2 instead of M_1).
7 Many monetary theorists see the money supply curve as vertical. Explain why an upward-sloping supply curve for money is reasonable.
8 Many monetary theorists see the money supply curve as vertical. Explain why a vertical money supply curve makes sense.
9 Explain the importance of the relative price elasticity (the slope) of the money demand curve in terms of central banking's ability to change interest rates.
10 Show, using the money market equilibrium in Figure 9.1, the effects of a monetary contraction on the interest rate on money and the quantity of money in the economy.

Suggested reading

For a review of money demand, David Laidler's book is a classic. *The Demand for Money: Theories, Evidence and Problems* (1993), New York: Norton Publishers.

10 Money, employment, inflation and expectations

Introduction

Monetary policy depends on many relationships in the macroeconomy working correctly for its transmission to be both efficient and predictable. Alan Greenspan, the immediate past chair of the Federal Reserve Board, was chastised many times by the press for being obstinate in his remarks about future monetary policy.[1] This opaqueness was purposeful, as Greenspan thought (and many economists do) that providing the financial markets with any true sense of policy's direction would begin a speculative frenzy surrounding every Federal Open Market Committee (FOMC) meeting. Such an announcement effect provides a press release with similar effects to actual policy changes. If the markets learned from these statements and the central bank shapes their statements correctly, the announcement effects can initiate policy before its actual occurrence and smoothly transition markets from one equilibrium to another. The US central bank has been famous for its design as autonomous from the American government, specifically autonomous with regard to fiscal policy and politics; autonomy enhances the predictability of central banker discretion to shock the economy if and when needed.

Certain central banks follow explicit monetary rules, such as New Zealand and Canada. In these countries, monetary policy is not only predictable but also completely transparent based on new macroeconomic data. The Reserve Bank of New Zealand publishes a monetary rule that follows inflation and unemployment, suggesting that unpredicted movements in either one of these two variables will initiate monetary policy.[2] A bandwidth exists around a certain, tolerated level of inflation and dictates policy changes. In Canada, a similar rule applies.[3] This index tracks the path of money and financial markets in Canada, providing a signal as to when new policy may occur. Because both Canada and New Zealand rely heavily on primary product industries and exportation, monetary policy is also concerned with an appropriate exchange rate as well as price stability.[4] In either case, a rule dictates the accountability and reliability of these central banks with respect to policy decisions.

Policy-makers are meant to create jobs and to keep prices in check. Chapter 11's model suggests a different way of looking at policy if prices are slow to move; this chapter's analysis focuses on aggregate demand and supply as a framework for understanding monetary policy in simple ways, and as a foundation for arguing for or against monetary policy rules. John Taylor of Stanford University has been associated with a rule that combines both inflation and unemployment in determining what a "target" interest rate should be. The Taylor Rule also incorporates expectations. Expectations, formulating conjectures about the future and acting upon them today, have become a centerpiece of both monetary theory and practice. In the early part of the twentieth century, economists and policy-makers agreed that markets provided all the necessary information to market participants, especially between workers and employers. Rational expectations suggests that labor markets would naturally come to equilibrium, and policies, such as the manipulation of the money supply, would have no effect on labor markets and real economic variables except to bid up nominal wages through inflation. Say's Law, that supply creates its own demand, was followed in policy circles as if a fact of nature; any labor supply surplus (unemployed workers) would create its own demand because the unemployed workers would accept lower wages; firms would gladly hire these now less-expensive workers. That idea works so long as labor and employers share information equally such that neither side has an information advantage, such as monopoly or monopsony power. The hypothesized relationship between inflation (y-axis) and unemployment (x-axis) is a vertical line in classical economics, vertical at some unemployment rate specific to that economy at full employment

An economist named A. W. H. Phillips (1958) published a study of the tradeoff between inflation and unemployment in the United Kingdom over 100 years of data that propelled the Keynesian revolution that was well under way in macroeconomics.[5] Phillips found that instead of no relationship between inflation and unemployment, there was in fact an inverse relationship. This function, subsequently called the Phillips Curve, showed a tradeoff for monetary policy-makers in pursuing offensive monetary policies to reduce inflation (endure more unemployment) or to boost employment (endure more inflation). Not only did researchers quickly estimate these curves for every country that had aggregate price and labor market data, they also sold this curve to policy-makers. This tradeoff was based on workers not possessing the same information set as the firms, where employers have two, parallel economic incentives to gain more information than workers. First, firms monitor policy and macroeconomic data to know how much they should charge for their goods and services and to take advantage of expected inflation not foreseen by workers. Second, if consumers drive a new economic boom, employers want to hire workers at relatively low real wages to maximize the profit of hiring more workers.

Adaptive expectations help explain the Phillips Curve's shape. Macroeconomics has two theories of expectations, two theories of the inflation–unemployment relationship, and potentially two categorical ways of making policy. Since Phillips (1958), most research in macroeconomics has been a combination of choosing a Keynesian or Classical framework in which to build models or to study which type of model best describes the data. Only recently has there been some unification, but the debate remains. This unification began in 1976 with the Lucas Critique, posited by Nobel Laureate Robert E. Lucas. The Lucas Critique partially synthesized Phillips's work and that of two other Nobel Laureates, Milton Friedman and Edmund Phelps.

This chapter has five sections. First, the AD-AS model is shown in brief; hopefully, this section is a reminder of work done in macroeconomic principles. This model begins our journey into understanding the macroeconomics of monetary policy. Second, a definition and explanation of inflation are provided. The economic problems of inflation are discussed, as well as issues in measuring inflation and the price indices used to track aggregate price changes. Next is an overview of unemployment. While labor economics has evolved away from macroeconomics, some simple ideas that combine both the microeconomic decisions of the firm and aggregate measures of labor markets show connections to monetary policy. Fourth is a section on expectations, how adaptive and rational expectations are defined in the context of inflation and unemployment. Finally, this chapter ends with a discussion of monetary discretion versus rules. Should monetary policy-makers have a choice as to when and how to manipulate the money supply? Should their choice be based on a macroeconomic rule instead? The most beloved way of studying macroeconomic effects from monetary policy is the IS-LM model which extends the AD-AS model.

The AD-AS model: a brief overview

A large amount of analysis can be done using this simple model, which aggregates both the supply and demand curves from the market for all goods and services throughout the macroeconomy. Aggregate Demand (AD) retains a downward slope in y-P space, where P is a measure of the average, aggregate price level for a household's consumption bundle and y is real GDP. Just like a market demand curve, the AD curve represents price–quantity combinations at which consumers are in "equilibrium", where marginal utility is equal to marginal cost. The Aggregate Supply (AS) curve slopes upward, at least a portion of it does, reflecting the profit incentives of firms to increase production as prices rise. The AS curve's shape, at its ends, reflects differences in expectations formation and firms' reactions to demand-side growth. Because the AD curve is less controversial, our analysis begins there.

The AD curve

Few economists debate aggregate demand basics. The consumer is the foundation of this curve, and the classic characteristics of demand drive both its slope and how it shifts. The slope is a reflection of opportunity cost. As prices fall, consumers have utility incentives to purchase more goods. This movement along the AD curve is due to changing supply conditions; as in economics principles, a movement along the demand curve reflects a supply curve shift. If firms face new production conditions that allow for lower prices, consumers recognize firms should reduce their prices and act accordingly. The reason consumers in the aggregate react to these supply changes, and resultant price changes, has been categorized three ways.

- The Real Balances Effect. As prices fall, the real value of current money demand, real balances from Chapter 9, increases in value. As real balances rise, the consumer has more purchasing power with the same amount of money, increasing incentives for consumption. As consumption rises, real GDP rises.
- The Interest Rate Effect. As prices fall, the real money supply rises in value. The real interest rate falls as a reaction to this change. As the real interest rate falls, investment rises, causing real GDP to rise. The main difference between the Real Balances Effect and the Interest Rate Effect is that the former acts on household consumption while the latter acts on the firm's choice of physical investment.
- The Foreign Trade Effect. As domestic prices fall, the relative price of exports falls. As export prices falls, more exports are sold, and fewer imports are sold. Net exports rise, and real GDP rises.

The AD curve reflects monetary policy when it changes. The AD curve retains a market demand curve's shape and its basic determinants: income, population, consumer expectations. However, shifters of market demand, such as the price of substitutes and complements, are not a part of our aggregate analysis. Further, income changes are specific to macro-economic policy. For our purposes, aggregate demand shifts for three major reasons.

- Macroeconomic policy: monetary, fiscal and trade policies
- Consumer confidence: partially expectations, partially opinion
- Population changes: change in the number of consumers, change in aggregate demand

Suppose the Japanese central bank decreased interest rates, as they did for much of the 1990s. The AD-AS model would show a shift of the AD curve to the right, increasing prices and real GDP simultaneously. Both of these results are intuitive from Chapter 9. First, the increase in real GDP comes from lower interest rates which provide utility-maximization incentives to households to consume more and save less; the lower interest rates also provide profit-maximization incentives to firms to increase real investment in physical capital. Real GDP rises in both cases. Prices rise because the monetary authority has increased the number of original dollars in circulation. Fiscal and trade policies work in a similar way. For example, if the government spends more money or reduces taxes, real GDP rises due to a combination of augmented consumption. If a new import quota is placed on a country, net exports rise. Both of these policies shift the AD curve to the right. Policies that reduce the level of real GDP shift the AD curve to the left: contractionary monetary policy, reduced government spending, new or higher taxes, or new trade policy that leads to more net exports. Prices and income move in the same direction as a result of monetary policy; unemployment moves in the opposite direction of price and income changes. The AS curve's shape dictates the speed and magnitude of these changes; this shape is one of the most debated topics in macroeconomics.

The AS curve: three possible sections

While the aggregate demand curve resembles simple market demand curves, the AS curve and its shape are not as connected to basic economics. The AS curve's slope has three possibilities and all three are tied to different views of expectations and price-setting by firms. Shifting the AS curve is connected to basic macroeconomics. There are three categorical reasons why the AS curve shifts to the right as examples, and none of them is expansionary monetary policy.

- A change in technology: any new technology that makes goods and services production more efficient (reduces costs) across the macroeconomy shifts the AS curve to the right, reducing the average price level and increasing real GDP.
- Capital accumulation: when firms accumulate capital, the amount of production possible increases, reducing prices and increasing real GDP by adding new capital to the capital stock.
- New resources and firms: more labor, capital, land, and entrepreneurship increase the number of firms that produce goods and services. Somewhat similar to population growth, this is the growth of firms. As more companies are born, prices fall and real GDP rises.

A common error is to think that aggregate supply includes the supply of money. Monetary policy is a demand-side policy, affecting the demand for goods and services and not their supply. Monetary policy indirectly affects the amount of real GDP by providing incentives to purchase idle resources (capital and labor not currently utilized but available), but does not provide incentives for the potential production level of the economy to rise at all prices.

There is a debate concerning the AS curve's shape, which is a focus of monetary theory and policy, and is over expectations formation. When an economy has relatively small levels of real GDP versus its potential, prices may have little incentive to change. As an economy matures and uses more of its capacity, competition over these more limited resources leads to increasing price pressure on inputs, such as labor and capital. Those price increases are passed on to consumers as well as possible by the firms. This pass-through leads to consumer price inflation. As the economy grows ever nearer its potential output level, the income level associated with full employment, the scarcity of inputs is exacerbated and prices begin to move more rapidly upward. Once the economy reaches its potential, as aggregate demand has increased to the point where all excess capacity has been utilized to satiate consumers, prices reach a tipping point where any more demand pressure upward creates only price increases. Macroeconomic policy, both fiscal and monetary, must be careful not to push the economy far beyond this point. The AS curve takes on three shapes to represent each of these price-setting situations. A flat AS curve represents the initial stages of an economy. The demand side of the economy has the ability to grow without inflation pressure.

Two related reasons lead to that possibility. First, firms are likely to have a large amount of monopoly power at this stage of the economy, which accounts for the idle capacity. If monopolies exist, there will be little incentive for these firms to change their prices as an increase in demand will not necessarily provide competitive pressure to reduce prices. Second, the assumption that prices do not move is because firms hold an information advantage over households in two ways. As workers, the household does not know what wage is to be paid and do not realize how scarce their labor hours are in the market. As demand increases and firms face input scarcity, the lack of a price change restricts the information signal that inflation is on the horizon; workers do not demand higher wages to compensate themselves for lost purchasing power because they do not know any better or cannot because they are engaged in nominal contracts with firms. The consumer, who is also the worker, faces the same quandary. Prices do not change right away because idle capacity has not yet given way to scarcity. This is the ultimate case of adaptive expectations where price-setting power resides with the firm's information advantage and translates into inflation-free growth for the macroeconomy.

That ability may be very short-lived. If the economy grows rapidly, the signs of inflation are more apparent, reducing the firm's ability to restrict information available to households. This does not mean, however, that the firm is suddenly going to raise prices and pass them directly along to the consumer. There may be costs involved in changing prices for the firm; staggered price-setting may take place because of "menu costs" involved with changing prices. These costs are associated with advertising new prices, deviating labor away from production to make necessary changes, and reduced revenue from changing prices to the new levels. Prices may initially grow very slowly from demand-side pressure, if the cost of changing prices outweighs the benefits for most firms. However, as demand continues to rise, firms have growing profit incentives to change prices alongside increasing production, as continued scarcity now outweighs any menu costs faced by firms. Firms recognize that nominal wage increases may be necessary to attract workers who remain unemployed, or retain their own workers in a more competitive labor market. The penalty for households demanding more production from firms is higher prices. Real GDP continues to grow along this portion of the AS curve because workers are paying more for goods and services than they are paid in wages, providing more but shrinking marginal profits. The AS curve's shape here is upward-sloping, representing the tradeoff faced by the macroeconomy as aggregate demand continues to rise.

In the final portion, the AS curve is vertical. The macroeconomy is in full employment, and prices adjust to new demand conditions during recessions (P falls) and booms (P rises). The key idea concerning expectations is that the economy's transition from the upward-sloping to vertical portions of the AS curve is a transition from adaptive to rational

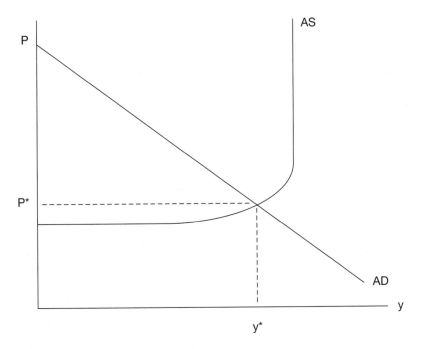

Figure 10.1 The AD-AS model.

expectations; households and firms now share and use the same information set about the macroeconomy. Any new policies are perfectly anticipated by firms and households, and their reactions deliver a new equilibrium. If demand continues to increase, prices rise to quell any real gains from the nominal changes; real growth is zero as a result of policy when the economy reaches its full potential.

Further, this vertical AS section relates two other, famous ideas in economics. First is the production possibilities frontier. The frontier represents the combinations of two goods' production levels at the maximum amount of production with a given state of technology. At the macroeconomic level, full employment or the potential production level of the economy is the result of equilibrium along this frontier. The vertical AS curve is positioned at a real GDP level that theoretically employs all the economy's resources. Second, because the vertical AS curve represents full employment of labor, this portion of the AS curve is similar to the vertical Phillips Curve of Friedman and Phelps. Perfect competition now reigns through Say's Law in dictating the macroeconomic outcomes. To increase the money supply at this point is to cause only inflation and not to reduce unemployment any further. To understand the Phillips Curve and its possible shapes, and why the focus of macroeconomic policy is to drive the economy, if stagnant, to the transition point between the upward-sloping and vertical AS sections as shown in Figure 10.1, a discussion of inflation and unemployment is needed.

Inflation: a reflection of scarcity

In any market, prices rise due to a good's scarcity. For example, if a good's supply is reduced, say a disease kills half of the annual wheat harvest in Russia, the price of wheat is going to rise from scarcity. If consumers find out that red wine is good for their health, the rising demand for red wine reduces its availability and prices rise. If both curves are moving in the same direction, one mitigating the price effects of the other, inflation can still occur if the inflationary change outpaces the deflationary change. The key is that any exogenous shock to a market is inflationary if scarcity results.

Two types of macroeconomic inflation can occur as a result of demand or supply shifts. The first type is called demand-pull inflation, the ultimate result of macroeconomic policies such as monetary policy, where the AD curve shifts to the right. Suppose the central bank reduced interbank lending rates. The reduction causes firms to recalculate present values and purchase more physical capital because the cost of borrowing is relatively less expensive. As macroeconomic investment rises, incomes rise for the owners of capital, triggering a multiplier effect on consumption. As consumption rises, more income is made and more goods are produced to satiate this new demand. Firms, as they produce the larger amount of goods now demanded, will face scarcity in inputs, and face higher input prices. Their reaction will be to increase prices at a rate that exceeds the input price change and profit. As a result, general prices rise due to demand pulling inflation behind it, an opportunity cost of demand-ing more goods with higher incomes. This inflation pressure is what classically slows down an economic expansion because supply cannot keep up with demand, and prices rise to naturally curb consumption.

The other possibility is called cost-push inflation, represented by an AS curve shift to the left. When a leftward supply shift takes place in a market, the cost of producing goods has risen and prices rise to compensate firms for exogenous change in costs that is economy-wide in scope. An increase in oil prices is also a good example, an input in most production processes for goods or services. From driving to work, to delivering goods to market, to the production of plastics (which are then used as an intermediate good in many manufactured products), oil has become an essential input for the world. When oil prices rise unexpectedly, the threat of cost-push inflation exists. What is most troubling about this type of inflation, and why its occurrence sends tremors throughout the macroeconomy, is that it is accompanied by a reduction in real GDP and employment. Another name for cost-push inflation surfaced in the late 1970s, stagflation, where inflation and unemployment rise simultaneously.

Central banks react to inflation by contracting the money supply when inflation is demand-pull. It is important that central bankers understand the reason why inflation is happening, which can be confusing when a mix of forces are working simultaneously on the economy. To temper central bank reactions, economists have worked long and hard on a definition of inflation that can be generalized across countries and provides some room for an economy to maneuver before a policy change.

Price indices and inflation's definition

Economists define inflation as a significant and persistent increase in the average price level. Notice that this definition has two parts, and while inflation may be significant (gas prices rising 10 percent in a week), the increase must also be persistent (lasting a minimum of two quarters). Policy-makers should react to any increase in prices on a case-by-case basis, as the surge may be short-lived or caused by forces that the central bank cannot easily change. Petroleum prices are a good example of an inflation-causing phenomenon that monetary policy cannot easily quell. For example, suppose oil prices rise steadily and gasoline prices rise even faster. These price increases cause primary product industries to face larger costs of delivering goods to manufacturers and retailers, and these firms begin to pass those costs on to their customers. Manufacturers, grocers and other retailers then pass those price increases onto final consumers or wholesalers. Monetary policy can reduce consumption behavior through increasing interest rates; the central bank faces a nasty tradeoff if it expands the money supply to save labor from being unemployed by making inflation pressure worse.

Significance is generally seen as annualized inflation that is greater than the annualized growth of real GDP. If inflation exceeds the long-term trend in real GDP growth, inflation erodes nominal GDP growth significantly and pushes real GDP below trend. If prices rise one percent in January and February of a given year, annualized inflation is 12.6 percent because of monthly compounding. This is exactly why economists also watch inflation's persistence. Suppose policy was initiated after two months of one percent inflation. In March, inflation may have been 0.2 percent, and in April 0.3 percent. This would reduce the annualized inflation forecast from 12.6 percent to 10.4 percent. Further, the significant price increase experienced in January and February may not be seen as persistent now that inflation has fallen over March and April.

It is important to recognize that while inflation may be the focus of monetary policy, central bankers do not look at inflation statistics alone to make judgments. Forecasts of many variables in the macroeconomy that are perceived to have an impact on inflation and its forecast are followed by central banks. Later in this chapter, we see that a common monetary policy rule uses forecasts of inflation, unemployment and real GDP to make decisions on interest rates.

Case study 10.1 Don't cry for me, Argentina: we need to cry for you

The post-war period in Argentina, much like the Chilean case in Chapter 9, is not a great story, and these neighbors had somewhat similar experiences sociopolitically. A book by Della Paolera and Taylor (2003), specifically Chapter 3, provides a detailed look at Argentina's economic history. Argentina's twentieth-century story is one of constant political upheaval, where democracy comes and goes and is replaced by a military regime in most cases. After World War Two, Argentina was a country of continuously rising fiscal deficits and used monetary policy to pay for these deficits. As a result of constant fiscal and monetary expansions, inflation in Argentina has been a constant problem.

Della Paolera and Taylor (2003) discuss seigniorage revenues paying for government debt as one of the main problems of Argentina's modern history (p. 73). Measures to reverse the inflation problem were short-lived as fiscal conservatism never took place. A slowdown in spending, which allowed a contraction of the money supply, was reversed because of political problems soon thereafter in almost every episode. The attempts generally coincided with cyclic downturns where inflation was naturally falling. In Argentina, mainly for political reasons, fiscal instability was the order of the day. Under military regimes, fiscal policy was used to provide for the police state, and then the money supply was increased to finance the spending. It has a history much like its Brazilian neighbor, where industrialization was geared toward replacing imports and reducing import dependence. Growth did come with industrialization, but inflation was an average of 26% per year from 1944 to 1974 in Argentina.

The first oil shock in 1973 hit Argentina hard, and caused rapid inflation. A trade surplus that had built up over the relatively booming 1960s was quickly erased, and currency devaluation came quickly thereafter. In 1976, Argentina had yet another military coup and after many years of democracy became a country with a military regime. Fiscal spending surged, as did monetary policy to cover the debt, and inflation became more rampant. Even though the junta was pro-business, its fiscal policies provided no long-term support to the peso or the economy. Wages skyrocketed to cover against inflation expectations, and Argentine debt accumulated to finance its taste for imports and became unsustainable; while maintaining a closed economy for the most part, black markets existed everywhere, exacerbating inflation.

In 1982, rapidly rising interest rates and sharply declining output and growth hurt the leveraged debt positions Argentina had accumulated, owed mainly to the United States in adjustable-rate loans; analogous to Mexico, refusing to pay the interest payments and default on the debt was seen as an easy solution (Lindert and Morton 1989). Furthermore, the Argentinean government ordered the invasion of the Falkland Islands, a British protectorate in the southern Atlantic Ocean, which caused a brief but devastating war between the United Kingdom and Argentina. After the war was lost and political turnover took place to a more moderate military government, inflation continued to rise rapidly.

Economic crises have plagued Argentina since 1983, regardless of political regime or relative economic prudence (Saxton 2003). Inflation was the main problem of the 1980s for Argentina, and the currency history table in this case shows that problem. In 1983, the new peso was 10,000 old pesos; in 1985, the Austral was 1000 new pesos. Notice that within two years, the new Austral currency was worth 10,000,000 old pesos! In 1992, a new, pegged currency was introduced that lasted nine years, and survived the Tequila Crisis of 1995, only to experience forced devaluation in 2002. However, the convertible peso was worth 10,000 Australs!

The latest economic crisis of widespread significance was in 2002. With the terrorist attacks came reduced spending in the United States, Argentina's main trading partner. Argentina's economy had recently opened its borders to international trade, and the dollars came in. As a result of this expansion of foreign reserves, and a pegged, convertible currency which was one dollar for one peso, Argentina accumulated dollars and used these dollars as if they were gold to print pesos. For each dollar that arrived in Buenos Aires, a new peso was printed. On the surface, this decision maintains the parity between the currencies. However, as we learned in Chapter 8, there is a money multiplier effect, where the actual number of pesos created would far exceed the dollars in foreign reserves. The 1990s were a relative boom period for the Argentinean economy, where new leadership had guided the country out of its military roots and into an emerging marketplace taking advantage of Argentina's vast resources.

In 2001, the emerged world began to slip into recession. As recession hit, the outlook for Argentina's economy also began to falter. Dollars stopped coming in at the same pace, and fiscal spending had continued assuming foreign trade and finance would partially pay for it. Monetary policy was easy and credit conditions were good for domestic businesses, but foreign investors were becoming somewhat worried. By December 2001, Argentina's stock market began a collapse and pressure built on the peso to be devalued. Ultimately, this was due to the pressure building behind the value of the peso, which gave a poor expectation of equity values in pesos as well as the economy's value. In early 2002, the peso was converted to a new peg and its economy fell rapidly. From 2003 to the present, Argentina has recovered somewhat, but commodity price volatility and leadership turnover makes the short-term outlook for

Argentina worrisome once again. The author of this text was in Argentina in July of 2001 when the stock market in Buenos Aires dropped 12 percent in one day. The next morning, there was a riot about 200 meters from the author's hotel, with about 50,000 people in attendance. It provided some serious perspective on getting excited over day-to-day movements in American markets.

Price indices

The "correct" price index central banks should follow has become a topic for much debate. Generally there are four indices available to macroeconomists. These indices are based on three essential items: a "basket of goods", a weighting system, and categorizing goods into subgroups to construct sub-indices. The first is the Producer Price Index (PPI), representing the average price or cost of a firm's set of inputs. This is the fundamental price index for any economy, assuming that if primary product producers (agriculture, mineral, forestry, fishery, labor, etc.) raise prices, manufacturers using these inputs will pass on any price increases. The next is the Wholesale Price Index (WPI), which measures a basket of wholesale goods and their costs. The Consumer Price Index (CPI) includes wholesalers' mark-ups when selling goods to retailers. The CPI is based on a basket of consumer goods which represents most major categories of markets. This basket is made up of sub-indices, and those sub-indices are specific to goods or industries. The CPI is the most watched and used inflation measure.

There are three debates over consumer price indices and their construction. First is the basket of goods. Many goods in this theoretical bundle do not go out of style or change technology, such as corn and milk. Others, such as tennis balls as a measure of sporting goods or CD players as a measure of music entertainment consumption, experience obsolescence. Second, the best way to measure price indices from a microeconomic standpoint is called the "Divisia" index, which compares a basket's price in previous periods to a basket's price today without holding price or quantity constant, regardless of the basket's composition. Because of the potential obsolescence of goods, a "Paasche" or "Laspeyres" index is used, holding price constant (Paasche) versus holding quantity constant (Laspeyres). Microeconomists can easily show that these latter indices are inferior to the Divisia index in terms of true measurement of inflation but easier to measure.

Should the entire CPI be used to measure inflation? Central banks may use a "core" CPI measure as their main yardstick for inflation. The core CPI excludes food and energy prices, considered relatively volatile as they can drive overall CPI movements because of short-term, episodic changes. Some argue that using the core CPI and excluding these sub-indices forces the analyst to forget that energy and food prices may drive other goods' prices in the CPI; excluding food and energy eliminates an important portion of a household's consumption decisions directly and indirectly.

The GDP deflator and the Personal Consumption Expenditures (PCE) index relate nominal and real GDP between the current and base year. All price indices are built around a base year, where the index is normally set equal to 100. If in the year following the base period there was five percent inflation, the index in the following year would be 105. Nominal and real GDP are the same in the base year by definition; if the same quantity of goods costs five percent more the following year, the GDP deflator would be 105 and real GDP would be the same. The other indices work the same way concerning the choice of a base year and construction of an index to represent the basket's cost.

The costs (and benefits) of inflation

Most economists and people would state that inflation is not a good outcome for an economy. Three reasons stand out as to why inflation is generally dreaded.

- Purchasing power erosion: real incomes fall as prices rise
- Bracket creep: if income taxes are assessed, taxes are on nominal not real income; tax burden rises without any new resources
- Consumer and firm uncertainty: when inflation takes place, prices are no longer stable and thus costs become unpredictable

These costs can be so pervasive and both politically and economically damaging that central banks are somewhat forced (if not by economic theory and logic) to focus their efforts on inflation. The most immediate of the concerns above is the uncertainty. It takes time for workers to realize their real wages are falling. The uncertainty can turn an otherwise stable economy into a vortex of chaos based on unanticipated, rapid inflation. Countries such as Argentina, Brazil, Chile, Mexico, Malaysia, Thailand, and Singapore have all experienced major inflations and financial collapse since 1970. Providing signals of inflation and its control by the central bank is essential to curbing fears. Demand-pull inflations are by-products of growth periods; in many cases, inflation episodes are simply a sign of growth; inflation is ultimately a reflection of scarcity and an opportunity cost of excess demand in markets or economies.

The erosion of returns to a worker's time makes for resentment and potential political strife. The link between unemployment and inflation is meant to curb this problem, as lower unemployment drives inflation rather than the other way around. However, much of that, as discussed above, depends on what is causing inflation. When inflation is driven by demand, and firms hire labor hours to produce more for household consumption of goods and services, inflation is a tolerable problem. To understand the other side of the Phillips Curve relationship, we now discuss labor force dynamics.

Unemployment: a difficult statistic to follow

The workers of the world come from a subset of the economy's population. Not every man, woman and child is expected to work. Notice the unemployed are part of the labor force, which may initially seem like a contradiction, but these folks are assumed to be actively seeking work. For this reason, the employed and unemployed make up the labor force; the labor force is either working or seeking work. Age determines eligibility for work in many countries. Some do not actively seek work; the official statistics on unemployment only count those actively in the labor force.

The unemployment rate is the percentage of the labor force not currently working; the employment rate is the percentage working. The exercise seems simple enough: count those working by either surveying firms or using data from payroll taxes, count those not working but actively seeking work by those collecting unemployment insurance payments, social insurance, and so on, where the payments are based on providing evidence of seeking a new job. Two specific problems arise. First, there are people actively seeking work by evidence, not necessarily actively seeking work in reality. These are called discouraged workers, those who are counted in the official statistics but are not active labor force participants. This overstates the unemployment numbers. The other issue is that there are people working at jobs that underutilize their skills, for example a PhD economist working as a janitor. That person takes away a job from someone who is trained to be a janitor and is not utilizing their education and skills as an economist. More production could take place if this person was employed based on their skill set, assuming a PhD in economics produces more value-added to the economy than janitorial service does. This is an example of underemployment, which understates the unemployment numbers. Both problems are a function of wages: if wage offers were large enough, the discouraged worker would be encouraged to actively seek work.

Workers become unemployed for two general reasons, one of which makes up the official statistics. Discouraged workers make up voluntary unemployment along with those who quit their jobs and walk away from the labor force. In most advanced countries, a worker cannot quit their current job and collect social or unemployment insurance. Obviously, especially for low-wage jobs, social insurance of any type provides incentives for workers to quit and receive income for not working ("leisure" in the terminology of labor economists). However, what makes a person quit? The specific reasons are vast in breadth and not always obvious. Economists have posited a clever explanation for a worker calling it quits: the current wage is too low. A worker will tolerate draconian bosses, poor work conditions, problems with fellow workers, and other job-specific problems if wages are high enough to endure these issues. If a worker volunteers to not work, we assume that the benefits derived from working (the wage received in the least) are less than the cost of working (a wage paid at another job plus the non-pecuniary costs of working that particular job). Because the former workers are not eligible for social insurance, they are not officially counted by labor-market statistics as unemployed, even though they may actively be seeking work in some cases. Economic theory comes to the rescue of this confusion in the aggregate by focusing on the other type of unemployment.

Involuntary unemployment

In contrast to voluntary unemployment, workers are fired because the wage they are being paid is not at least equal to the benefit derived by the firm for the worker's labor hours, from the firm's perspective. This is a simple relationship from microeconomic theory. When a firm hires a worker, the marginal benefit to the firm is known as the marginal revenue product of labor (MRP_N), the revenue derived by one additional hour of labor being employed. The cost is the nominal wage (W), the money a firm must part with per hour to employ the worker. In the aggregate, the MRP_N is the average price level multiplied by the change in real GDP or a quantity of goods produced because a worker was employed an additional hour; this quantity is also known as the marginal product of labor (MP_N). Equation 10.1 shows the relationship economists assume firms are using to decide on the profit-maximizing number of labor hours to employ, where

$$MP_N = \frac{MRP_N}{P}.$$

$$MP_N = \frac{W}{P} \qquad\qquad (10.1)$$

If MP_N is greater than the current real wage ($\frac{W}{P}$), the firm has an incentive to hire more labor hours. As the firm hires more labor hours, the MP_N falls because of diminishing marginal returns; assuming the real wage remains constant, the firm continues to hire until the MP_N

and real wage are equal. This equality is equivalent to marginal revenue and marginal cost: the firm is maximizing profit from labor hires when Equation 10.1 holds. There are four ways to be involuntarily unemployed from basic macroeconomics.

- Seasonal unemployment: the time of the year dictates the demand for labor hours
- Cyclical unemployment: the business cycle dictates labor hours demand (recession or goods demand contraction leads to a reduction in labor demand)
- Structural unemployment: the worker's labor hours are replaced by technology, or the worker's position is lost to obsolescence
- Frictional unemployment: the worker is simply between jobs and was fired for some other reason

There is an important distinction between frictional unemployment and voluntary unemployment. While many workers who quit actively seek work immediately after walking out on their current job, not collecting social insurance eliminates them from the statistics as described earlier. Economic theory suggests that if worker and firm incentives connect correctly, no one will quit, they will only be fired. Since the aggregate wage can only be at one level, wages will be held artificially too high versus too low with respect to equilibrium; involuntary unemployment is probably the reason why someone in the labor force is not working. These are the only unemployed workers counted. The voluntary unemployed are considered to be a statistical anomaly.

Classic labor market theory, espoused by market purists and those who believe in rational expectations, posits that the labor market will solve any temporary wage differential faced by the firm and worker. Because both firms and workers know the labor market conditions with the same information in classic economics, they will agree on an appropriate wage as if by an invisible hand. Policy is not necessary to draw these sides of the labor market together. Full employment, in this context, is the natural outcome; any deviation from it, whether recession or boom, is simply a transition period between long-run equilibria. How does such a theory explain the problems of persistent unemployment faced by most European nations since the Second World War, or by the United States in the Great Depression or the 1970s stagflation?

First is the existence of nominal wage contracts, where wages are frozen over a specific period because the firm and worker have agreed to a wage above equilibrium. This contract also insures the firm against rising costs, providing the firm with incentives to agree to such a wage. Further, higher wages may lead to more productivity, a gamble taken by the firm in some cases. The higher wage reduces the demand for more worker hours, and attracts more labor hours than will be demanded. As a result, involuntary unemployment exists and persists. Another reason may be the use of efficiency wages. This idea suggests that firms pay workers higher wages specifically to be more productive, and must incur a cost to monitor workers because workers have an information advantage over the firm as to their effort level as a function of wages. This extra cost reduces the demand for work hours at current wages; labor supply exceeds labor demand, which leads to involuntary unemployment. Other reasons include an insider-outsider hypothesis, where current workers have an incentive to block new market entrants, and a concept known as hysteresis. Hysteresis is an idea that suggests unemployment begets more unemployment because the labor market itself is pressured and cannot break that pressure of new labor supply.

Monetary theory is based on involuntary unemployment being affected by policy. A simple, Keynesian transmission mechanism from a monetary policy shock to a change in real

GDP and prices is as follows. Assuming the economy is not at full employment and prices are sticky but partially mobile, a monetary expansion (M^S shift to the right) puts pressure on general prices to rise. This price pressure provides firms with a profit incentive to hire more labor hours because firms know workers face sticky wages and household incomes are about to rise through either the increase in real GDP coming from larger levels of real investment (which the firm also intends to make) or lower interest rates creating a wealth effect on consumption or both. The larger demand for labor hours by firms ramping up production to meet these new demands increases the level of real GDP. Both prices and real GDP rise as a result of monetary policy. Without a pool of surplus labor, involuntarily unemployed workers who possess labor hours waiting to be employed and willing to accept lower real wages initially, this transmission mechanism would not work. Because historical data support such a simple path from monetary tool to goal, the Phillips Curve discussed in Chapter 9 has been used as a model for policy.

The inflation–unemployment tradeoff

The Phillips Curve is a theoretical relationship between inflation and unemployment. For our purposes, it is better to see this as a relationship between unemployment and expected inflation, as we can assume that firms and workers are going to react to changing expectations rather than wait around for the change to actually take place. Figure 10.2 shows the short-run version of this curve; Equation 10.2 shows the Phillips Curve in a mathematical form. The downward slope represents the inverse relationship and the opportunity cost of pursuing lower inflation or unemployment as an explicit goal of monetary policy.

$$\dot{P}^\varepsilon = \dot{P}^* + \beta(U_t - \overline{U}) + \varepsilon \tag{10.2}$$

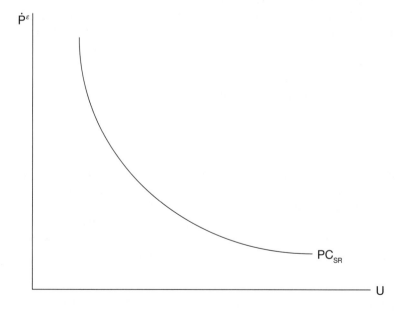

Figure 10.2 The short-run Phillips Curve.

Equation 10.2 shows the relationship between unemployment and expected inflation, where the difference between the current unemployment rate and the natural rate of unemployment determines the amount of expected inflation, including a positive trend and error.[6] The parameter β represents the sensitivity of expected inflation to a marginal difference in current unemployment from the natural rate; $\beta > 0$. The larger the value of β, the more sensitive the relationship is between unemployment and inflation (steeper Phillips Curve); the less positive β's value is, the flatter the Phillips Curve and the less sensitive inflation expectations are to changes in unemployment.

The transmission mechanism discussed earlier helps understand how sensitive expectations can be. Suppose expansionary monetary policy took place. The relationship between the change in unemployment and the subsequent inflation would depend on how fast both firms and workers reacted to the new policy. The faster both sides react to new inflation expectations, the steeper the Phillips Curve should be. Notice there is no mention of unemployment expectations, only prices. This idea connects back to aggregate demand: when monetary policy changes, aggregate demand changes and creates incentives for more production or real GDP. The fact that more employment (less unemployment) is a result of monetary expansion is not debated, i.e. the aggregate supply curve is either flat or upward-sloping when the economy is not in full employment. Whether it is flat or upward-sloping depends on how workers and firms react to their price expectations.

Adaptive and rational expectations: a brief overview

Before the long-run version of the Phillips Curve is discussed, a brief digression and overview of adaptive and rational expectations is needed. Forming adaptive expectations, in many ways, is the cornerstone of the Keynesian world. If expectations are rational, markets react with a large degree of precision and speed to macroeconomic policy. When expectations are adaptive, forecasts of future events are not perfect and have systematic errors within them: forecast error is due to a lack of information on the part of the prognosticator. Because error is endemic in the way expectations are formed, markets cannot clear easily or with precision (the economy remains at employment levels below full) and prices move sluggishly because certain parties (firms) hold an information advantage over others (households) concerning price setting. Expectations are formed by only taking the current set of information into account (or a subset of the full amount available), making a systematic error in their forecast. Equation 10.3 shows the typical equation for inflation forecasts.

$$\dot{P}^{\varepsilon}_{t+1} = \dot{P}^{\varepsilon}_{t} + \gamma_t z_t + \gamma_{t-j} \sum_{j=1}^{J} z_{t-j} + \varepsilon_t \tag{10.3}$$

This equation shows that expected inflation formed in time $t + 1$ is a function of current prices and other variables (z), where t = today, and past variables $(t - j)$, where j represents known information, from the previous period $(j = 1)$ to some period in the past $(j = J)$. γ is a forecast parameter that dictates the importance of current and past information in the forecast. In adaptive expectations, we assume that $\gamma = 0$, and $z_t = \dot{P}_t$ only. As a result, the error term is equal to the difference between the actual and forecast inflation rates. There is going to be some error on average; because not all the information is used, the error is different from zero on average.

Suppose γ was greater than zero and the error term was assumed to be zero on average. Under these conditions, the forecast would be true on average or a self-fulfilling prophecy.

This is the basic idea of rational expectations. When a household uses all the available information and the error term is white noise or zero on average with a known, finite variance, whatever the household predicts for inflation in the next period will come true. Perfect foresight on average propels the economy to full employment, as firms and workers both react with the same information and any individual error is simple white noise. Forming rational expectations has been studied in vast articles and volumes, and is generally the starting place of macroeconomic modeling.[7]

The long-run Phillips Curve is based on rational expectations. With perfect foresight, neither workers nor firms have an information advantage to exploit. An aggregate demand change, such as monetary policy, does not create any more real resources if the economy is in full employment. Because no information advantages exist, perfect competition reigns over all markets. Say's Law now returns, and labor supply creates its own demand again. If demand rises for some exogenous reason, consumers pay more for the same number of physical goods that existed before the policy change.

Perfect foresight of workers and firms leads increasing prices to be completely matched in nominal wages; wages and prices are no longer sticky. Workers know the economy is at full employment and there are no surplus labor hours. Because firms have no available substitutes for inputs, the firm passes on any price increases directly to workers in the form of larger nominal wages. The end result is no more labor hours hired and only inflation. This was Milton Friedman's warning that inflation is always a monetary policy phenomenon: if the money supply increases, and policy-makers mistakenly believe the economy is not fully employed when it is in reality, the policy will create nothing except for inflation. The Quantity Theory of Money provided this prediction in Chapter 9; the idea of rational expectations is simply an extension of the Quantity Theory in the context of monetary policy. Looking very much like the vertical AS curve, its close cousin, the long-run Phillips Curve is vertical at the natural rate of unemployment ($\bar{U}$) (Figure 10.3).

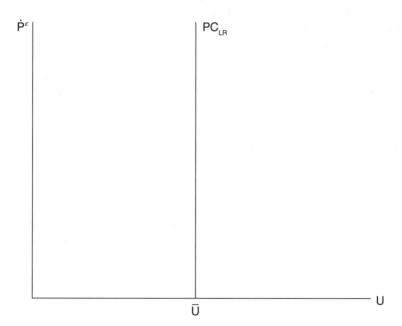

Figure 10.3 The natural rate hypothesis.

This natural rate of unemployment is also known as the non-accelerating inflation rate of unemployment, as it represents a steady-state equilibrium. The labor market clears, is in full employment, and has no demand-side reason to change. In conclusion concerning expectations, policy-makers generally believe the economy is not at full employment, however close the economy may be to this theoretical maximum. Instead of striving for this potential GDP level, central banks strive for balance between inflation and unemployment while trying to maintain the economy on the edge of inflation. If expectations are rational, policy will need to be unanticipated to have any impact; if expectations are adaptive, policy can be either anticipated or unanticipated and have real effects. The Lucas Critique provided the beginnings of a bridge between the adaptive and rational expectations worlds, and continued into the formation of monetary rules based on the expectations-augmented Phillips Curve of Equation 10.3. The expectations debate in monetary theory has become one of how to conduct monetary policy.

Discretion versus rules

John Taylor of Stanford University has been associated with the most famous, foundational idea on monetary rules since the IS-LM model of John Hicks in 1937.[8] Taylor suggested that the Phillips Curve provides a way to shape monetary policy where a balance was struck between inflation and unemployment. Consider a central bank that has multiple monetary tools at their disposal. Ultimately, these tools either manipulate the secondary government debt market through open market operations (OMOs), change the rate at which banks borrow from their central bank or the rate at which banks borrow from each other, or change the reserve requirements. Since central banks rarely change reserve requirements, a monetary rule normally dictates the need for an interest rate or a monetary aggregate to change and satisfy an optimization function for monetary policy. The challenge is to decide how important inflation is versus unemployment to the economy and then pick a monetary tool to use. A rule can tell the public when the money supply will change as a result of new data and expectations. The optimization function tells the public how much of a change to expect under the new policy conditions.

The choice of interest rates or monetary aggregates has been a hotly contested debate. Recently, the focus of policy has been on short-term interest rates, specifically the interbank overnight rate (the Federal Funds Rate in the United States). Using the manipulation of interbank lending rates as the monetary tool, an example of a Taylor rule is shown in Equation 10.4.

$$r_t^{IB} = r_t^{IB*} + \alpha_p (\dot{P}_t^\varepsilon - \dot{P}_t) + (1 - \alpha_p) \cdot (\bar{U} - U_{t-1}) + \varepsilon \tag{10.4}$$

The Taylor Rule simply equates the policy-set rate for interbank loans (called r_t^{IB} here) to a combination of the assumed long-run, real interbank rate, the percentage difference between inflation expectations and the optimal inflation rate, and the difference between the current unemployment rate and the natural rate. The percentages added together tell the central bank what to do with interest rates, and thus money supply. Expectations play into this rule through inflation. The larger the expectations of inflation, the more pressure there is on interest rates to increase, as α_p is greater than zero (the weight on inflation in central bank decisions). As unemployment rises, relative to the long-run rate, $\bar{U}$, interest rates will fall to mitigate the recessionary forces.

Notice the similarity here to the Phillips Curve. If expected inflation is rising, unemployment should be falling. When this happens, the central bank will have unambiguous

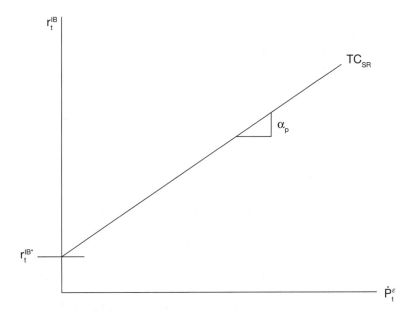

Figure 10.4 A simple Taylor rule for interbank rates.

pressure to increase interest rates. When expected inflation is falling and unemployment is rising, the central bank has unambiguous pressure to decrease interest rates. The Taylor Rule could be expressed as a "Taylor Curve" (TC) following expected inflation. Figure 10.4 shows a hypothetical Taylor Curve, where the interbank rate target, r_t^{IB}, is on the vertical axis and expected inflation is on the horizontal. Notice that the slope of this relationship is the central bank weight placed on expected inflation, α_p.

Case study 10.2 Monetary rules in practice: Norway and New Zealand

A monetary rule is a quantitative way of conducting monetary policy. For example, an economy may be worried about inflation (as is true in almost every economy). Information about actual or expected inflation can trigger a monetary policy response. If an explicit rule exists, the central bank reacts as the economy's fiduciary to relieve that inflation pressure. These rules are concerned with deflation as well and instead of increasing interest rates, the central bank decreases rates to fight this pressure. Price stability is the general, single goal of central banks that utilize monetary rules. Two countries that use monetary rules in slightly different ways are Norway and New Zealand.

In Norway, expected inflation is determined by the central bank and those expectations trigger a monetary response (Norges Bank 2009). If inflation expectations exceed an annual inflation rate target, it is an immediate signal that Norwegian monetary policy is likely to change. Since 2008, this idea of holding the line on inflation has been tested. As financial stability became a larger question for central bankers worldwide, countries like Norway are also looking at providing liquidity and partially abandoning inflation stability in the future for economic stability now. Of course, given that Norway is primarily a country that exports goods for the bulk of their income, as world commodity prices have fallen due to global demand contractions, the Norges Bank is looking at deflation as the driving force behind lowering interest rates. In part, the current monetary stance of Norway is following the inflation rule in reverse, exactly as it should be.

In New Zealand, a similar idea is at work but the room for movement is much larger than Norway's. New Zealand also publishes an inflation target as its quantitative rule. However, instead of a hard inflation target, a bandwidth for annual inflation is given, currently between one and three percent. From a central banking standpoint, that is a wide margin for error, but it reflects the difficulty in tightly controlling inflation.

As in Norway, New Zealand is exposed to export contractions as a result of worldwide demand changes, specifically China, the United States and western Europe. To maintain price stability, New Zealand uses a macroeconomic model that is similar to the United States and has 30 explanatory variables. In Chapter 11, we examine the IS-LM model which is at the core of this system of equations. At the beginning of 2009, the model suggested that worldwide demand for New Zealand's goods and services would contract, and that as other economies began to reduce interest rates in earnest to provide incentives for business investment, New Zealand must follow suit to reduce pressure on the carry trade and other global currency movements affecting New Zealand's economy further. Mishkin (2006) provides parallels between Canada and New Zealand's inflation targeting strategies.

Summary

If inflation is rising too rapidly, the monetary authority may choose to increase interest rates and slow down economic growth. As a result, higher unemployment takes place in lieu of higher inflation pressure. This tradeoff is known as the Phillips Curve. This tradeoff depends on two related issues. The first is the flow of information between parties in transactions, specifically the exchange of labor for wages between households and firms. Whether the household controls this transaction or the firm does leads to problems in monetary policy affecting employment. If the firm controls the labor market, due to an ability to see the coming of policy changes before the household, policy can have real effects on wages; prices will move faster than nominal wages. If the household controls this transaction, or is equivalent to the firm, real wages are probably unaffected by nominal policies. The second issue is how this information restricts the movement of nominal wages. If expectations on prices and income are adaptive, the firm has the advantage. If expectations are rational, the firm and household are equal. The inverse relationship between inflation and unemployment depends on adaptive expectations; rational expectations, in their pure form, suggest monetary neutrality. The Lucas critique, which began a synthesis between these philosophical endpoints, posited the idea that unanticipated monetary policy was the key to having real effects, and that anticipated policy acted as rational expectations would predict.

The Lucas critique helped to put a final shape to the aggregate supply curve, where there are three theoretical sections for monetary policy to move along. The first is flat, reflecting adaptive expectations and no movement of prices to shifts in aggregate demand. Shifts in aggregate demand begin to generate momentum in consumption of goods and inputs such that inflation must rise with growth at some point. As it does, the tradeoff in the Phillips Curve begins. As full employment grows nearer, only unanticipated monetary policy has real effects. The Taylor Rule is one way to view the predictability of policy, where central banks set price stability as a goal and monitor how close the economy is to full employment as the signal to change policy. An economy running too fast will cause inflation and is a signal for monetary contraction. An economy running too slow causes unemployment, which is a signal for monetary expansion. Rule-based policy makes policy more anticipated, but leaves room for policy discretion.

Key terms

1 Adaptive expectations: a way to form expectations of the future where only the most current information is used to make a forecast; errors in forecasts are assumed to be different from zero in adaptive expectations, allowing for profits.
2 Announcement effect: the effect of announcing monetary policy is going to change the macroeconomy.
3 Cost-push inflation: inflation caused by a leftward shift in the aggregate supply curve.
4 Demand-pull inflation: inflation caused by a rightward shift in the aggregate demand curve.
5 Discouraged workers: workers who have stopped actively-seeking work.
6 Employment rate: the percentage of the labor force which is employed.
7 Expected inflation: the inflation rate currently expected for a future period.
8 Inflation: the rate of change of prices, or a persistent and significant increase in the aggregate price level.
9 Involuntary unemployment: the amount of workers unemployed due to firms choosing not to hire labor hours.
10 Labor force: the sum of the employed and unemployed workers in an economy.
11 Marginal revenue product of labor (MRP_N): the additional revenue generated by hiring one more hour of labor, or the price of the good produced multiplied by the marginal product of labor (MP_N).
12 Natural rate of unemployment: the rate of unemployment that represents the productive capacity of the economy.
13 Nominal wage: the stated hourly payment to labor in the labor market.
14 Non-accelerating inflation rate of unemployment (NAIRU): the natural rate of unemployment, where inflation is stable.
15 Rational expectations: a way to form expectations of the future where all the available information is used to make a forecast; errors are equal to zero on average, which makes rational expectations the same as perfect foresight.
16 Real wage: the nominal wages less inflation.
17 Social insurance: government transfer payments based on an event, such as the loss of a job; unemployment insurance is an example.
18 Steady state: the long run in macroeconomics, where the macroeconomy reaches equilibrium in its goods, money and labor markets simultaneously.
19 Underemployment: the underutilization of skills at a job such that productive capacity is not maximized.

20 Unemployment: the condition of not working, but actively seeking work.
21 Unemployment rate: the percentage of the labor force not working, but actively seeking work.

Questions and problems

1 Explain why inflation must be both persistent and significant for economists to react.
2 Compare and contrast demand-pull and cost-push inflation. Which is caused by monetary policy? Explain.
3 Discuss two problems with the methodology of constructing the unemployment rate.
4 Explain how monetary policy can have an effect on labor markets.
5 What is the equilibrium decision of the firm concerning the hiring of labor? Why is this decision an equilibrium condition? Explain.
6 Compare and contrast adaptive and rational expectations.
7 Expected inflation is decided upon in the previous period. Explain why that would affect both current and future decisions.
8 Expected inflation is decided upon in the previous period. Explain why a household or firm would not use all the information available to make decisions.
9 Describe the inverse relationship between inflation expectations and the unemployment rate depicted in the Phillips Curve.
10 Give two reasons the Phillips Curve might shift toward the origin.
11 Give two reasons the Phillips Curve might shift away from the origin.
12 Contrast monetary discretion and monetary rules.

Websites

See the Bank of Canada's website: www.bankofcanada.ca/en/index.html.
See the Reserve Bank of New Zealand's website: www.rbnz.govt.nz/.

11 Money and the macroeconomy

Introduction

The European Central Bank (ECB) has become as much a focus of world financial markets as the Federal Reserve. The ECB represents the extent to which the European Union (EU) has evolved politically to date, the frontier of monetary unions in practice. The interplay between the ECB and the EU member countries is difficult to surmise; thousands of pages of research have tried to explain these connections. What may have kept countries such as the United Kingdom, Switzerland, and Sweden out of the monetary union was a loss of control over central banking, an inability to individually confront domestic economic problems through monetary policy. While each European Currency Union country retains its individual fiscal policy measures, monetary policy has been centralized. For countries wishing to retain policy freedom, the choice of joining this economic bloc is a difficult one. Money, and monetary policy, is now the centerpiece of world economic policy. It speaks and all stand up.

The ECB has a relatively short history. The Maastricht Treaty, which outlines European Union (EU) membership rules, is based on inflation targeting and control. Each country, before joining the currency union, must satisfy the following five criteria:

- inflation rates of no more than one and a half percentage points above the average of the three lowest-inflation countries;
- nominal, long-term interest rates are not to exceed, by more than two percentage points, the average nominal, long-term rates of the three countries with the lowest inflation rates;
- no exchange rate realignment for at least two years after joining the European Currency Union (ECU);
- a country's fiscal budget deficits cannot exceed three per cent of GDP;
- the gross debt to GDP ratio of the country is not to exceed 60 percent.

Many of the current nations in the currency union and those striving for acceptance struggle to meet all five of these criteria annually. Each member country focuses on fiscal policy and domestic labor and capital markets not to exacerbate inflation. The latter two criteria reflect fiscal policy issues; the first two criteria are concerned with inflation effects on goods and capital markets. The third criterion is that the multilateral agreement concerning member nations' fixed exchange rate to the euro cannot be changed for two years once the country converts currency.

The ECB provides support on the monetary side in an attempt to optimize the EU economy as a whole. Monetary policy is predictable and has known effects on the individual nations.

Second, monetary policy has similar effects on countries that meet these criteria and does not bias against or toward any one country. Finally, monetary policy channels do not upset countries satisfying these five criteria such that monetary policy acts like an unfunded mandate. Each of these tasks is a major challenge for a central bank that does not face representative fiscal policy, labor or capital markets. How monetary policy affects a macro-economy is the focus of Chapter 11.

This chapter is split into five major sections, each of which examines how money enters the macroeconomy through monetary policy. First, the basic Keynesian macroeconomic model is introduced. The domestic money market is connected to its sister, macro markets, the domestic goods and labor markets. To understand these connections, we must first examine how macroeconomists envision an economy. The IS-LM model is introduced as a way of analyzing macroeconomic dynamics. By shifting away from aggregate demand and aggregate supply analyses and focusing solely on the AD curve, the IS-LM model examines interest rates and income instead of prices and output. Prices are assumed to be "sticky" and policy has real effects. The fourth section of Chapter 11 is devoted to policy examples which prime the reader for Chapter 12's focus on open-economy macroeconomics. These examples are simple, graphical examples of both monetary and fiscal policies. The intent is to educate the reader on IS-LM basics, illustrating that any macroeconomic policy can be examined in this framework. The final section briefly discusses the transition to price movements, when the AS curve is sloped upward, a segue to Chapter 12. Throughout the chapter, examples of monetary policy focus on the EU to understand the challenges of conducting monetary policy. Chapter 12 opens the economy up to international forces and slightly complicates matters by doing so.

Case study 11.1 Worldwide policy aggression – deflation fears become inflation realities?

In a test of policy and economic integration, many of the world's leading economies witnessed their central banks in the fourth quarter of 2008 and early 2009 lower interest rates in attempting to stave off deep recession. The worldwide movement toward lower interest rates provided a signal that many economies, not just the United States, United Kingdom and the euro area, were in an economic downturn. The problem to be solved initially was one of deflation rather than inflation; however, inflation pressure is building worldwide.

Deflation, in contrast to inflation, is when prices are falling significantly and persistently. Inflation's problems are somewhat reversed under deflation, which makes the worries over deflation somewhat quizzical. On the surface, deflation enhances real incomes, reduces bracket creep, and provides more certainty in consumer budgets, it erodes the incentives for businesses to hire as their revenues are falling due to falling prices. When consumers contract their spending, business revenues contract as prices fall; hiring then ceases and firing begins.

Deflation is feared in countries where exports are the driving force. Obviously, every economy wants to export and derive income from outside their own borders; economic theory and common sense tell us that such a strategy is good. Price instability, regardless of direction, is deleterious to an economy because it leads to uncertainty. For companies with long-term debt, the real interest rate to be paid rises with deflation. This is the beauty of fixed interest rates when inflation is expected; the real interest rate falls as inflation rises because the nominal rate of interest is locked. Deflation benefits the lender that made the fixed interest rate loan, hurting the borrower. Because developed economies have rarely experienced persistent and significant deflation episodes, fixed interest rates sell themselves in terms of passing that inflation risk onto the holder of debt. As real interest rates rise, there is a reduced demand for long-term, fixed-interest debt which reduces investment and reduces GDP growth. So, even though prices are falling and consumers are happy, businesses suffer through deflations because of lower revenues and rising costs in terms of credit balanced partially by lower input costs, including wages.

Figure 11.1 shows the United Kingdom's, the United States' and Japan's deflation episodes since 1980. It is a rare occurrence, and generally on the heels of a severe recession. In 2009, deflation is likely to take place for a relatively short time.

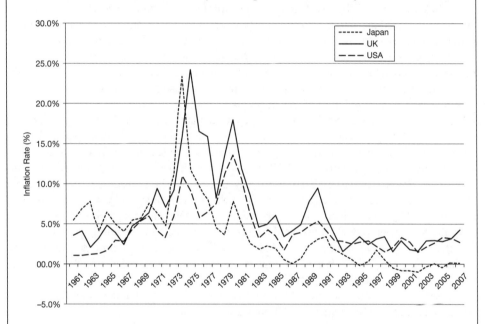

Figure 11.1 Inflation and deflation, Japan, UK, and US, 1961–2007.
Source: World Development Indicators, World Bank, 2009.

The basic Keynesian model: the goods market

In Chapter 9, money demand was described as a function concerning individuals holding money as cash, where incentives to change the amount of non-interest-bearing money held come from changing interest rates or income. From those ideas, money demand acts as a bridge between changes in policy and the choice to consume or save; in monetary economies, money's medium of exchange characteristic is manipulated by both fiscal and monetary policies. The quantity of money supplied to the domestic market is affected by two forces, the central bank (which determines the money supply in total based on policy) and the banks (which determine the quantity of money supplied based on market incentives).

The goods market is where aggregate supply (AS) and aggregate demand (AD) come together, as discussed in Chapter 10. However, in the Keynesian model, this equilibrium takes place assuming prices are initially not very mobile. If prices are stable during periods of policy changes, for example after a monetary expansion, the aggregate demand curve shifts to the right, creating incentives for a larger amount of output; prices may change very little or not at all when a large amount of productive capacity is idle. The Keynesian assumption of sticky prices is based upon the idea that an economy which is not at full employment has little incentive to increase prices after a policy change. Issues such as the costs of changing prices (menu costs), monopoly pricing and sticky wages all contribute to the assumption of sticky prices. Hence, the economy operates in the flatter portions of the aggregate supply (AS) curve

This price immobility assumption is one of the largest controversies in macroeconomics. After Keynes published *The General Theory of Employment, Interest and Money* in 1936, John Hicks interpreted that work in a famous article which introduced the IS-LM model and revolutionized the way macroeconomic courses were taught and policy was conducted; macroeconomics split into two distinct camps as a result.[1] These camps have shifted, reformed, renewed, and continue to this day. Regardless of your school of thought concerning macroeconomic policy and outcomes, most accept the Keynesian goods market model as the way to describe economies concerning decisions to purchase goods and services.

The second major deviation of the Keynesian world from mainstream economics at the time was the reversal of Say's Law. Aggregate demand was now built upon aggregate expenditure (AE), prices no longer the focus of the model due to price stickiness; AE is at a given level of aggregate prices. Aggregate supply reacts to satiate aggregate demand, as if demand creates its own supply; real GDP is considered the measure of aggregate supply. This reversal of Say's Law is another reason why prices may be considered sticky. For our purposes here, demand dictates all the goods market movements: policy, whether it is fiscal or monetary, flows through the goods market demand rather than through production initially, as in the Keynesian model. Household and government demand changing provides profit incentives for firms to produce more goods. Figure 11.2 shows the goods market, also known as the "Keynesian Cross", where aggregate expenditures (AE) and real GDP (y) are the vertical and horizontal axes respectively.

AE is made up of four variables, the same four that make up the famous definition of gross domestic product (GDP). Equation 11.1 shows this formula.

$$AE = C + I + G + NX \tag{11.1}$$

Only in equilibrium is AE equal to real GDP. GDP represents the value of final goods and services produced and sold within an economy's borders within one period; real GDP (y) ultimately represents the income available to the macroeconomy after inflation is taken into account.

There is some meaning for the macroeconomy when AE ≠ y. Suppose spending was greater than income, such that AE > y. In this situation, the macroeconomy would have an incentive to borrow. As borrowing takes place, savings rises to fund the borrowing as interest rates rise, and AE falls until equal to y. If y > AE, interest rates fall, which drives more borrowing and spending until y equals AE again. Any difference between AE and y leads to changes in interest rates that bring the goods market back to equilibrium. A market involving

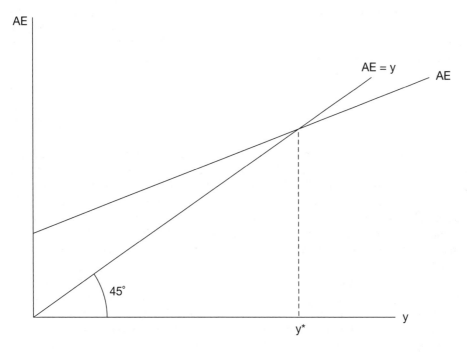

Figure 11.2 The domestic goods market equilibrium.

interest rates exists parallel to the goods market and reacts along with the goods market, moving the macroeconomy toward general equilibrium. To understand how interest rates become involved in the goods market, the dichotomy of consumption and saving needs more discussion.

Consumption vs. saving

In Chapter 2 we learned that the individual's income is either consumed or saved; the amount of income consumed or saved is a function of interest rates. The Keynesian model begins where no income is derived from the economy, where the households consume endowments, natural resources that could be used for production inputs otherwise, to survive. The implication is that these households "dissave", or borrow from future income by doing so. If income is derived by combining endowments in certain ways, to make goods for example, this income provides larger amounts of consumption and savings simultaneously. Consumption rises and dissavings falls (the amount of borrowing falls) until consumption equals income. In this single equilibrium, AE = C = y, total savings is equal to zero.

While this dynamic is somewhat unrealistic, it showcases the interest rate's role in augmenting savings as expenditures are greater than income. If C > y, then the households must borrow to pay their bills. As they borrow, consumers attract the requisite amount of savings to satiate their needs (in this case, reduce their dissavings or endowment consumption to zero). Once the amounts of borrowing and savings are the same, the macroeconomy is in equilibrium by implication, as the incentives to either borrow or save from the goods market not being in equilibrium no longer exist; therefore, the goods market must also be in equilibrium.

A positive amount of consumption takes place with or without income in theory: humans must consume to survive. Saving, by implication, begins as a negative value and rises toward zero as income increases. Consumption and saving have functional forms in the basic Keynesian model as shown in Equations 11.2 and 11.3 respectively.

$$C = C_0 + mpc \cdot y \tag{11.2}$$

$$S = -S_0 + mps \cdot y \tag{11.3}$$

Consumption and savings begin at a constant level (C_0 and S_0) and progress at some rate of change based on the movement of income. The "mpc" is also known as the marginal propensity to consume; the "mps" is the marginal propensity to save. Their sum is equal to one, where the assumption is that every new euro of income induces both consumption and savings but nothing else. We will assume that these propensities are cultural constants of the macroeconomy and not easily subject to change. Once the income level is known, if consumption is greater than income, the interest rate begins to act on savings until consumption equals income.

It is important to understand why the interest rate would become involved if no banks exist and no financial markets exist in this theoretical economy. Net borrowers and savers make decisions about the future when they decide to spend more than they make in income or to save current income for future consumption. This rate of return on saving (an opportunity cost of consumption) is fundamental to not only how a macroeconomy works, but how monetary policy transmits its effects to households. The building block of any macroeconomic model is the household, as the household provides labor to firms, provides the funds by which firms borrow to invest in physical capital, and the provides demand for goods produced.

Investment vs. savings

Once firms are added to the macroeconomy, a synergy takes place between the household and the firm. A circular flow connects households and firms in two ways. First, households provide firms with labor, and firms exchange wages and salaries with the households in return for their time, which is the labor market. Firms also provide goods and services for households, and the household purchases of these goods provide firms with revenue. This is the goods market.

There is a third way in which these two sectors of the circular flow interact. The households, if firms provide them the incentive to do so, save part of their income to financially invest in the firms. Before firms are formed, households that were net savers simply did not consume as much of their natural endowments, what we can now call wealth, as net borrowing households did. Firms can now provide savers with income from interest or dividend payments earned by either lending to the firm or owning the firm outright. For simplicity, we will assume that households ultimately own firms in the macroeconomy, where dividends are part of income, so the only financial market of interest is the loanable funds market.

Firms make physical, real investment in capital, equal to "I" in Equation 11.1. Firms attract household funds through the promise of interest payments. These interest payments are generated by the profits firms make. The augmentation of real GDP is derived from income through wages and salaries to households that are employed, as well as interest payments to those households that chose to save. For both households and firms, the net savings of the macroeconomy is assumed to be completely borrowed by firms. The reasoning is simple. When looking at the households, some are net borrowers and some are net savers. Once firms arrive, any additional consumption is driven by real investment. The new equilibrium is $AE = C + I$; for simplicity, we assume that the level of real investment is exogenous of income.

Investment is determined by the interest rate. In a monetary economy, the household has two choices: it can hold money or save money in excess of money needed for consumption. The more money households save, the more the interest rate on savings is reduced through the law of diminishing marginal returns. This reduced rate provides two incentives: a lower interest cost for firms to make capital purchases and for households to consume more. The interest rate continues to fall until equilibrium is struck. The economy now has two entities demanding money: firms and households. The goods market is in equilibrium again where $AE = y$.

$$AE = C + I = C_0 + mpc \cdot y + I \tag{11.4}$$

Earlier in this text, firms financed their decisions to expand productive capacity through a mix of equity and debt financing; this optimal decision-making was considered to be one of the key ways financial markets showed dynamics. In fact, the interest rate faced by the firm is called the "cost of capital". This cost of capital is generally seen as an opportunity cost, where the firm could have invested in a variety of options, and must make a certain level of revenue to cover this opportunity cost. The present value of capital purchased is the discounted expected cash inflow. If interest rates rise, the firm must make more revenue to cover this "cost", reducing the firm's demand for such a purchase; other opportunities have a better expected rate of return. Accumulation of new inventories and purchases of new capital goods by firms are inversely related to the nominal interest rate.

$$I = f(r + \dot{P}^\varepsilon) \tag{11.5}$$

Households face the opposite challenge with interest rates; saving is directly related to interest rates, reflecting a larger enticement for more savings as interest rates rise. Equation 11.6 reflects the goods market equilibrium, setting Equation 11.4 equal to y.

$$y = C + I = C_0 + mpc \cdot y + I \tag{11.6}$$

Household decisions

The household has income equal to real GDP, and consumes and saves from that income assuming the households own the firms; real GDP is equal to consumption and savings in equilibrium also, as the household must choose between those two acts in the form of a budget constraint.

$$y = C + S \tag{11.7}$$

Setting Equations 11.6 and 11.7 equal to each other suggests a relationship between savings and investment in equilibrium, assuming there is no government and no international trade as of yet: $S = I$. The equality of savings and investment in equilibrium can be also thought of as financial market equilibrium. Much like the equality of AE and y in equilibrium, the supply and demand for loanable funds must also be equal to stabilize the macroeconomy. Suppose S > I. In simple terms, this inequality implies household savings cannot find a home at the current rate of interest, given the output level in the economy. If the interest rate were to fall, savings would be reduced and investment would rise simultaneously; as if by an invisible hand, the financial markets would find equilibrium through interest rate movements, or alternatively as the price of assets changed to bring buyers and sellers together. If S < I, the opposite movement would occur; the interest rate would rise until enough savings were drawn from households to fund the firm's excess demand for borrowing. Interest rate movements, given a level of income, dictate the level of consumption and savings as a measure of time preference. Monetary policy ultimately travels through this relationship to manipulate interest rates.

What interest rate should the firm use to determine its optimal investment level? The concept of opportunity cost is of major importance here, as the firm has myriad choices. Much like the household, the firm decides between "consumption" and saving when it purchases physical capital; this purchase is investment in the aggregate model. If the firm is not engaging in investment, it may also not be saving. In net, firms that purchase capital are assumed to fund that investment from the net savings of households because each sector of the economy has profit incentives to act on each side of this market. Once government is added to the model, households have an alternative to saving with the firm; this alternative changes the equilibrium condition of S = I and how monetary policy transmits its effects to the macroeconomy.

Government spending vs. savings

When adding government to the macroeconomy, the household is assumed to fund the government's actions through a variety of taxes. The three categorical taxes in our model will be lump-sum taxes, proportional taxes and inflation taxes. Lump-sum taxes are taxes not associated with a specific level of income. Proportional taxes are tied directly to a certain level of income; an income change leads to a change in taxes paid by the household. This should not be confused with marginal taxes, the additional tax paid with an additional dollar of income made. Taxes can be flat, regressive or progressive (not change as income rises, fall as income rises, or rise in tandem with income respectively). An inflation tax takes place when the government funds itself through asking its central bank to print money to pay for spending beyond its lump-sum and proportional tax receipts. The printing of money leads directly to some seigniorage income for governments. This income reduces the value of the current money stock, and leads to inflation pressure as discussed in earlier chapters.[2]

Governments borrow to fund expenditures taxes cannot cover. There is a simple budget constraint for the government, with the sum of all taxes receipts equal to T, the interest payments on past debts equal to $R_{t-1}B_{t-1}$, and the new borrowings equal to B_t. B is the local currency amount of bonds issued by the government to finance any current borrowing. Equation 11.8 shows this budget constraint for period t.

$$G_t = T_t + R_{t-1}B_{t-1} + B_t \tag{11.8}$$

To simplify our discussion here, let's suppose that the government has no outstanding debt ($B_{t-1} = 0$), because the government pays off its outstanding debts completely as part of G at the beginning of each year. The government's budget deficit, G – T, is now simply equal to the amount of borrowing to balance the fiscal budget each period: G – T = B.

The addition of the government to the macroeconomy has three effects. First, the amount of government spending, G, reflects the government as another macroeconomic sector acting like a consumer. The government, if G > T, must attract household savings to purchase its debt, like any other borrower. One simple way a government attracts household savings is to issue debt at lower prices than similar debt instruments, and thus at higher effective rates of return. Naturally, there will be marginal households that will purchase these instruments, and a reduction in consumption takes place as interest rates rise. Once the government decides how much to spend and tax receipts are known, the financial markets gear up for a change; once a fiscal budget deficit is known, the financial markets anticipate the sale of any new government debt securities to pay for any overspending. As seen in the examples later in this chapter, the central bank may be called on to pay for these deficits with new money printing, effectively raising tax receipts (through the inflation tax) to match spending rather than imposing other tax increases or issue new debt.

The central bank and fiscal policy

This interplay between the central bank and government's budget is a crucial one. Consider the European Union's situation. Central banking functions are centralized, while fiscal policy decisions are not. Suppose each country's government in the European Union spent more than their respective tax receipts. The sale of euro-denominated bonds would change interest rates throughout Europe, entailing worldwide savings to fund these changes. It is quite possible that an Italian budget deficit would be funded by German household savings but without any exchange rate pressure. Suppose further that the European Union, for other reasons, did not want interest rates to rise. By expanding the supply of euros, the ECB could reduce the interest rate effect of all these budget deficits by effectively purchasing the debt through an inflation tax. If the ECB signaled to its member countries a proclivity to fight interest rate instability upward, EU countries may have incentives to run budget deficits and enjoy the fact that the inflation pressure from ECB action to combat the interest rate pressure will spread itself across multiple nations and thus have a reduced effect on any single nation. How tenable such an arrangement is remains to be seen, especially with the inflation-fighting focus of the ECB.[3] Households are assumed to pay taxes to the government in all forms. Thus, the total tax receipts of the government are added to the consumer's budget constraint, Equation 11.9.

$$y = C + S + T \Rightarrow y - T = C + S \tag{11.9}$$

Equation 11.9 can be seen in either form; the latter form reveals something about how all economists view the payment of taxes. Households pay taxes before consuming or saving, where household income is now after taxes; disposable income is equal to $y - T$. In Chapter 3, the after-tax return on assets was described as the focus of financial planning, portfolio analysis and how investors should track their decisions. Disposable income is the same idea at the macroeconomic level. Taxes will come from income made before any other expenses take place. We assume that government spending is exogenous and not a function of income; taxes are a function of income generally, but for our purposes taxes are seen as lump-sum to reduce the technical nature of this analysis. Equations analogous to Equations 11.6 and 11.7 to describe the new macroeconomic equilibrium are shown in Equations 11.10 and 11.11.

$$y = C + I + G = C_0 + mpc \cdot y + I + G \tag{11.10}$$

$$y = C + S + T \tag{11.11}$$

Equation 11.10 describes the expansion of aggregate expenditure and household sources and uses of income as a result of adding government to the economy. There is an augmentation to the income derived by the country's economic activity; the household adds an expenditure line to its budget, the taxes to partially fund the government's spending. In equilibrium, the income available to the household is equal to the income derived from the production and sale of goods and services to the households, firms and government, which implies the following relationship, what we will call leakages (S + T) and injections (I + G) from here.

$$S + T = I + G \tag{11.12}$$

Savings and taxes are seen as leakages; each reduces the economy's ability to consume domestic products. Investment and government spending augment the economy's ability to consume domestic products and are called injections. While simple on the surface, Equation 11.12 is one of the most important algebraic statements in all of macroeconomics. In equilibrium, the sum of savings and taxes must equal the sum of investment and government spending for the same basic reasons that savings equaled investment when there was no governmental or international sector. This equality is a description of financial market equilibrium, another way to say aggregate supply equals aggregate demand through the connection between the interest rate and income.

Before we move away from the effects of adding government to the economy, two more characteristics of this model need clarification. First, the entrance of government changes the composition of household asset portfolios. When budget deficits exist, and subsequently new debt certificates are issued as described above, the government competes directly with firms for net saving households. As a result, the amount of investment demand falls; as interest rates rise through both the higher demand for money because of the government's budget deficit and the necessary bond price pressure to sell that debt (which are two ways of describing the same event), firms face increased opportunity costs of physical capital purchases. Savings rise due to higher interest rates and investment falls; the government budget deficit has effectively "crowded out" the investment opportunities of private firms. The larger savings level takes place due to the multiplier effect on incomes from government spending and higher interest rates.

As fiscal deficits rise, or even with balanced budget spending, the macroeconomy is stimulated to grow. From the equilibrium conditions above, the change in real GDP as a result of a spending increase can be easily estimated. Equation 11.10 can be solved for real GDP (y) in equilibrium, in terms of those variables considered to be unaffected by income.

$$y^* = \frac{C_0 + I + G}{1 - \text{mpc}} \tag{11.13}$$

Equation 11.13 shows that as G rises, y rises. However, there is a multiplicative effect of an increase in government spending; an additional dollar of government spending increases income itself, and then initiates more consumption which further expands the amount of income. Income creates income stimulated by augmented spending. Some of the growing income is saved. The injection of government spending, G, increases both consumption and savings. This continues until the increase in G is equal to the total increase in both T and S combined, less the crowded-out investment level, I. Equation 11.14 shows the multiplier effect on income; because mpc is less than 1 by definition, any change in government spending creates more than 100 percent of itself in the new equilibrium.

$$\Delta y = \frac{\Delta G}{1 - mpc} \tag{11.14}$$

Let's combine these two ideas, crowding out and the multiplier effect, and show how the leakages and injections equality of Equation 11.12 is affected by fiscal policy. If G increases and T remains constant, the algebra suggests that savings (S) must rise, investment (I) must fall, or both; the crowding out and multiplier effects. As government spending rises, savings are created through larger incomes. However, savings are also created from higher interest rates as the government sells its new debt on the open market, assuming there is a government deficit. As interest rates rise, investment is reduced; the combination of S rising and I falling continues until Equation 12.12 is in equilibrium again. If a deficit does not exist, such that G increased while G < T and now G > T, savings are still created and will rise until the additional savings matches the amount of new government spending.

The importance of these results is twofold for monetary policy. Monetary policy affects the level of investment by changing the opportunity cost of holding money. For example, if monetary policy is expansionary, investment rises as interest rates fall. The lower interest rates signal a lower cost of the government's financial leverage, financing asset purchases by issuing debt, and also reduced opportunity costs of consumption because the return on saving today and not consuming has fallen. If a fiscal expansion is taking place, monetary policy can either accommodate the effects on income, effectively "crowding in" private investment from where it was once crowded out, or exacerbate the interest rate instability by reducing the money supply at a time when money demand is on the rise because of enhanced government expenditures versus taxes. Fiscal policy, for this reason, leads to conundrums for central banks.

Further, the multiplier effect works with monetary policy also. Because investment is a function of the interest rate, and the interest rate (as determined in the market for money) is a function of monetary policy, the level of investment in the goods market is a function of monetary policy. When monetary policy is expansionary, for example, interest rates fall and investment rises in the quintessential Keynesian model. This change, much like expansionary fiscal policy, increases the amount of real GDP by more than the initial increase. The additional income created triggers more consumption and savings. This process ends, with a multiplicative change to income as a result of a given change to investment, when leakages equal injections again, and the new investment level is matched by newly induced domestic savings and taxes as income rises.

Savings have been considered "domestic" to this point. In the final sector of the goods market, international trade and financial markets round out the circular flow and further complicate the way the macroeconomy works. However, this complication provides a great deal of insight into other ways monetary policy affects the macroeconomy and how the world really works.

Net exports and savings

To complete the Keynesian model of the macroeconomy, we add the international sector. Net exports (NX) are equal to exports less imports; this difference represents the current account

(CA) of the balance of payments (BOP) from here. We assume that imports (IM) are a function of domestic income and act much like the consumption of domestic goods, C. Exports (EX), like investment and government spending, are exogenous of domestic income levels; exports are a function of exchange rates and foreign income levels instead. The subtraction of imports is a critical idea. Real GDP is reduced by the amount of imports (IM), the consumption of foreign goods and services; imports represent domestic income that is leaving the domestic economy and being paid to foreign firms and households. This change to aggregate demand does not create its own supply; in fact, imports reduce the incentives for domestic producers to increase output. So far we have assumed that NX = 0. Countries may strive to have incomes made from export sales cover their purchases of imports, which somewhat nullifies the detrimental aspects of imports much like the way in which tax receipts and government spending are related.

There is another similarity between net exports and fiscal deficits. As imports rise, for example, there is marginally more income flowing away from the domestic economy than flowing into it from exports. When imports exceed exports, disposable income is reduced because of international trade; the domestic household's spending is now part of another country's GDP. As a result, expenditures are greater than income, which leads to borrowing. What is different about this borrowing versus a fiscal deficit is when government spending is greater than taxes, more domestic income is generated from which new savings are partially derived. In the case of net exports being negative, domestic savings may not exist to fund these import expenditures; households may borrow from abroad to pay for imports, the only other source of net savings available. If exports exceed imports, the reverse is true; when net exports are greater than zero, domestic incomes rise and provide for an expansion of net savings where domestic households now fund foreign borrowing.

By adding net exports to this model, the equilibrium conditions expand in simple ways. First, household expenditures are unaffected and remain as shown in Equation 11.11. What changes is the income available to households. Equation 11.15 shows this final relationship, where NX is equal to exports (EX) less imports (IM).

$$y = C + I + G + NX = C_0 + mpc \cdot y + I + G + EX - IM \tag{11.15}$$

By setting this equation equal to Equation 11.11, we find the leakages and injections relationship that encompasses the entire circular flow.

$$S + T + IM = I + G + EX \tag{11.16}$$

The basic Keynesian model focuses on investment as the bridge between the money and goods markets. Monetary policy affects investment, by manipulating rates of interest and the supply of money, changing the amount of injections. Suppose the ECB lowered interbank lending rates and the money supply in the euro area subsequently increased. The lower rates of interest that would follow the interbank rate would increase investment demand. As investment demand increases, the right-hand side of Equation 11.16 would increase, assuming monetary policy was the only change and the economy was in equilibrium pre-policy. As a result, injections would exceed leakages, indicating that more income would be generated in the euro area as aggregate demand increased. In Chapter 10, we discussed this as the "interest rate" channel of monetary policy.

As investment and income rise in tandem, the sum of savings, taxes and imports must change (assuming G and EX are constant). If taxes are proportional and increase with income, taxes rise as investment increases; savings also rise as incomes rise through the multiplier effect. Imports should also rise with income if modeled analogous to consumption. Notice that when monetary policy acts on one side of Equation 11.16, a mix of the other variables (specifically those on the left-hand side) reacts until both sides are equal again. As explained earlier in the chapter, this balancing act is a function of equilibrium in markets: as demand rises, the supply side has incentives to rise and match. In this case, the interest rate moving downward conflicts with the income increase on changing domestic savings until the global supply and demand for finance is in equilibrium. In Chapter 12, we will see that the responsiveness of foreign savings to domestic interest rate change adds another layer to this analysis.

The short-run macroeconomy: inflation not a factor

With the goods market and its equilibrium defined, we now introduce the IS-LM model, which combines the domestic goods and money markets, to analyze the macroeconomy. This combination allows central banks to investigate and track changes from monetary policy. To understand this model, the user must first state assumptions that limit the economy to certain locations along the AS curve. For example, this model works best when there is no inflation (flat portion of AS curve) or when inflation is relatively slow-moving (upward-sloping portion of AS curve). Effectively, the assumptions made restrict the analysis to either prices not moving or general prices moving faster than input prices (wages and interest) such that real effects can come from monetary policies. This "price stickiness" assumption of the macroeconomy was a gigantic leap away from conventional economics when the IS-LM model was introduced by Hicks (1937). The three assumptions are:

1   the macroeconomy is not in a state of full employment (current U > U*);
2   prices are "sticky" downward, and input prices are more sticky than general prices in their movements;
3   expectations are adaptive on average.

Each of these assumptions is important to how the IS-LM model works, and the assumptions are linked. The assumption that the economy is not fully employed is because some market friction keeps the labor market from achieving equilibrium, from labor supply and labor demand becoming equal. Possible reasons for this wage and price stickiness were discussed in Chapter 10. If firms have market control over price-setting, prices will be slow to move as a result of new policies. If firms are maximizing profit at the current price level, firms have little to no incentive to change those prices. Changing prices may also have a large cost involved, so-called menu costs as discussed in Chapter 10. The glacial movement of prices is critical to real effects resulting from policy. When expectations are adaptive, there is an information advantage in the financial markets, and this slow response to new market signals through policy also holds nominal interest rates steady while real interest rates and inflation change. Because expectations are adaptive, both firms and households do not react optimally to new market signals, keeping labor markets from clearing; hence the macroeconomy is not at full employment.

These three assumptions continue with us throughout the policy examples and typify the "short-run", flat portion of the AS curve. Because the IS-LM model investigates sticky price macroeconomics, the focus here is on real interest rates, real wage levels and real GDP as the focus of output. In an environment where prices are not moving at all, the difference between real and nominal input prices is small. It is when prices begin to move that this model becomes more difficult to use, though adjustments are suggested after our policy examples. Let's first build the model.

The IS curve

The goods market is described by this curve, where each point along the IS curve is equilibrium between AE and y. Though this curve resembles the aggregate demand (AD) curve, and is related to it, the real interest rate is the "price" of aggregate expenditure. In the AD-AS model, the average price level of the macroeconomy, whether it is the GDP deflator or the consumer price index, represents the price of aggregate demand. Given a real interest rate, the interplay between injections ("Investment" in the Hicks model) and leakages ("Savings" in the Hicks model) delivers goods market equilibrium, the IS relationship. The production and sale of goods and services depend on financial market equilibrium, hence the equilibrium of savings and investment to describe the goods market. Figure 11.3 shows this curve.

Movements along the IS curve are due to changes in real interest rates, policies and other macroeconomic occurrences other than a goods market shock. For example, when central banks initiate monetary policy, the policy changes interest rates, driving goods market changes as described above through investment. Shifting the IS curve (the direction of the shift is in parenthesis with a possible cause) is due to goods market shocks, such as:

- fiscal policy (expansionary policy, rightward; contractionary policy, leftward)
- trade policy (trade-surplus causing, rightward; trade-deficit causing, leftward)
- consumer confidence (more confident, rightward; less confident, leftward)

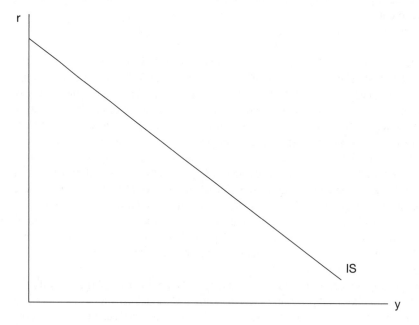

Figure 11.3 The typical IS curve.

Any shift of the IS curve moves interest rates and income in the same direction. Suppose there was a fiscal expansion, such as an increase in government spending. This policy would increase income through the multiplier effects and also increase interest rates by an increase in money demand. How much interest rates and income would rise is due to the money market relationship between r and y, the LM curve.

The LM curve

The money market, as discussed in Chapter 10, can also be illustrated in y–r space. The money market is a simple equilibrium on the surface, determined where money supply equals money demand. Money supply is by the domestic central bank, where the banking system determines the quantity of money to be in circulation through their asset allocation. In a sense, the bank does not determine this quantity alone; household savings also help determine the overall amount of money in circulation. In Chapter 10's model of the money market, the supply and demand for money came to equilibrium because savers and borrowers agree on a quantity of lending and borrowing at a specific interest rate. Because money demand is a function of interest rates, its slope is negative (the interest rate is the price of demanding money) and money demand shifts as macroeconomic income changes.

Assuming the goods market is in equilibrium at a given level of real GDP, y*, this amount of income is taken into consideration by households in determining the level of optimal money demand. The more income made by households, the more consumption by these households, the more money is demanded to pay for consumption. As money demand shifts, it reflects aggregate expenditure (the households, firms and government in total) reacting to new income levels. The LM curve is upward sloping because interest rates and income move in the same direction as money demand shifts along the money supply curve; as income rises, for example, interest rates rise to reflect scarcity of the current money supply due to enhanced money demand. If income changes from its given level, money demand shifts and the interest rate change follows as money demand moves along money supply.

The LM curve is the key to macroeconomic policy for two reasons. The slope of the LM curve reflects how changes to fiscal and trade policy affect rates and income, acting like the money supply curve shifts as central bank policy changes. Its upward slope represents the profit incentives of banks and households to provide loans (banks) or savings (households) in response to new demand signals from aggregate expenditure changes. Figure 11.4 shows the LM curve in y–r space[4].

Short-run macroeconomic equilibrium

Combining these two curves shows a "market" similar to any depiction of supply and demand. The IS curve, as an analogy to money demand, represents the goods market while the LM curve represents the money supply. The IS curve is downward sloping in the real interest rate and shifts as a result of goods market shocks. The M^D curve is downward sloping as a function of the real interest rate and shifts as a result of aggregate expenditures changing, where a change in spending and money demand takes place at all interest rates. The LM curve reflects the money supply curve directly, shifting due to monetary policy and financial innovation, where monetary policy is the dominant force. Why, if the IS-LM model is ultimately reflective of money supply and money demand, do analysts and policy-makers not use the money market to determine macroeconomic equilibrium? The answer lies in the slopes of each curve.

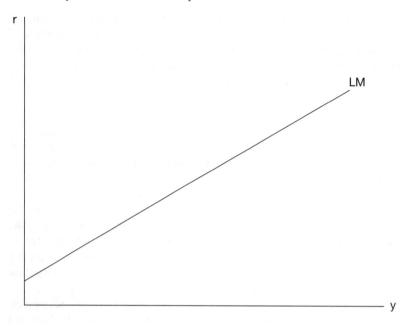

Figure 11.4 The typical LM curve.

The IS and LM slopes

The equality of injections and leakages, which has money demand within, is represented by the IS curve. When monetary policy changes, investment is where that shift in money supply first enters the goods market. When fiscal policy changes, the resultant change to aggregate expenditures enters the money market through money demand. Both investment demand and money demand are part of the injections–leakages equality, where investment is an explicit component and money demand is summarized by the injections overall.

The IS curve's slope reflects how much income can be generated by a change in the money supply; how responsive the goods market is to a change in real interest rates. The steeper the slope of the IS curve, the less reactive income is to a change in real interest rates; the flatter the IS curve, the more a change in monetary policy can affect real GDP. There are two ways to view this relative slope. First, the IS slope reflects the interest elasticity of investment demand, or how much the quantity of investment changes as a result of a change in real interest rates. The other way to view this slope is to consider the goods market multiplier from Equation 11.4. If the money supply increases, investment reacts as a result of the lower interest rates. How much the change in investment drives a new level of real GDP depends on the multiplier's size: the larger the mpc, the larger the multiplier and the flatter the IS slope. The flatter the IS curve's slope, the more potent monetary policy is in changing real GDP at a small cost in the interest rate.

For fiscal policy, the LM curve's slope provides a way of tracking policy potency, or how much manipulating government spending can change bank incentives to provide more financing. When fiscal policy is expansionary, the IS curve shifts to the right, a reflection of increasing money demand. The quantity of new money to be released for consumption depends on how much the money demand curve shifts and how steep the money supply curve may be. The steeper the LM curve, the less reactive banks are to new demand incentives from

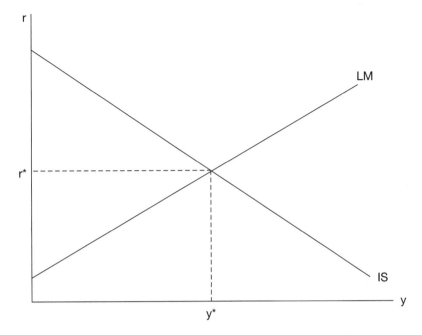

Figure 11.5 The short-run macroeconomy.

aggregate expenditure to release funds for lending. The flatter the LM curve, the more potent fiscal policy is in changing real GDP at small changes to interest rates. The interest elasticity of income is the quantification of this slope. The further importance of the LM curve's slope is shown in Chapter 12.

Figure 11.5 shows the short-run macroeconomic equilibrium. The intersection of the IS and LM curves defines the goods and money markets in equilibrium, while the labor market is not in equilibrium by assumption of the short run. It is important that the reader remembers that the goods market is defined as AE = y and AD = AS, not just AD = AS. Inflation expectations are inside real interest rate calculations, and assumed to be slow-moving.

Policy cases focused on monetary policy

The following cases are examples of simple policy shocks and their effects on the macro-economy using the IS-LM model. The policy examples here are focused on monetary policy. Because we have been talking about fiscal policy, one example will include expansionary fiscal measures, while the final of these first four examples focuses on how the central bank may react to expansionary fiscal policy if control of interest rates is a concern for the economy. The first two examples are monetary policy, expansionary then contractionary.

Case 1: expansionary monetary policy

When a central bank increases the money supply by one of its policy tools discussed in Chapter 9, the policy unleashes new signals upon the financial markets. The larger money supply tells the financial markets that interest rates are about to fall. Firms also recognize the new signal and begin to plan expansion and capital expenditures based on the expectations

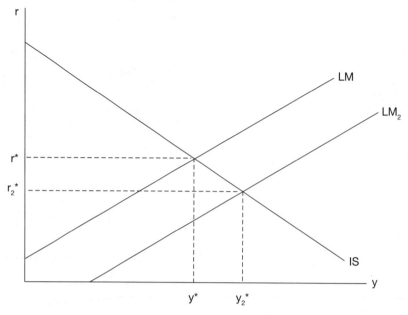

Figure 11.6 Case 1's initial policy shock.

of lower interest rates. The lower interest rates are achieved through the financial interactions of banks, consumers and firms. The initial new funds come from the central bank, providing banks with more funds through new incentives to lend, by the central bank buying government debt held by the banks, for example. If firms can find financing at the lower interest rates, the firm initiates purchases of capital, expanding the economy's productive capacity, increasing real GDP. The resulting increase in GDP provides a larger incentive to save (through larger income levels), and continues to increase until the interest rate reaches equilibrium in the money market at a new, lower rate. When this is achieved, the goods market comes to equilibrium using the new interest rate to determine investment and savings levels, and a new IS-LM equilibrium is struck. Figure 11.6 shows the shift in the LM curve that represents a monetary expansion.

On the surface, the new equilibrium (y^*_2, r^*_2) is like any other market movement after an exogenous change. As if by an invisible hand, the LM curve shift to the right begins market movements toward more loans, more investment, reduced interest rates and increased real GDP. However, because of the final short-run assumption, adaptive expectations, the transition from the original equilibrium to the new y-r couplet is not due to a direct market movement along the IS curve. Only if information was perfect, such as a rational expectations framework, would that smooth transition take place. Instead, this model makes the case that monetary policy takes a more circuitous route from one equilibrium to the other. This route, as in Chapter 10, is the liquidity effect.

The liquidity effect and adaptive expectations

The monetary expansion in Case 1 leads to an immediate change in expectations that reduces interest rates, and induces an immediate increase in both investment and income. This is the Keynesian interest rate channel of policy. The central bank, knowing that only expectations have changed, must reduce rates below the expected, new equilibrium. If adaptive expectations exist, the interest rate overshoot is necessary to provide signals to the macroeconomy. Once market actions take place based on these signals, such as banks beginning to lend more as well as firms and consumers borrowing more, the interest rate actually increases until it reaches equilibrium. This upward movement of the interest rate depends on the IS curve's slope. If the IS curve is relatively flat (steep), the liquidity effect is relatively large (small).

The liquidity effect is really the effect of demanding money, which is ultimately related to the multiplier effect. When the central bank supplies more money to the macroeconomy, policy-makers assume the money will be demanded. The money supply expansion provides incentives for more demand. Concerning the movement of interest rates, however, the central bank is at the mercy of consumers. If consumers spend a large percentage of each additional euro of income earned because the ECB lowered the interest rate and increased investment, interest rates will move very little. This is because interest rates, while initially falling to attract the newly available funds, rise as a result of an increase in money demand. If both the lenders and borrowers in these new loans had full information about their respective positions in these transactions, there would be a fluid movement along the money demand curve. Because of our assumption of imperfect information here, interest rates drift back to equilibrium slowly and indirectly. As consumers, firms and governments become willing to be more liquid (to consume or invest in capital); the interest rates remain out of, but move toward, equilibrium. This implies that central bank actions lead to disequilibria initially, causing financial market volatility until expectations and reality come together.

Figure 11.7 summarizes the movements of both interest rates and income from start to finish in this Keynesian model. The symbolic logic of these movements is Equation 11.17.

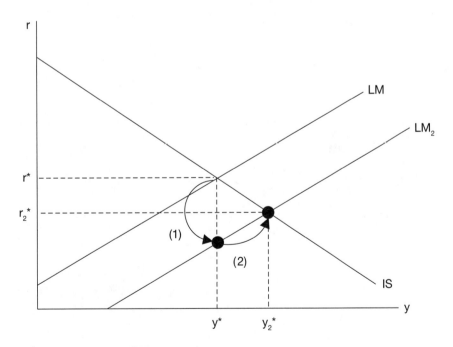

Figure 11.7 Case 1's policy movements.

$$M^S \uparrow \Rightarrow r \downarrow \Rightarrow I \uparrow \Rightarrow y \uparrow \Rightarrow Q_M^D \uparrow \Rightarrow r \uparrow \Rightarrow I \downarrow \Rightarrow y \downarrow \qquad (11.17)$$

The net effect of these movements on r and y is for interest rates to fall and real GDP to rise. The movements after the initial increase in real GDP ($Q_M^D \uparrow \Rightarrow r \uparrow \Rightarrow I \downarrow \Rightarrow y \downarrow$) are the liquidity effect in sum; notice that these effects are led off by an increase in the quantity of money demanded to match the new quantity of money supplied at current interest rates. The central bank needs this increase in quantity to deliver increased real GDP through the multiplier effect. In Figure 11.7, movement (1) is the initial effect of policy and movement (2) is the liquidity effect.

Case 2: *contractionary monetary policy*

There are many international examples of inflation control where central banks increase interest rates in an attempt to slow down consumer spending. This monetary contraction signals an increase in interest rates and a decrease in real investment and income, the opposite effects of a monetary expansion. There is also an "illiquidity effect", the reverse of the liquidity effect in Case 1. Using the same logic of adaptive expectations and that the central bank merely begins a process that ends in the interaction between the goods and money markets, the initial increase in interest rates overshoots the final destination to provide a large enough signal to motivate necessary market actions to move the macroeconomy to a new equilibrium. Equation 11.18 provides a logic analogous to Equation 11.17 and Figure 11.8 illustrates the movements graphically.

$$M^S \downarrow \to r \uparrow \Rightarrow I \downarrow \Rightarrow y \downarrow \Rightarrow Q_M^D \downarrow \Rightarrow r \downarrow \Rightarrow I \uparrow \Rightarrow y \uparrow \qquad (11.18)$$

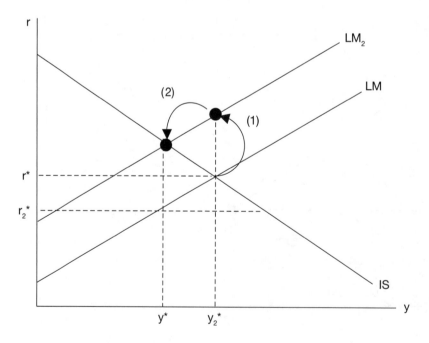

Figure 11.8 Case 2's policy movements.

The net effect of these changes is to increase interest rates and decrease income. Once again, the slope of the IS curve dictates how much (or how little) interest rates and income change as a result of monetary policy. When the money supply is reduced, interest rates rise and provide a signal to goods markets to contract aggregate expenditure. This contraction leads to a reduction of incomes, which begins to slowly reduce interest rates. The reduction, after the initial increase, of interest rates provides investment incentives on the margin and mitigation of real GDP's decrease. The net effects are the opposite of the monetary expansion as expected. The role of adaptive expectations here remains front and center: equilibrium is found only after a drift of interest rates into disequilibrium, which provides the correct signals to initiate market actions sought by the central bank. In Figure 11.8, movement (1) is the initial effect of policy and movement (2) is the illiquidity effect.

Case 3: expansionary fiscal policy

The euro area faces a struggle with fiscal policy decisions throughout its member countries' disaggregated fiscal policies. A central bank must worry about expansionary fiscal policy for two reasons. First, when governments spend more money, they act like consumers and increase the amount of income made by the macroeconomy. As a result, households reap the multiplicative benefits of that policy and enhance their own consumption (as well as their savings). In both cases, money demand rises as a result of the spending increase, and upward pressure builds on interest rates in financial markets. Second, if the government does not have enough tax receipts to fund its spending, there is a need to issue new debt to cover this spending deficit. If this is the case, not only will money demand increase through more government and household spending, but real investment will suffer as increased interest rates reduce the firm's ability to afford new, real investment. Also, if the government must issue debt, the government is also asking households to shift their savings to purchases of government debt securities rather than investing in the firm (banks are assumed to follow suit). The resulting increase in interest rates provides incentives for savings to shift away from the firm and toward the government, crowding out real investment.

This crowding-out effect is the initial opportunity cost of a government running fiscal deficits funded by new debt issued. The crowding-out effect only takes place if the macroeconomy shifts savings from one sector (the firms) to another (the government). If new government spending is completely funded by tax receipts, the amount of household savings necessary to fund the current amount of investment remains the same. This is a subtle point. Interest rates still rise under either scenario, a balanced-budget or deficit-producing fiscal expansion. However, if the increase in interest rates uses the financial markets to fund government spending, a shift in savings is necessary to deliver equilibrium. In both cases, the firm reduces its real investment level because interest rates rise. The difference is how profound that change is, a function of how the fiscal spending is funded.

Figure 11.9 shows the fiscal expansion in the IS-LM model. Instead of the LM curve shifting, the IS curve now shifts to the right because fiscal policy is a goods market shock (a government spending increase changes aggregate expenditure, and thus incomes, at all interest rates). Initially, interest rates are unchanged. It is only when incomes are made from government spending that interest rates begin to rise. This logic is once again tied to adaptive expectations. Because markets do not have perfect information, households and firms need signals that an expansion in government spending (or the reduction of taxes) delivers an increase in income. Once income has increased, and more money is demanded at all interest rates to fund the new aggregate expenditure, interest rates react to these changes. Once again,

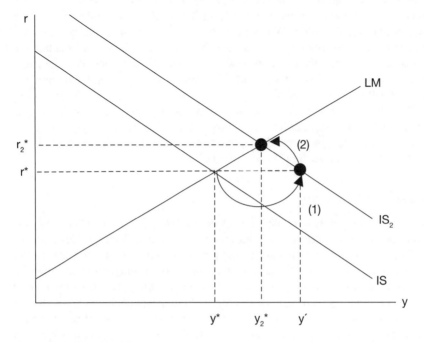

Figure 11.9 Case 3's policy movements.

even if the new spending is fully funded by taxes, money demand will rise. Whether this is due to crowding out or to more savings depends on how the government funds its deficit. Equation 11.19 shows the logic of the macroeconomic effects

$$G \uparrow \text{ or } T \downarrow \Rightarrow y \uparrow \Rightarrow M^D \text{ shift to the right} \Rightarrow r \uparrow \Rightarrow I \downarrow \Rightarrow y \downarrow \qquad (11.19)$$

A subtle difference between this policy and the monetary expansion of Case 1 is that instead of the quantity of money demand changing to meet the new money supply, the entire money demand curve shifts as a result of fiscal policy. In the case of monetary policy, the money supply shift is a movement along the money demand curve, and simply seeks to provide incentives for a larger quantity of money to be demanded to meet the new supply. In fiscal policy, the government is demanding more money to pay for its expenditures (regardless of borrowing or having the tax receipts to pay for the expenditures) at all interest rates, a shift of money demand. The slope of the LM curve now dictates how much the interest rate must change to attract the requisite funding to clear the money market once the money demand curve has shifted.

The injections–leakages equality also showcases changes from a fiscal expansion. If government spending rises, but $G < T$, savings remains less than investment, just at a smaller difference. In this way, investment is not crowded out per se, it is just reduced due to the higher cost of making the purchase (r rising). However, if $G > T$, $S > I$ is necessary to deliver equilibrium, assuming that $NX = 0$. This is the crowding-out effect seen from a slightly different angle.[5] The net effects of a fiscal expansion in the IS-LM model are to increase interest rates and to also increase real GDP through the multiplier effects, where movement (1) is the initial effect and movement (2) is the "crowding-out" effect of interest rates rising and reducing real investment.

The loss of investment due to either the balanced-budget or deficit-financed fiscal expansion is caused by the increased interest rate. This slows the income that otherwise would have been earned had the interest rate remained the same. Because more spending is driving this income growth, the larger interest rate reflects a type of "inflation", where the cost of purchasing real capital is rising due to aggregate expenditure and money demand rising; the interest rate increase reflects the scarcity of money.

Case 4: fiscal policy accommodation or crowding in

In this chapter's final case, fiscal expansion occurs again, but with monetary expansion layered over the top. The idea here is that the central bank may be called upon to "purchase" the new government deficit to stabilize interest rates. Imagine that the ECB knew that every country in the euro area had cut taxes. This stimulus would put pressure on region-wide interest rates and begin some destabilization of financial markets. As a result, the ECB may be asked to stabilize interest rates by increasing the money supply juxtaposed to fiscal expansion. On the surface, this seems like the best prescription for macroeconomic policy: we have just learned that both fiscal and monetary expansions increase income. Using them simultaneously should have an amazing, boom effect on the macroeconomy. Further, the ECB could simply print money to pay for the government debt, which would eliminate the increase in what each member government owed to itself or the rest of the world. Right?

While this mix of policies may seem very appealing on the surface, especially while prices remain sticky, it is important that the reader understands that prices will not remain sticky forever, especially if a government were to pursue dual policies that were each inherently inflationary. Before diving headlong into an explanation of an economy moving from a flat AS curve to an upward-sloping one and how inflation can come quickly to an unaware economy, let's first go through the mechanics of this final case.

When a fiscal deficit is paid for by its central bank, the economic logic is the same as if the reader simply laid Case 1 over Case 3. The fiscal expansion is assumed to happen first, giving the central bank either the signal or mandate to initiate parallel monetary measures to keep interest rates stable. Then the monetary expansion takes place. This use of seigniorage, or revenue from printing money, eliminates the government deficit in one of two ways. Either the new money pays for the deficit directly or the central bank buys the new debt issued by the government as if the central bank was a financial market participant. Regardless, the central bank has created the money needed to eliminate the crowding-out effect of interest rates rising, which crowds investment back in. Another opportunity cost of initiating so much spending and production is that the economy moves from price stickiness to price mobility very quickly. Each portion of this case has a logic already described above. Equations 11.20 and 11.21 show this logic again to match the diagram of Figure 11.10.

$$G \uparrow \text{ or } T \downarrow \Rightarrow y \uparrow \Rightarrow M^D \text{ shift to the right} \Rightarrow r \uparrow \Rightarrow I \downarrow \Rightarrow y \downarrow \tag{11.20}$$

$$M^S \uparrow \Rightarrow r \downarrow \Rightarrow I \uparrow \Rightarrow y \uparrow \Rightarrow Q_M^D \uparrow \Rightarrow r \uparrow \Rightarrow I \downarrow \Rightarrow y \downarrow \tag{11.21}$$

The net effect of these policies depends on their respective magnitudes. If fiscal policy has a smaller impact on income, then the interest rate will fall; if fiscal policy is more potent in its effect on income, interest rates will rise. These relative magnitudes take into account the

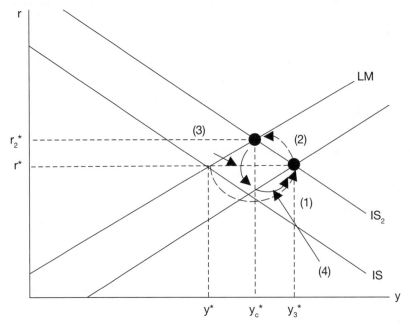

Figure 11.10 Case 4's policy movements.

multiplier effect of government spending on real GDP and the interest elasticity of income to know how much money demand will change as a result of new government spending (the shift of the IS curve mimics the M^D shift).

For illustrative purposes, assume the magnitudes are the same for the two policies, such that the change in the interest rate should be about the same and net to a negligible change from the rate's initial equilibrium. Fiscal policy has its initial effect on income, and then the shift in money demand moves interest rates up. The higher interest rates reduce investment and mitigate income growth. As a reaction, the central bank expands the money supply, putting downward pressure on interest rates, and expanding investment. It is here that the crowding-out effect on investment is abrogated, and investment is crowded back in. The larger income levels and lower interest rates lead to the liquidity effect, and interest rates and income move toward their new equilibrium as if interest rates did not change. In fact, if the central bank coordinates its actions with the fiscal policy-makers, the financial markets will not experience much of a change, if any, as a result of policy. In a sense, the macroeconomy will have growth free of the opportunity cost of higher interest rates.[6]

At some point, however, we must relax the sticky price assumption somewhat and allow prices to move. Demand-side growth with no inflation is short-lived. We assume that real interest rates face a tug-of-war between nominal interest rates and expected inflation. Any expansion will put upward pressure on inflation; the respective policies are hypothesized to have real effects because nominal interest rate effects are slower to change when prices begin to move as nominal wages move slowly.

This is known as the "medium run" in macroeconomics; labor markets are still not clearing, but both general prices and input prices are moving, where general prices move with larger magnitudes in percentage change than do nominal wages and interest rates.

The medium run

In each of the four cases above, the general price level, P, has been assumed to be completely sticky such that the inflation rate is zero. This was the extreme case of our second assumption of the short run. It is important that this limiting assumption of the short-run model be relaxed to understand how the IS-LM works in inflationary economies. Suppose prices were still relatively sticky, but beginning to move. In Cases 1 and 3 (p. 171 and p. 175), expansionary monetary policy seems like a worry-free recipe for policy success: lower interest rates and an increase in real GDP result simultaneously. If we add the layer of changing prices to these cases, the opportunity costs of pursuing such policies rise. The AD-AS analysis of Chapter 10 showed this tradeoff, but how does the IS-LM model show this tradeoff by focusing on interest rates and income instead of prices and income?

The Fisher Equation, $R^\varepsilon = r + \dot{P}^\varepsilon$, provides some insight. We have assumed to this time that with $\dot{P}^\varepsilon = 0$, $R^\varepsilon = r$. However, it is more revealing to define the real interest rate as $r = R^\varepsilon - \dot{P}^\varepsilon$, where the real interest rate is the residual of the current market's expected rates and expectations on inflation. When the money supply rises, nominal interest rates fall and expected inflation begins to rise once we allow a situation different from complete price stickiness.

As prices become more flexible, and the economy moves closer to full employment, banks begin to lose market power over controlling interest rates. The central bank no longer has an incentive to change the money supply because no more real growth can come from the macroeconomy. Many intermediate macroeconomic theory texts use vertical LM curves to describe the money market at all times (which implies a vertical money supply curve). The multiplier effect is somewhat suppressed in real terms because of inflation, and completely suppressed in the long run as the price movements eliminate any real gains. If the money supply expands in the medium run, the initial LM shift is matched by an incomplete movement back toward the original LM curve because of inflation rising. This is because the value of money, real balances, is falling as inflation rises.

The labor market is assumed to work in a similar way. The real wage is the ratio of nominal wages to the price level, and the percentage change in real wages is simply the percentage change in nominal wages less inflation. The real wage is what remains from the nominal wage after the removal of inflation. If the money supply increases, nominal wages are assumed to be more sticky than the general price level; prices are assumed to move immediately once the money supply has increased and reduced the value of every euro in circulation. Given the lower cost of labor (a lower real wage) to the firm, the firm has an incentive to purchase more worker hours from the labor market. This increase in demand may not change the nominal wage, but will increase real GDP to create more overall wage income as more hours are worked. An increase in nominal wages will take place at some point along the AS curve when workers realize that their hours are scarcer and their real income is being slowly eroded by inflation.

The medium-run model simply allows for input price changes, which mitigates the changes in real GDP when policy is expansionary and stabilizes interest rate changes. Since the directional effects of the short and medium runs are essentially the same, any differentiation here is simply to infer the magnitude of changes from one run to the next.

Case study 11.2   The meaning of central bank independence

Monetary theory has struggled to decide whether central banks should be independent of government budget processes and edicts about how monetary policy is to be conducted, versus a central bank that reacts to legislative arrangements. As many new central banking systems are either being formed soon (the Eco in Africa as an example) or being considered (an Asian monetary union is gathering support), the tie of those institutions to governmental processes remains an open question. This question is also of importance as many central banks are becoming very aggressive on reducing their interest rates and providing monetary stimulus in the midst of global recession since 2008. Is it possible to account for cross-country differences in inflation and output by investigating the independence of central banking decisions?

Economists initially approached this question by generating a measure of central bank independence. A recent article by Cukierman (2008) provides an outstanding survey of both the literature and data in measuring independence. Central banks in Latin America and in former communist nations in Europe have been allowed more independence in a legal way. The governments explicitly separate the monetary policy powers from both the fiscal budget and electoral processes. An index, as in Bade and Parkin (1984), is the indicator of central bank independence. This index is based on a coding of 16 different characteristics of central bank charters about authority over monetary policy, procedures for conflict resolution between the central bank and its government, the relative importance of explicit inflation targets stated in the law, legal limitations on central bank lending, and how appointments and dismissals of central bank leadership take place. The index generally ranges from zero to one, where one is complete independence and zero is complete control by the government or perfect congruence with the fiscal process.

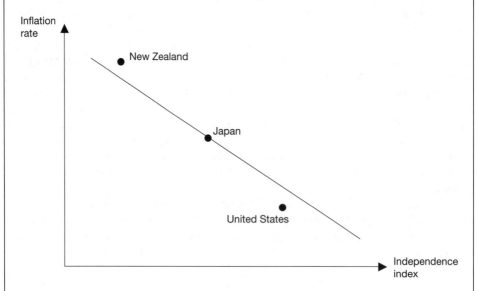

Figure 11.11 Typical depiction of central bank independence and inflation.

Figure 11.11 shows the typical tradeoff between inflation and the independence index, which is a downward-sloping function of independence: the higher the independence level, the lower inflation is likely to be (Carlstrom and Fuerst 2009). While Figure 11.11 is simply the typical structure, there is no finality on this question. It is generally accepted that the more independent the central bank, the lower is the long-term inflation.

Summary

This chapter used Chapter 10's model of the macroeconomy and drilled down into the aggregate demand curve. Inside aggregate demand lie two distinct markets, buttressed by a third. The goods and money markets are where firms, households and government interact. The basic Keynesian theory suggests that relationships exist between consumption, investment, government budgets, and net exports that provide a way to measure and predict economic activity. This picture of the goods market assumes that for each new unit of disposable income (income after taxes) made by households, a portion is consumed and another portion is saved. When households satiate their needs for consumption and borrowing, net savings seek out rate of return opportunities with the firms, government, and foreign economies. This search ends when the balance between savings, taxes and imports equals investment, government spending and exports. The leakages from the ability to consume domestic goods are equal to the injections to that ability when the goods market is in equilibrium. The idea that "savings" equals "investment" simply suggests that macroeconomic supply equals macroeconomic demand, where both savings and investment are expanded to include government spending ("investment") and taxes ("savings") and the foreign sector (where exports are injections and imports are leakages).

The money market is the other half of aggregate demand, and this market helps determine the level of both savings and investment. Following the model from Chapter 9, money supply equals money demand when the equilibrium quantity of non-interest-bearing cash is determined. The central bank controls the supply of money, and both banks and households control the quantity of money supplied to the markets given currency in circulation. Money demand can change based on new fiscal policy, consumer confidence, and changes in the availability of credit. As money demand shifts, interest rates change and affect the savings and investment decisions of households and firms respectively. The goods market determines the level of real GDP and the money market determines the equilibrium interest rate.

The IS-LM model allows a determination of both real GDP and the interest rate simultaneously by combining these markets. The IS curve represents all equilibrium combinations of the interest rate and real GDP where leakages equal injections. The IS curve shifts as a result of new fiscal or trade policies, or changes in consumer confidence. The LM curve represents all equilibrium combinations of the interest rate and real GDP where money supply equals money demand. The LM curve shifts as a result of new monetary policies. In this framework, assuming the economy is not at full employment, prices are sticky downward and adaptive expectations exist, allows a policy analysis to take place in the flat or upward-sloping regions of the aggregate supply curve. Because of adaptive expectations, changes in monetary policy may force slow reactions in the market place to determine the new equilibrium. This liquidity (or illiquidity) effect is an important component of the Keynesian macroeconomic model.

Fiscal policy, especially when deficit spending takes place, provides another challenge to monetary policy-makers. The crowding-out effect, where savings are shifted toward the government instead of the firm, increases interest rates. The monetary authority may be asked to stabilize interest rates such that new monetary policy crowds this lost investment back in through monetary expansion. Inflation pressure can build quickly under such a scenario, breaking out of pure price stickiness, such that exchange rates can also be affected. Chapter 12 adds the international economy more explicitly to this model.

Key terms

1 Consumption: the act of not saving from disposable income.
2 Crowding out: the effect of a fiscal expansion where interest rates rise and savings is diverted to government debt from funding private, real investment at firms.
3 Disposable income: personal income less taxes.
4 Endowment: an initial stock of wealth for any entity, including natural resources.
5 European Central Bank (ECB): the monetary authority for all economies in the European Currency Area.
6 Exports: goods and services sold to another economy from firms in the domestic economy.
7 Goods market: the market for tangible products.
8 Government spending: the expenditures of the government portion of the macroeconomy.
9 Imports: the purchase of goods and services produced in another economy by the domestic economy.
10 Injections: the sum of real investment (I), government spending (G) and exports (EX).
11 Investment: the purchase of new plant and equipment, housing and inventories by the macroeconomy.
12 IS curve: the locus of combinations of given interest rates and associated equilibrium values of real GDP in the goods market.
13 Leakages: the sum of savings (S), taxes (T) and imports (IM).
14 LM curve: the locus of combinations of given real GDP levels and associated equilibrium interest rates in the money market.
15 Net exports: the difference between exports and imports of goods and services.
16 Taxes: the revenue of governments.

Questions and problems

1 Why would a central bank worry about fiscal policy if it controls monetary policy? Explain.
2 Explain the connection between the goods and labor markets. Do they come to equilibrium at the same time? Explain.
3 Explain the interest rate channel of monetary policy.
4 As the slope of the IS curve gets steeper, what is happening to the potency of monetary policy to affect real GDP?
5 As the slope of the IS curve gets steeper, what is happening to the potency of monetary policy to affect real interest rates?
6 Does the "run" of the macroeconomy make a difference as to monetary policy's potency? Explain.

7   As the LM curve gets steeper, the crowding-out effect of fiscal policy worsens. Why?

8   When the central bank provides seigniorage income to the government, why is this considered an "inflation" tax? Explain.

Suggested reading

Keynes, John Maynard (1936) *The General Theory of Employment, Interest and Money.* London: Macmillan (reprinted 2007).

12 Monetary policy in the open macroeconomy

Introduction

When the United States' Federal Open Market Committee (FOMC) meets, they publish that meeting's minutes. With bated breath, the world waits for these minutes to arrive on the internet or to be summarized in various news sources elucidating why any change or no change to the federal funds rate target was made. Why should the world await this news so intensely? In Chapter 11, the domestic effects on various markets from a monetary shock were discussed. This chapter focuses on monetary policy effects, the exchange rate, and connections between economies.

In 2007, and into 2008, the value of the American dollar fell rapidly versus most major currencies. The link between the expansionary monetary policy of the Federal Reserve and this downturn was corroborated by the international financial market's activity. In 2008, the lower dollar value caused commodity prices to rise rapidly, especially oil, which began to have a detrimental effect on imports. There was also a positive effect on exports, which helped the American economy through the summer of 2008 not to experience a technical recession in the midst of sagging residential construction investment because of falling housing prices.

When thinking about how monetary policy in one economy affects others, it is important to recognize how countries are economically linked. The balance of payments (BOP) provides an accounting of how exchange rates and the flows of both capital and trade are all tied together. The way monetary policy shocks in one economy have effects on other economies may not be as clear-cut as Chapter 11's models assume. The BOP basics begin this chapter, where interest rate parity acts as an explanation of why exchange rates fluctuate. This chapter provides an extension of the IS-LM model to investigate how the balance of payments, exchange rates and policy are tied to each other. Simple rules that students can follow decipher the effects of domestic monetary policy on international finance within the context of this extended model. Finally, an economy's movement toward the long run is briefly discussed. The transition from sticky prices to more flexible prices changes policy outcome expectations internationally.

The international macroeconomy

The exchange rate, defined as the number of foreign currency units that one domestic currency unit buys, acts like the price of domestic currency in other countries. In the United Kingdom, if the exchange rate between the Japanese yen (¥) and the British pound (£) is 60, this means that it costs ¥60 for £1. As the Japanese currency weakens (or the British pound gets stronger), this exchange rate rises because more yen will be needed to buy the same British pound. The value of the British pound rises. The opposite is also true: as the yen strengthens against the British pound, the exchange rate falls. Notice the directional changes hold true only if we define the exchange rate as above: $e = \dfrac{\yen}{\pounds}$. The Japanese economy defines its exchange rate with the United Kingdom in the inverse way as the yen would now be the domestic currency.

We learned in Chapters 10 and 11 that a money supply expansion reduces the value of domestic currency and increases expected domestic inflation. There are ultimately two connected reasons why we should expect the exchange rate to fall from a monetary expansion. First, if domestic prices are expected to rise as the money supply expands, the relative price of imports will fall, providing domestic consumers incentives to purchase more imports and foreign consumers to purchase fewer domestic exports from the newly inflationary economy. These new trade incentives lead to an increase in the supply of domestic currency and a reduced demand for the same currency internationally. The exchange rate, therefore, should unambiguously fall.

Second, as the money supply increases, expectations on interest rates change to reflect lower domestic rates. A reduction in real rates of return domestically, due to the expected inflation to come from an increased money supply, initiates the same currency movements as depicted above from increased terms of trade. As domestic currency flows out to foreign countries with relatively higher rates of return on assets, foreign demand for the home currency is simultaneously reduced, and the exchange rate must fall to bring supply and demand back together again. The sum of these two parts tells us that expansionary monetary policy leads to unambiguous balance of payments deficits.

For this reason, an economy's BOP and exchange rate with other economies are linked. What is confusing for many students of international finance and macroeconomics is the order of operations for the BOP imbalance, be it surplus or deficit, and subsequent exchange rate movements. Policy first shocks the balance of payments, and the exchange rate reacts to bring the BOP back to equilibrium. To understand this more clearly, we now briefly discuss the structure and rationale of BOP accounting, followed by its relationship to Chapter 11's model.

BOP structure

When studying the international macroeconomy, the BOP structure provides both insight and detail. To understand the basics, students must recognize three key points about the BOP. First, it is based on a double-entry accounting system, where debits (outflows of cash) equal credits (inflows of cash) for every transaction. For example, if a British medical-device manufacturing company purchased microprocessors from Japan, the receipt of microprocessors would be the "inflow" and the payment of cash would be the "outflow". For this reason, British imports rising would cause a balance of payments deficit or a net outflow of cash. Had this transaction been paid for using credit originating in Japan, the net flow of cash would have been zero as no cash changed hands; the inflow of credit paid for the imports and the BOP would remain in balance. If credit was not used, the net outflow of cash would cause exchange rates to fall, attracting a net inflow of cash to drive the BOP back toward its equilibrium value of zero.

What is critical for our story here is the linkage between the BOP and the exchange rate. The BOP has two categorical accounts, the current account (CA) and the capital account

(KA). The current account summarizes trade flows between two economies, net factor income inflows and transfers between the home economy and another economy. The capital account is for net capital flows (loans, equity purchases) and foreign direct investment (FDI), were FDI is the purchase of at least ten percent of a company. Thinking about the import example above and its connection to the exchange rate, a simple rule can be followed by students to track a policy shock to the exchange rate.

> *Rule*: Any net inflow (outflow) of cash between the home country and other countries results in a BOP surplus (deficit) and the exchange rate will rise (fall).

The exchange rate simply moves to bring the BOP back into balance, which is the exchange rate's function macroeconomically. The exchange rate achieves this by acting as the price of the domestic currency outside the economy's borders. If there is a net outflow of domestic currency, the value of that currency falls. It is that simple.

The connection between CA and KA is an easy one to understand from our basic macroeconomic model. When the BOP is in balance, its value is zero. This describes an equilibrium condition between the two subaccounts, CA and KA. Below is a BOP definition that represents equilibrium because debits equal credits for all international transactions.

$$BOP = CA + KA \qquad (12.1)$$

If there was a BOP surplus, $CA + KA > 0$, the economy with the BOP surplus would have a net cash inflow to equalize debits and credits. From our example above, imports paid for with cash would be a net debit for the outflow or payment of cash. Our macroeconomic model shows the BOP equilibrium under certain assumptions. Let's assume that net exports (EX − IM) represent the current account. Further, let's assume that net household savings (S) purchase three types of debt overall: government debt (S_G), business borrowing (S_C) and a mix of international debt (S_{Int}), such that

$$S = S_G + S_C + S_{Int} \qquad (12.2)$$

We know from Chapter 11 that an equilibrium condition for the macroeconomy is when leakages equal injections, where savings are used only domestically. From this equation in Chapter 11, we can equate 12.2 above with its analog:

$$S = S_G + S_C + S_{Int} = (G - T) + I + (EX - IM) \qquad (12.3)$$

If S_G is the consumer's savings that purchase new government debt, then $(G - T)$ equals S_G. If domestic, real investment is funded by the consumer's purchases of corporate assets (or bank's loans drawn from consumer savings in bank accounts), then S_C equals I. Thus, in equilibrium, the amount of net international savings for the households, or total net credit flows provided by the domestic economy to others, equals the trade balance in absolute value: a trade deficit equals net credit inflows to the home country or $-CA = KA$, which implies $BOP = 0$.

While this equality to zero rarely occurs in the real world, what Equation 12.3 implies is that a macroeconomist can analyze the effects of monetary and fiscal policy on the open macroeconomy by recognizing changes in Equation 12.3 as the tendency of the macro-economy's reaction to policy. A policy change shocks the BOP and thus exchange rates, and any exchange rate movement can be linked now to the BOP changing; the BOP moving away from equilibrium, from any economic forces, triggers subsequent changes in exchange rates to reverse the BOP imbalance. We assumed thus far that EX = IM for simplicity, which we now relax. When monetary or fiscal policies take place, simultaneously or otherwise as described in previous chapters, there are predictable results on the BOP and exchange rates. To understand policy effects, we need to discuss two topics first: exchange rate regimes and interest rate parity.

Exchange rate regimes and interest rate parity

Countries can choose to have either fixed or floating exchange rates. A fixed exchange rate is when two or more countries agree to a currency's value based on another's currency value, the value of a "basket" of currencies, or the value of an internationally traded commodity such as gold or silver. Historically, gold has been both the anchor of currency values and a "hard" or vehicle currency for international transactions: gold by weight acts as money everywhere under a gold standard. In 1870, an official gold standard began, where major currency values were tied to an amount of gold. Through the first seven decades of the twentieth century, an analog of the gold standard remained, where major differences included the establishment of the Bank of International Settlements (BIS), where BOP deficits were cleared by exchanging an internal currency called a Special Drawing Right (SDR). By 1973, the gold standard ended and was replaced by major currencies allowing market forces to dictate exchange rates and many smaller countries free to choose to tie their currency to the array of floating regimes.

Central banks in nations that choose fixed exchange rates are asked to monitor their economy's BOP situation and "defend" their fixed exchange rate with monetary policy. Of course, such action is not necessary for a floating rate. The need to defend a fixed exchange rate becomes the sole occupation of the defending central bank, an occupation that forces a central bank to abandon other, potentially stimulative policies. The linkage between the domestic money market, as described in Chapter 9, and the foreign money market as in Figure 12.1 reflects both global conditions in the currency's supply and different conditions for currency demand. For example, if the central bank increases the money supply, then the money supply curve will shift in both the domestic and foreign money markets. This monetary expansion drives both interest rates and exchange rates down. Under fixed exchange rates, such monetary expansion should only happen as a reaction to combat rising interest rates after a goods market shock to relieve pressure on the current peg.

A floating exchange rate is where the foreign supply and demand for the currency determines its exchange rate with another currency. The supply of the home currency in foreign markets is due to capital outflows and demand for imports originating at home; domestic purchases of foreign goods and foreign assets supply the domestic currency to satiate a simultaneously demanded foreign currency. The demand for the home currency in foreign markets is for the opposite BOP reasons: exports and capital inflows. Thus, BOP shocks imply changes in the exchange rate due to shifting supply (BOP deficit activity) or demand (BOP surplus activity) conditions for currency. Figure 12.1 shows the equilibrium in the foreign money or exchange market. The exchange rate is represented by e and $Q_\$$ represents the amount of domestic currency in a specific foreign market.

The implications of choosing fixed versus floating exchange rates are discussed soon, but let's again consider the connection between the macroeconomy and the exchange rate. In the model above, excess savings beyond domestic firms and governments were assumed to find a home in foreign asset markets. Why? In a simple sense, it must be due to foreign interest

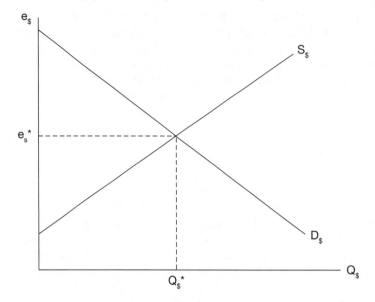

Figure 12.1 Equilibrium in the foreign money market.

rates being relatively higher than domestic rates. At a world interest rate that exceeds the domestic equilibrium, savings will exceed both the domestic investment demand of firms and the domestic government's fiscal deficit, assuming those markets clear at the domestic equilibrium interest rate. The differential between foreign and domestic interest rates provides a signal of profit opportunities.

That opportunity immediately diminishes due to market activity and exchange rate fluctuations. As domestic savings move toward foreign asset markets in pursuit of a relatively higher interest rate, the exchange rate falls; a higher supply of the domestic currency in foreign markets reduces its international value, $e_s\downarrow$. The exchange rate depreciation then triggers incentives for foreign consumers to buy more of the domestic economy's exports, slowing down the exchange rate's depreciation. As the cost of lending to foreign countries rises due to the currency depreciation, excess savings are smaller as the effective interest rate differential is reduced by falling exchange rates. This is the essence of interest rate parity (IRP) theory: interest rate differentials between countries dictate profit opportunities that become BOP imbalances and exchange rate fluctuations until the interest rate differential is eliminated in real terms and brought back to parity. In a world where IRP rules the foreign exchange market, trade imbalances are simply by-products of asset market activity.

Case study 12.1 The loonie goes loony – late 2008 and the Canada/US exchange rate

In late 2008, with American monetary policy becoming very aggressive in the midst of high oil prices and forecasted recession, the Canadian dollar (known as the "Loonie") began to surge to levels unseen since both Canada and the United States left the gold standard in 1973. The Canadian economy was enjoying a surge in exports and commodity prices, specifically oil, feeding the economy's growth. As a test of how resilient the Canadian economy was, monetary policy in Canada did not move quickly to stem a coming recession. Much like other economies that depend on exports of primary products, when commodity prices shifted direction in late 2008, so did the Canadian economy's forecast. The Canada–US exchange rate's movement followed the expected movements in Canada's macroeconomy; for a few weeks, the US dollar and Canadian dollar were at par. By March 2009, the exchange rate was 1.295 Canadian dollars per US dollar. Canadian monetary policy reacted slowly and speculators were now betting that the Bank of Canada was going to expand the money supply. A second factor was how exposed the Canadian economy was to a change in commodity prices, specifically oil. Finally, the connections between the United States and Canada became very apparent in late 2008, and reminded economists that the United States still drives many economies.

Figure 12.2 shows how Canada's exchange rate with the US dollar and oil prices in the United States have followed each other over the last 30 years. It shows little if any effect of changing oil prices on Canada's exchange rate, with a –0.04 correlation which is insignificantly different from zero.

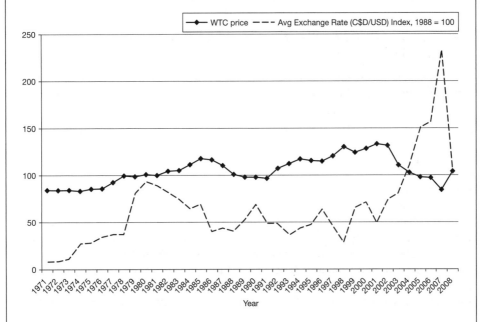

Figure 12.2 Canada's exchange rate and oil prices.
Source: Economagic.com.

If oil prices rising were not the driving force behind the Canadian dollar's surge against the US dollar, what explains the change? Purchasing power parity (PPP) suggests that the exchange rate between two countries is determined by the relative money supplies in each country in question (Figure 12.3).

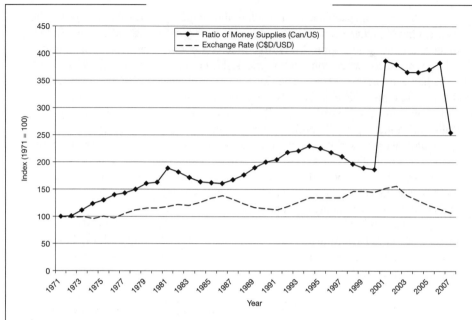

Figure 12.3 PPP calculation and exchange rate, Canada/US, 1971–2008.
Source: Economagic.com.

No matter the reasons why the Loonie moved quickly in late 2008 and into 2009, the obvious connections to expected monetary policy movements in both countries contributed to the uncertainty.

Interest rate parity

Interest rate parity is a model to explain fluctuations in exchange rates due to international financial market incentives changing. Suppose a trade deficit exists in an economy with a floating exchange rate. There would be pressure on the exchange rate to fall to create net capital inflows and exports, as well as lower imports, such that the BOP deficit would be reversed. However, under fixed exchange rates, this natural downward pressure on the exchange rate will simply build up rather than naturally release through a changing exchange rate. The defending central bank reacts by reducing the money supply, which increases domestic interest rates, and the exchange rate pressure goes away as net capital inflows take place.

The concept of interest rate parity is that exchange rates fluctuate because of interest rate differentials between two economies, specifically rates of return on low-risk governmental debt. If exchange rates are floating, any difference between US Treasury securities rates of one-year maturity and their UK one-year counterparts are likely to drive international monetary movements which change US–UK exchange rates. Suppose US interest rates increase due to a monetary contraction, and UK rates remain the same. This would make US Treasury bonds relatively more attractive to British investors, increasing the UK demand for US dollars, forcing dollar spot exchange rates to rise. As dollar spot exchange rates rise, the initial advantage that the rising US interest rates provided would diminish due to the US dollar's appreciation. Investors will slow their purchases of dollars and Treasuries accordingly until the asset and currency markets are in equilibrium again.

In a fixed exchange rate regime, a similar theory exists. If pressure exists on the exchange rate to fall, a monetary contraction defends the pressured exchange rate's value, but at the cost of higher domestic interest rates in the defending country. Defending a fixed exchange rate means manipulating monetary policy when trade or fiscal imbalances pressure the current exchange rate's par value to move. Fixed exchange rates can be adjustable pegs or crawling pegs, where the concept of a "peg" comes from the idea that two countries put a "peg" at a certain value and agree for that peg to remain in place. The crawling peg can move within a bandwidth around the negotiated exchange rate daily without a call for overt adjustment. An adjustable peg is where the fixed exchange rate moves between new par values within a bandwidth around the original peg. However, once beyond the bandwidth's bounds in either case, the defending central bank must react. Why would interest rate movements dominate exchange rates versus trade flows? An assumption of interest rate parity is that real interest rate differentials between nations dictate exchange rate movements.

Interest rate parity also assumes that prices are somewhat sticky, as in the IS-LM model of Chapter 12. The only way the trade balance may change is through exchange rate fluctuations or the pressure on exchange rates to change because of the inequality between the BOP subaccounts. What about fiscal policy or a change in consumer confidence? Let's suppose there is either a fiscal expansion or an augmentation to consumer confidence. In either case, interest rates and income will have pressure to rise. Interest rate parity suggests that the increase in domestic interest rates causes upward pressure on exchange rates by the attraction of foreign capital. However, this exchange rate pressure is going to be buttressed by deficit-creating activities of income rising domestically, causing more imports and capital outflows. Whichever BOP effect dominates then dictates the final change in exchange rates and is dependent upon the responsiveness of net capital flows to domestic interest rate shocks in this model.

That is the essence of interest rate parity: macroeconomic shocks that change the real interest rate force an imbalance in the KA that dictates exchange rate changes to clear the BOP through subsequent changes in both the KA and CA. To see how the foreign market for money affects domestic interest rates and incomes, we now add a third curve to the IS-LM model, the EE curve, following the Mundell–Fleming (1961, 1962) extension of IS-LM.[1]

The IS-LM-EE model

The long run in economics is characterized by the real growth of income and interest rates becoming equal to zero. The IS-LM family of models are shown here in terms of the short and medium runs. The short run has no price growth as demand rises and the medium run trades real GDP growth for inflation on its way to full employment. Further assuming that prices are sticky and expectations are adaptive, the IS-LM-EE model allows an analysis of shocks to the macroeconomy in many possible ways, under different exchange rate regimes, and interest rate elasticity assumptions such that the international effects of any macroeconomic policies can be analyzed. First, a brief description of the EE curve is needed.

The EE curve

There are two distinct markets for every currency, domestic and foreign. Both have similar dynamics. In Chapter 10, the domestic market for money showed the relationship between interest rates and the quantity of money demanded and supplied. Much like any other good or service, money market equilibrium provides signals concerning the "price" and "quantity" of money. Foreign exchange markets are not that much different. The major difference lies in that the foreign exchange market's price is an exchange rate, but still describes equilibrium between the supply of and demand for money; the interest rate is the domestic price of money while the exchange rate is the foreign price of the same currency in specific, foreign markets.

The EE curve is built on the same principles as the LM curve from Chapter 11. The LM curve was considered to be upward sloping because the central and private banks create or supply money. Central banks provide currency while private banks allocate currency by lending cash. Private banks create money based on market incentives. If money demand increases due to income expectations rising, banks can create more money by releasing reserves for loans as the interest rate rising provides a profit incentive to do so. The EE curve suggests the same is true in international currency markets. As the demand for the domestic currency rises, domestic banks have a profit motive to supply foreign citizens with domestic currency. A new equilibrium is struck when supply satiates the new demand, at a higher exchange rate. Both the LM and EE curves are upward sloping and their location on a graph, such as Figure 12.2, is dictated by the current amount of money supplied by the central bank. The key geometric difference between the LM and EE curves represents a potential difference between domestic and foreign money market reactions to changing demand for domestic currency, which connects IRP theory to macroeconomic policy modeling. Figure 12.4 shows, equilibrium where all three curves cross. The real interest rate, r, and real GDP, y, are the same as in Chapter 11.

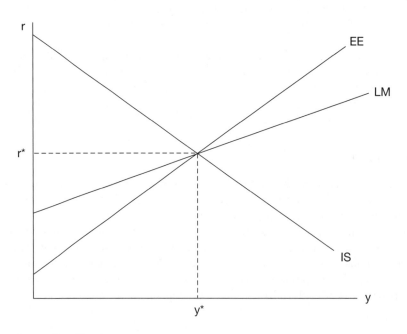

Figure 12.4 The short-run macroeconomy.

The LM and EE curves and their slopes

How responsive the domestic and foreign money markets are to shocks in income depends on how banks react to new domestic versus foreign demand for currency. With a set amount of currency provided by the central bank, private banks in the domestic economy choose to release funds based on profit incentives originating from interest rate changes. The less profit to be made from domestic lending, the less elastic domestic money supply is to interest rates changing (LM relatively steep). The same holds for foreign money supply: the less profit banks see from international lending, the less likely they will be to react to new interest rate signals by supplying more currency in exchange for foreign reserves (EE relatively steep). We can compare these two curves; their relative slopes tell us something about the BOP surplus or deficit created from policy changes. First, let's look at the easy case of monetary policy shocks in the open macroeconomy, when the relative slopes of EE and LM initially have no meaning.

Monetary policy in an open macroeconomy

As stated above, monetary shocks flow through the domestic asset markets to the foreign exchange markets in predictable ways. Under fixed exchange rates, monetary policy can cause permanent BOP imbalances unless reversed by accommodating fiscal policies or new, opposing monetary policy. This uninteresting policy case harkens back to the idea that once an economy chooses to fix its exchange rate, it does so knowing the international financial markets will assume that using monetary policy as a tool for macroeconomic growth is no longer available for that economy.

The more interesting case is when exchange rates are flexible. Let's suppose the Japanese economy expanded the money supply by lowering its discount rate. The Bank of Japan understands that the yen's exchange rates will be globally affected by this policy shock. Assuming no other shocks take place, the result will be a depreciated yen worldwide. An increase in the Japanese money supply is going to send a worldwide signal that circulating yen is going to be worth less than it was before the policy change. Japanese interest rates are going to fall to reflect a reduced domestic value of the yen. Yen exchange rates are then going to depreciate to reflect a lower international value of the yen. Both interest and exchange rates fall until their respective markets are back in equilibrium.

Interest rate parity, because we are assuming prices are sticky, provides us with an event chain between the policy decision and resultant exchange rate depreciation. As interest rates fall in Japan due to a monetary expansion, net capital outflows take place as Japanese investors seek higher profit opportunities in foreign financial markets and foreign investors are less attracted to the Japanese financial markets as a result of lower real rates of return. The capital account moves toward deficit; as incomes are expected to rise from the lower interest rates in Japan, imports are also expected to rise, causing a current account deficit simultaneously. In sum, the BOP begins to move toward deficit, forcing exchange rates to fall to bring the BOP back toward zero. The exchange rate continues to fall until that equilibrium is established again by BOP surplus activities. A simple rule can be followed by students when their country chooses to engage in monetary policy.

> *Rule*: When the domestic central bank expands (contracts) the money supply, domestic interest rates fall (rise), the BOP moves toward deficit (surplus) and exchange rates fall (rise).

Geometrically, the expected shift in the LM curve moves the domestic equilibrium between the new LM curve and the original IS curve "below" the EE line (to its right geometrically), a signal of a BOP deficit. The EE line begins to move toward the domestic equilibrium to reflect a depreciating currency. Exports are stimulated by this change, and the IS curve begins to move again. The EE and IS curves move toward each other until they intersect along the new LM curve where the BOP is again equal to zero. Figure 12.5 shows this movement from the original equilibrium. The numbers in parentheses represent the chain of events: (1) is the monetary policy; (2) is the exchange rate reaction; and (3) is the IS curve shift due to more exports triggered by lower exchange rates.

Monetary policy is the simple case because there is no ambiguity about the currency's value domestically or internationally after the central bank's policy shock. It is in fiscal policy and other aggregate demand shocks, where ambiguity exists and the relative interest rate elasticities of both the domestic and foreign currency markets must be compared.

Fiscal policy and other IS shocks

Using fiscal policy as an example of a macroeconomic shock acts as a generalization for other events such as consumer confidence changing, new trade policies and other shifters of the IS curve as discussed in Chapter 11. Let's assume that UK fiscal policy is expansionary, say to pay for a war. As the United Kingdom's fiscal deficit rises, domestic demand for British pounds is going to rise. This is true whether the British government has to borrow the funds or not. As domestic money demand increases, UK interest rates begin to rise as British pounds become more scarce internationally. Interest rate parity suggests that capital inflows rise as a result of domestic interest rates rising, attracting foreign financial flows and acting

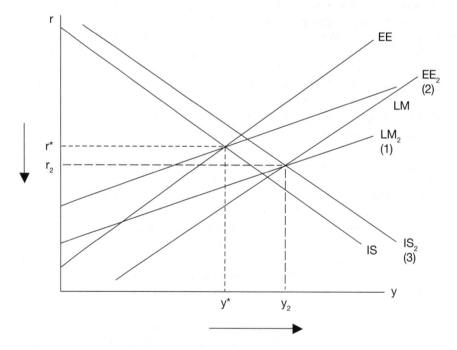

Figure 12.5 Monetary expansion with flexible exchange rates.

as a disincentive to domestic investors to seek foreign financial opportunities. However, the larger fiscal spending by the British government also stimulates more domestic consumer spending as a result of the multiplier effect. As incomes rise, imports also rise in tandem with the net capital inflows. The BOP effects are ambiguous as a result.

Resolving the BOP ambiguity of fiscal policy

The relative slopes of the EE and LM curves provide an answer to this ambiguity. If the EE curve is relatively steeper than LM, an interest rate increase from a goods market shock leads to more BOP deficit activities than the BOP surplus activities expected from higher domestic interest rates. If the EE curve is less steep than the LM curve, net capital flows rise very quickly and outweigh the increase in domestic money demand and imports that also result. A rule for fiscal policy can be posited to help summarize these ideas, if exchange rates are floating.

> *Rule*: When the EE curve is more (less) interest elastic than the LM curve, the EE curve is geometrically less (more) steep, and an IS shift or positive goods market shock causes the BOP to rise (fall) and exchange rates to rise (fall).

This rule works in reverse if the goods market shock is negative, a reduction in consumer confidence for example. To summarize, the BOP and exchange rate effects of IS shocks depend on the relative slopes of the EE and LM curves or the relative interest elasticities of currency demand in the foreign (EE) and domestic (LM) currency markets. The exchange rate effects are dictated by the BOP effects, and are meant to drive the BOP back toward zero as the macroeconomy moves back toward equilibrium because of interest rate parity. In the case of floating exchange rates, the EE curve will move toward the domestic equilibrium, and the IS curve will further move toward the EE curve, reflecting a changing trade balance in reaction to e_S changing. The new equilibrium is established along the original LM curve, as monetary policy is assumed to not be changing or needed to clear the BOP under floating exchange rates.

We can geometrically show the IS curve moving to the right, reflecting the fiscal policy shock. If the EE curve is relatively steeper than the LM curve, net capital flows have a slower response than domestic banks to changing interest rates. If the LM curve is relatively steeper than the EE curve, net capital flows are more responsive than domestic currency markets to domestic interest rates changes; Figures 12.6 and 12.7 show these two cases respectively.

The case of fixed exchange rates and IS shocks

IS shocks are made more complex when exchange rates are fixed. Suppose the UK government ran a fiscal deficit, as described above. The responsiveness of capital flows would rule the direction of the BOP change, which would then dictate exchange rate pressure to change, not actual fluctuations. Because BOP pressure would be building, the announcement of UK fiscal deficits would signal an expected BOP imbalance to the world; the UK central bank would be forced to defend its fixed exchange rate by changing the money supply. In the case of expansionary fiscal policy, the only case shown here, expansionary monetary policy (e_S pressure to fall) would be used if capital flows were relatively responsive (G↑ leads to r and y both rising, which lead to BOP rising because KA effects dominate CA effects, which under flexible exchange rates lead to e_S rising) to countermand the exchange rate pressure

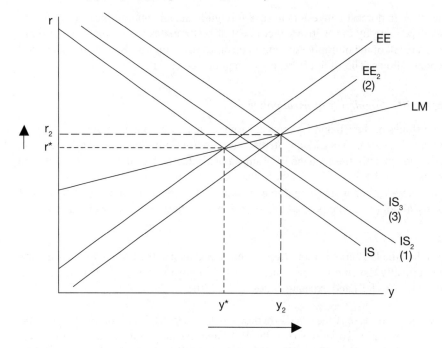

Figure 12.6 Fiscal expansion with unresponsive capital flows and flexible e_S.

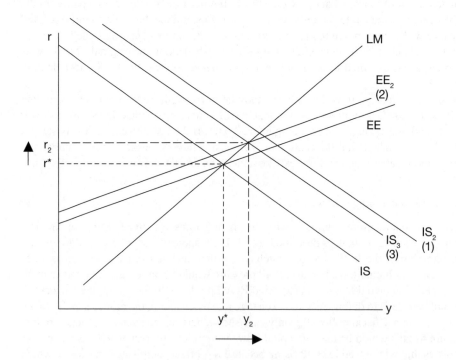

Figure 12.7 Fiscal expansion with responsive capital flows and flexible e_S.

and cause a BOP deficit against the fiscal-policy-created BOP surplus. The opposite is true if capital flows are relatively unresponsive versus domestic financial markets. Figure 12.8 shows the exchange rate being defended after fiscal policy creates a BOP surplus; Figure 12.9 shows the case of a BOP deficit being defended.

Exchange rate defense elucidates the role of relative responsiveness and how monetary policy reacts in either case. If net capital inflows are relatively responsive to interest rate signals from the domestic market, monetary policy must make purchasing domestic assets less attractive for foreign investors. By expanding the money supply, the domestic central bank provides disincentives to foreign purchases of domestic assets by stabilizing interest rates. In the case where net capital flows are relatively unresponsive, a monetary contraction enhances the profitability of domestic assets by exacerbating the instability of interest rates. A final rule for monetary policy action as a result of BOP pressure can be posited under fixed exchange rates.

> *Rule*: When the EE curve is more (less) interest elastic than the LM curve, the EE curve is geometrically less (more) steep, a positive IS shift or income-augmenting goods market shock causes the BOP to rise (fall) and pressures exchange rates to rise (fall). The domestic central bank that defends the fixed exchange rate, to relieve that pressure, expands (contracts) the money supply, pressuring exchange rates to fall (rise).

When a central bank is forced to defend exchange rates, it must abandon any other direct and indirect goals of monetary policy as discussed in Chapter 10. The indirect goal of stabilizing interest rates may not continue if domestic fiscal policy is expansionary while foreign capital does not respond to new interest rate signals. The reasons net capital flows may be inelastic differ from nation to nation. Two general reasons stand out. First, the transaction costs to a

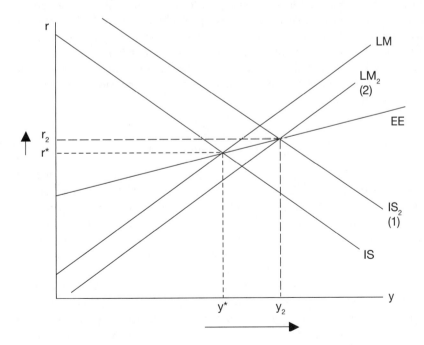

Figure 12.8 Fiscal expansion with responsive capital flows and fixed e_S.

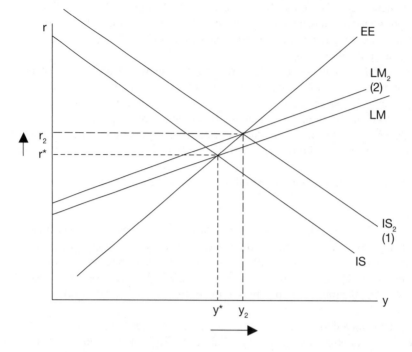

Figure 12.9 Fiscal expansion with unresponsive capital flows and fixed e_s.

foreign citizen may be large, providing disincentives to purchasing assets from certain markets. Also, the domestic nation may have barriers against foreign ownership of financial assets. This also reduces the amount of inflows the domestic economy should expect from goods market shocks. The direct goal of predictable and stable inflation, as discussed in Chapter 11, is assumed so far to not be abandoned by the nature of sticky prices. What happens to the scenarios above if the central bank either lacks precision or drives the economy faster toward full employment?

Case study 12.2 Brazil: economic calamity and growth

Brazil's economy, much like Chile's and Argentina's described in earlier cases, has had a tumultuous history since the Second World War. Like other South American countries, it suffered from civil unrest, political turnover, military governments wasting resources, and economic instability at the hands of both sociopolitical inefficiencies and economic retardation. Brazil, as an economy and society, is a polychotomous place. On its east coast is an industrial metropolis, ever growing in numbers of people and highly cyclic in its economic output. In the west is the Amazon rainforest, which is a place of many primary products and ever-changing political issues. Historically, the Brazilian economy has been one of primary product industries, using the vast resources at Brazil's disposal to drive economic growth. However, misuse of these resources politically and questionable monetary policies along the way caused Brazil's currency, the *real* (pronounced ree-all), to devolve on three separate occasions due to massive inflation and be reconstituted as the "new" *real*. This history is interesting because the future of South America's continental economy probably rests in Brazil's hands.

Brazil's problems with hyperinflation and currency devaluation began brewing in the mid-1960s. The currency of Brazil at that time was the *cruziero*, and had undergone a currency replacement in 1967, one thousand old *cruzieros* for one new. Brazil's economy grew at a modest rate until the oil shock of 1973. As oil prices surged, Brazil received loans to grow that industry and help finance its growing current account deficits. The new *cruziero* surged in value during this time, putting further pressure on the Brazilian current account deficit. The military regime at the time was also spending furiously. Industrialization begin to replace Brazil's dependence on foreign manufactured goods, which transformed Brazil's economy from one that much like Argentina's into one that was ready to become a world leader. Unfortunately, inflation came with growth in the late 1970s, stagflation in early 1980s, and the debt that Brazil had accumulated under its military regime was inherited by its new democratic regime. Fiscal reforms began, but the Brazilian currency suffered greatly in the last half of the 1980s.

By 1986, the *cruziero* was replaced by the *cruzado*, one of which was worth 1000 *cruzieros*. By late 1987, Brazil's government defaulted on its foreign debt, after multiple attempts at fiscal reform. In 1989, a *novo cruzado* was introduced as currency reformation, one of which replaced 1000 *cruzados*. Within three years, the Brazilian *cruziero*, the currency during 14 years of growth in Brazil, was replaced by a currency that was 0.000001 of the old currency value! Stagflation then began again, as it did in other economies such as Mexico earlier in the 1980s, as the result of debt default. A new president, elected rather than from a military regime, came into office in 1990.

By 1993, the Brazilian economy was still stagnant and inflation continued to rage, even in the face of domestic economic growth. Because most of the growth was in consumption rather than efficiency gains, Brazil faced yet another currency battle. In 1993, the *real* was introduced, which traded at one thousand per one *novo cruzado* from 1989. It would take one billion *cruzieros* to buy one *real* in 1994! The *real* came with a dollar peg, which was removed in the late 1990s due to investors selling off *real*-based assets in the wake of the Asian flu and with a flight to developed equity markets. Argentina's problems in 2001 were seen as contagious, and Brazil suffered another bout of foreign investor confidence crises in 2002.

Since 2002, the Brazilian economy has grown with little inflation and has been the star of South America. In the current financial crisis, Brazil is fairly well situated, and has some of the same characteristics it did during the mid and late 1970s. Its industrial production has grown steadily, as has its GDP. Brazil's economic and monetary history does not provide a large amount of long-term confidence in its nascent emergence as a leading world economy.

The medium run and overshooting

This chapter's final section discusses the latest models in open economy macroeconomics as well as the transition to the medium run. These are tied to each other as moving from the short to medium run forces a change in price expectations; expectations can drive otherwise precise monetary policy toward imprecision and the creation of macroeconomic volatility. The idea of overshooting exchange rate targets using monetary policy was investigated by Rudiger Dornbusch in a famous article called "Expectations and Exchange Rate Dynamics" published in 1976.[2] Dornbusch's paper has been the seminal article in bridging the Mundell–Fleming idea to modern macroeconomic theory.

We saw in Chapter 10 that monetary policy will be neutral in its real effects in the long run; monetary neutrality is a key characteristic of the long run. Output grows more slowly through policy expansions and prices become more flexible. In a sense, expectations concerning output in the short run give way to expectations in the medium and long runs because price expectations are now changing. A major debate in macroeconomics is how fast prices adjust to monetary policy in both directions; a related question concerns the shape of the aggregate supply (AS) curve. When monetary policy is expansionary and accommodates fiscal expansions, as in the case of responsive net capital flows and fixed exchange rates, pressure on prices to rise builds quickly. What happens to this model when prices begin to rise? This model experiences the same reactions as in Chapter 11 with the added layer of real exchange rates now being dominated by trade flows rather than capital flows. As the economy moves toward the long run, the EE curve naturally becomes the LM curve, which naturally becomes more vertical. As this happens, capital flows become less responsive to domestic monetary policy because real differentials in foreign and domestic investment rates of return are becoming smaller. As prices are expected to rise, especially after both fiscal and monetary expansions, real returns on both assets and currency both fall.

Dornbusch (1976) suggested that to achieve a targeted exchange rate, the defending central bank had to overshoot the equilibrium exchange rate because of changing expectations. Much like the (domestic) liquidity effect shown in Chapter 11, there is an international liquidity effect in the foreign exchange market from monetary policy. Rates depreciate from their initial level beyond the new, expected equilibrium, which ensures the markets of adjusting to fulfill the prophecy of the monetary expansion. Just like the Keynesian liquidity effect, the Dornbusch liquidity effect has volatility as a by-product. The size of that volatility is a function of, once again, how responsive capital flows are to changes in interest rates. The more sensitive or responsive financial markets are to interest rate changes, the more volatile the asset markets. The more volatile the asset markets, the faster prices will become flexible, lose their stickiness, and usher the macroeconomy toward the long run. If net capital flows are less responsive to IS shocks, the macroeconomy crawls from the short to the medium run, and the price paid for slow inflation is slower output growth, constrained by the unavailability of foreign funding to finance rapid growth in domestic money demand.

Summary

This chapter extended the IS-LM model to include international markets. The open economy model adds the balance of payments (BOP) to the monetary policy-maker's view, and forces central banks to account for changes in the exchange rate as a result of monetary shocks. The BOP derives directly from the equilibrium equations of GDP and the leakages–injections equilibrium of Chapter 11. Instead of assuming exports equal imports, allowing a trade imbalance leads to many interesting possibilities concerning policy effects. The interplay between the BOP's current and capital accounts can be described by interest rate parity theory, assuming prices are sticky.

The Mundell–Fleming (1961–62) model extension of IS-LM simply places a third curve on this system, representing the foreign currency market equilibria at specific interest rates. Much like the LM curve, the EE curve represents what happens to interest rates as a result of demand-side shocks due to changes in net capital flows. When all three curves cross each other, the macroeconomy is in equilibrium and the BOP equals zero. The position of the EE curve represents a specific exchange rate; if the exchange rate changes, so does the position of the EE curve in y–r space. As defined, exchange rate depreciations and devaluations lead to rightward movements of the EE curve; appreciations and revaluations lead to leftward movements. The link between interest rates and exchange rates is now complete. The domestic interest rate is the domestic price of the home currency, while the exchange rate is the foreign price of the home currency.

Monetary policy has predictable effects on the exchange rate. As the money supply increases, a floating exchange rate falls to reflect a lower currency value; monetary contraction leads to an appreciation. The central bank uses monetary policy to defend fixed exchange rates, a defense that may come as a result of goods market expansions or contractions. Domestic financial market activity begins a process that pressures exchange rates to move, regardless of the activity's source. In floating regimes, the exchange rate moves freely to release that pressure. In fixed regimes, the monetary authority has exchange rate defense as its sole policy goal.

The BOP and subsequent exchange rate fluctuations from fiscal policy or any goods market shocks are dependent upon the relative responsiveness of foreign capital to domestic interest rate expectations. As interest rates rise, net capital inflows are expected, but the rate at which they arrive to domestic government, firms and consumers may not outpace new trade imbalances from changes in expected income. If the CA effects of an IS shock dominate the KA effects, the BOP follows the new CA balance; if the KA effects dominate, because the EE curve is flatter than the LM curve, representing a more elastic foreign than domestic currency market, the BOP follows the KA balance. Monetary policy may overshoot the intended exchange rate when defending a fixed rate because price expectations will slow the progress of the economy toward equilibrium.

The choice to enter a currency union or to fix currency values to major economic powers has grown considerably since the Bretton Woods system expired in its initial formulation in 1973. Chapter 13 explores these choices in more depth, and in the context of the policy implications of those choices.

Key terms

1   Adjustable peg: a fixed exchange rate which moves discretely between possible exchange rates.
2   Balance of payments (BOP): a double-entry accounting system for international transactions, the sum of the current (CA) and capital (KA) accounts.
3   Capital account (KA): the sum of net capital inflows and foreign direct investment in the macroeconomy.
4   Crawling peg: a fixed exchange rate which moves continuously between possible exchange rates within a bandwidth agreed upon by the international financial system.
5   Current account (CA): the sum of the trade balance, net factor income from abroad and unilateral transfers in the macroeconomy.
6   EE curve: the locus of combinations between given interest rates and real GDP levels such that the foreign money market is in equilibrium.
7   Interest rate parity: a theory that suggests exchange rates fluctuate due to asset markets trading currency such that interest rates on similar assets in two economies are equalized.

8   Purchasing power parity: a theory that suggests exchange rates fluctuate due to goods markets trading in reaction to changing prices until the prices of goods are the same in two economies.
9   Special Drawing Right (SDR): the internal currency of the World Bank.

Questions and problems

1   Explain why the balance of payments (BOP) is equal to zero in equilibrium.
2   Explain why the exchange rate moves when the BOP is not equal to zero.
3   Explain how interest rate parity is different from purchasing power parity as an explanation of exchange rate fluctuations.
4   The EE curve is a representation of the foreign money market for a currency. Explain the similarities to the LM curve.
5   The relative responsiveness of capital flows dictates the exchange rate response to IS shocks. Why does it not make any difference to the exchange rate fluctuations for monetary shocks? Explain.
6   Explain why the EE curve would be steeper than the LM curve.
7   Explain the overshooting idea and why it is considered an issue of rational expectations rather than adaptive.

Websites

BOP manual from IMF: www.imf.org/external/np/sta/bop/BOPman.pdf.
BOP details from Boston FRB: http://www.bos.frb.org/economic/special/balofpay.pdf.
Bretton Woods system: http://www.polsci.ucsb.edu/faculty/cohen/inpress/bretton.html.
Gold Standard article: http://www.econlib.org/library/Enc/GoldStandard.html.
New York Federal Reserve on foreign exchange markets: http://www.newyorkfed.org/education/fx/foreign.html.

13 The world economy and monetary policy choices

Introduction

The introduction of the euro revived a debate about countries joining their economies together in ways that were beyond agreeing to fixed exchange rates. While a currency union has fixed exchange rates as its foundation, the explicit amalgamation of monetary policy differentiates a currency union from other agreements. There are also intermediate currency unions, dollarizations or euroizations of nations that simply abandon domestic currency in lieu of a major trading partner's legal tender. Chapter 12 focused on choices facing central banks when exchange rates have the ability to adjust to new market information. A common misconception with fixed exchange rates is that foreign exchange markets are no longer market-driven. The residual effects of trade and financial flows between two countries is not seen in the official exchange rate, but pressure builds behind a fixed exchange rate due to market activity that triggers monetary reactions to alleviate that pressure.

This chapter examines some issues in global economics concerning central banking, the flows of goods, services and assets between economies, and choices made to be or not to be in currency unions of any type. First is a brief history of the international financial system since 1900. This history is based on international agreements: a gold standard gave way to a pound standard, which became a dollar standard, and finally floating exchange rates. Future choices are within the confines of this history; a gold standard, a currency standard or floating exchange rates are the possible choices. Second is a brief description of how fixed exchange rates work, why they are chosen and how they can break down. Third is the idea of forming a currency union, including a brief history of the euro. Expanding on this idea, we consider the possibility of other currency unions throughout the world, especially in emerging markets such as southern and eastern Asia as well as Africa. Finally, this chapter concludes with a discussion about the reformation of a global gold standard and whether one currency for the world, possibly gold, is a true possibility. We begin by looking briefly at the past.

Crosses of gold and pounds and dollars

Since William Jennings Bryan's speech to the Democratic National Convention in 1896 is seen by many as the beginning of the debate whether commodity money should be used, a question persists: why was gold chosen as the world's currency? Because many international transactions come with exchange rate risk when floating exchange rates prevail, gold and certain currencies have been historic triangular trade currencies. For example, if a retail store in Madagascar wanted to buy goods from Chile to sell to tourists, the Chilean exporter is likely to want the Madagascar retailer to pay in Chilean pesos. However, there may not be a market for an exchange between Chilean pesos and Madagascar's ariary. Without a market, it is difficult to tell how much currency is needed for the exchange and this may inhibit transactions between these countries. To solve this problem, a third currency establishes markets for other currencies. The retailer converts ariary to dollars, for example, and the dollars are then converted to Chilean pesos. Also, the exporter may accept US dollars in lieu of pesos to reduce the retailer's transaction costs.

Gold, at the beginning of the twentieth century, served this role. However, gold can be hoarded and is not easily replicated. After the First World War, one reason the British pound sterling became the world's new vehicle currency was due to its ubiquity and ability to expand in supply easily. England's trade dominance, territorial ownership and ties to British gold holdings made it a currency that acted just like gold. A gold standard forces other economies to find, seize or buy gold in order to print their domestic currency. Currencies are set to an exchange rate based on each currency's price of gold. For example, if in the United States gold costs $1 per ounce and in England gold costs £0.5 per ounce, the exchange rate between the dollar and pound sterling is $2 per £1. Parity was ensured by the gold standard, where the gold price is fixed and maintained by a multilateral, international agreement. By maintaining parity through central bank policy defending the fixed rate, the central bank was de facto fighting inflation.

This inflation reduction promise led to rules that dictated parities. As we have learned, exchange rates move away from equilibrium in reaction to BOP imbalances. As the French BOP moved toward surplus, the French franc appreciated in value. Because a fixed exchange rate was in place during the gold standard, the French Franc did not realize a larger market value; pressure simply built underneath the franc's international value. The French central bank would be forced to increase the franc's supply to relieve this pressure, or France would reduce its gold holdings (a way to implicitly increase the money supply). A BOP deficit had the opposite effect and called for a monetary contraction to relieve the currency's depreciation pressure. Having a lot of gold on hand allowed countries to run large BOP deficits, where gold acted as a way to pay for and relieve BOP deficit pressure without changing the actual value of domestic currency.

This BOP rule was also meant to keep larger economies, which were often net exporters to the world, from hoarding gold. As a BOP surplus caused appreciation pressure on the exchange rate, gold could flow to the surplus nation, forcing the surplus nation to increase its money supply and relieve the exchange rate pressure. However, the surplus nation would have more gold. If a country had too much gold, its domestic prices should rise to naturally slow down its exports and increase imports, shift comparative advantage to other economies on the margin and move international reserves back to their original place. To reduce the physical flow of gold between countries, many countries adopted a policy of paying for exports with imports and bundling transactions such that no net gold flowed and thus zero net pressure existed upon exchange rates to change. While good in theory, the gold standard depended too much on the physical possession of gold to back currencies, and both world wars showed, among many other losses of innocence, that holding gold was a difficult cross to bear.

The interwar and Bretton Woods systems

The period between 1919 and 1944 was one of first financial turmoil throughout much of the world and then one of repeated worldwide warfare. Between 1919 and 1939, a pound standard existed, where the British pound's value was tied to gold and other remaining currencies had values tied to the pound. The interwar system was similar to the gold standard except the British pound was accepted as equivalent to gold. From the ashes of World War I rose many new countries throughout the former empires of Austria-Hungary, the Ottomans, Germans, Russians, and Italians. These new countries needed foreign reserves to engage in international trade and finance, where gold was just too costly and there was a lack of willingness on the part of the victors to let go the golden spoils. The pound standard allowed new countries, such as Poland, to use holdings of British pounds to act as the foundation for the zloty, the Polish currency. The worldwide depression beginning in 1929, and subsequently World War II, shifted economic power to the West; the Bretton Woods system was born in 1944.

The Bretton Woods system was similar to the pound standard in that clearing the balance of payments could be done by equivalent gold or currency flows. However, the pound lost its status as a reserve currency and the US dollar became that currency in practice. In theory, there were organizations created specifically to manage the fixed exchange rate system and to act as a bank for all nations: the World Bank. The World Bank had an internal currency, the Special Drawing Right (SDR), a weighted amalgam of major world currencies. This SDR acted as equivalent to gold, based on set parities, and moved from one country's account to another as a reaction to BOP imbalances.

Three major financial entities were created underneath the World Bank's umbrella. The first was the International Monetary Fund (IMF), a financial intermediary for the world. The IMF has become both famous and infamous for brokering major loans to emerging nations since its inception. The second was the International Bank for Reconstruction and Development (IBRD), where its task was to focus on emerging market lending and to broker the use of SDRs to fund economic expansion, trade and finance with new and developing countries after World War II. The initial IRBD foci were central Europe and Japan; much of Germany and Japan's rise to economic power in the last 60 years from the shell left behind by World War II can be attributed to initial funding from the IBRD. Finally, the Bank of International Settlements (BIS) is where the BOP was physically cleared by a transfer of SDRs or gold or dollars from one economy's account to another.

The BIS function can be confusing at first. Consider the following example. Suppose Mexico had a BOP surplus with Canada, and thus Canada had a BOP deficit with Mexico. In the old systems, gold or the British pound would flow in net toward Mexico from Canada to make up Canada's BOP deficit. This flow would force Canada to reduce its money supply to keep the Canadian dollar at par with gold's value, and the Mexican economy would have to expand its money supply due to the increase in gold holdings. Instead of forcing central banks to constantly act upon new BOP data, the BIS was formed to simply transfer deposited gold or SDRs from one economy's account to the other such that neither the deficit nor surplus country must ask their respective central banks to act. As long as accumulated BOP deficits remained under the value of the country's SDR balance, the deposit covers any needs. Further, this allowed international trade to dictate new flows rather than having them stifled by reactive central banks. If Mexico ran continuous surpluses with Canada, the price of Mexican goods would rise in Canada and Canadian substitutes or a third country's goods would gain a comparative advantage, naturally reducing the Mexico–Canada BOP surplus from Mexico's standpoint. This redistribution would have to come with a new promise: the economy's BOP would be zero in the long run. Because of the inflation implications of running large BOP deficits, countries became careful in their net export balances.

By the late 1960s, after two decades of worldwide growth and stable inflation, the American economy experienced two key changes. First, fiscal policy expanded quickly on both social programs and national defense. This expansion began a Keynesian growth pattern and inflation quickly caught up with the American economy. Second, many countries lost their SDR balances through continuous BOP deficits. Economies began to seek and use American dollars as a way to complete transactions. The United States became the central location for both trade and finance worldwide. As the American economy experienced domestic growth, it also experienced current account deficits. These deficits forced the United States to increase money supply and reduce its SDR balances. Because the BOP deficits were mounting quickly, and the entire SDR balance of the United States was threatened, holders of dollars became worried that a devaluation of the dollar would lead to major financial losses worldwide. A small devaluation took place in 1971, followed by the United States abandoning the gold standard completely; in January 1973, the dollar began to float and the dollar price of gold surged as the American currency's value was pushed quickly downward in value. Other major countries followed this flexibility and international finance as we know it now was born. This decision effectively ended worldwide fixed exchange rates and ushered in the Bretton Woods II system, where the dollar still (though just barely) acts as the world's vehicle currency.

Understanding exchange rate fluctuations

A gold standard came with the promise of low inflation due to the theory behind it. Exchange rate fluctuations were explained in classic economics by a theory called purchasing power parity (PPP), discussed briefly in Chapter 12. This idea suggests that exchange rates fluctuate to equate prices (or purchasing power) between two economies. *The Economist* magazine runs a "Big Mac" index semi-annually to test this hypothesis, and has found mixed results. Equation 13.1 shows the basic idea.

$$P_{dom} \times e_S = P_{for} \Rightarrow e_S = \frac{P_{for}}{P_{dom}} \tag{13.1}$$

Notice that as domestic prices rise, the exchange rate would fall. As domestic prices increase, imports are now relatively less expensive. The demand for foreign currency, parallel to the supply of domestic currency on the foreign money market, puts downward pressure on exchange rates. The reverse is true when foreign prices rise, as imports become relatively more expensive. In a world where the trade of goods and services dominates international economic connections between two economies, this theory makes sense.

When the exchange rate is fixed, maintaining price stability is tantamount to maintaining the stability of exchange rates. If domestic prices rise, the money supply should contract domestically to control inflation. If PPP works as described above, the inflation control will also stabilize exchange rates and maintain the gold standard for the economy in question. If the exchange rate was flexible, it opens up speculation to changing exchange rates; with a credible commitment to a gold standard, speculation on currencies should also be at a minimum, making national currencies feasible and providing predictability in their interrelationships.

Enter interest rate parity

We discussed interest rate parity (IRP) in Chapter 12 also, and used it to define the way in which fluctuations in the macroeconomy were connected to the exchange rate changing or building pressure to change in the case of a fixed exchange rate. Interest rate parity assumes that asset markets, rather than goods markets, are the driving force in exchange rate fluctuations. Much like PPP, IRP believes that exchange rates fluctuate to equate prices across economies. Instead of those being goods prices, they are instead the price of assets. Equation 13.2 defines interest rate parity in its "covered" form.

$$\frac{e_f - e_s}{e_s} \approx (r_{for} - r_{dom}) \tag{13.2}$$

This equivalency recognizes that the relationship is not a perfect equality, but also recognizes that the relationships provide a guide to how exchange rates will react to changes in relative interest rates. The variable e_f is the forward market rate for currency, e_s is the spot rate as in Equation 13.1. Suppose the domestic rate of interest, r_{dom}, increased versus the foreign rate of interest, r_{for}, on corporate debt on average for both economies. As the domestic interest rate increases, there will be a larger demand for domestic currency to purchase domestic assets with relatively higher rates of return, which increases the spot exchange rate. Because those assets will mature, or have an expectation of being sold at a future date, many investors will choose to cover against the exchange rate risk and engage in a forward contract to sell the domestic currency back for their home currency to complete the transaction. This will increase the supply of domestic currency in the forward market (the sell positions for domestic currency in these contracts), and the forward rate will fall. Notice this is unambiguously predicted by the algebra of Equation 13.2 if r_{dom} rises relative to r_{for}.

Flexible exchange rates and currency risk

Currency traders use Equation 13.2 as the basis of their work, a transaction called the carry trade. By borrowing currency where interest rates are relatively low, and then lending where interest rates are relatively high, an investor can take advantage of changes in interest rates before exchange rates fluctuate via interest rate parity. In many ways, this is the same as demanding currency where asset returns are relatively higher. The key to the carry trade is the exposure to exchange rate risk. Once the loan and borrowing are set, the exchange rate will begin to fluctuate and reduce the profit of each position (the borrowing is short and the loan is long in their respective currencies), nullifying the point of the carry trade in the first place. By taking a forward contract in the lending currency, the investor can cover themselves against the exchange rate risk. If the loan is for six months, the forward contract should also be for six months and for the amount of interest and principal to come from the loan. In the borrowing currency, a forward contract will also cover against more cost when that loan is paid back, specifically by the asset purchased in the lending currency.

For example, suppose a trader in Germany saw a breach in Equation 13.2 between the Swiss Franc and the Canadian dollar. If this breach left the right-hand side of Equation 13.2 larger than the left-hand side such that Canada had higher interest rates, the trader would borrow in Swiss francs, then lend in Canada, thus owing Swiss francs and owning Canadian dollars. Even though the home currency is the euro, the trader would still want to take a forward contract to sell Canadian dollars for Swiss francs, which eliminates the exchange rate risk on the eventual trade coming in six months when both the loan in Canada and the loan in Switzerland mature. The carry trader has thus insured the profit from the interest rate differential.

As a result of all those movements, which can be as much as a trillion dollars in one day for the American currency, exchange rates can suffer from violent swings in value. As a result, many countries try to avoid speculation on currency through asset markets by fixing their currency to a nominal anchor.

Case study 13.1 The carry trade: follow the leader

As described in Chapter 13, the carry trade is where investors attempt to borrow in relatively low interest rate economies and purchase assets in relatively high interest rate economies using the debt incurred in the low-rate economy to make those asset purchases. The interest rate differential is the pursuit, much like the use of any other financial leverage. However, the idea behind the carry trade is simple but flies in the face of standard interest rate parity theory. The difference between two interest rates on similar assets, say government bond rates, is the percentage difference between the future spot rate when assets represented by the two interest rates mature and the current spot rate. By borrowing and then supplying the low interest rate currency, its value falls; by purchasing the high interest rate currency, its demand and value rises. Assuming an exchange rate exists between the two currencies, the exchange rate is predicted to adjust based on these movements to bring the currencies closer in value. The demand for the high interest rate currency reduces that currency's rate of return; the larger supply of the low interest rate currency increases its rate of return. So standard interest rate parity predicts low or zero profits from the carry trade due to the exchange rate fluctuations that follow the pursuit of an interest rate differential.

The carry trade is nothing more than another way for speculators to make money. By mixing positions in these currencies, the investor is attempting to take advantage of a market failure for profit. Since 1995, the Swiss franc and the Japanese yen have been low-rate currencies used worldwide for the carry trade. They are used against more volatile currencies, such as the US dollar, Australian dollar, and the euro. Much like the dominant theories in macroeconomics, there is a long-run and a short-run story here. According to Feenstra and Taylor (2008), from 2002 to 2006 the cumulative return on the carry trade between the Japanese yen and the Australian dollar was 15 percent (p. 928). However, from 1992 to 2001 the cumulative profit on the same transaction was zero. Theory suggests that in the long run profits will be zero; in the short run, information advantages can lead to profit. The problem is ten years and five years may both seem like the "long run" to certain investors (Cavallo 2006).

Using a nominal currency anchor

A modern currency standard, much like the Bretton Woods system, is employed by many countries around the world. The choice of fixed exchange rates is discussed later in this chapter. The set-up and mechanics of fixed exchange rates showcase two characteristics of international finance. First, fixed exchange rates reduce the use of future and forward markets on currency, and thus reduce speculation. Fixed exchange rates do not eliminate these markets. If pressure builds on a currency to revalue (increase the current, fixed exchange rate to a higher rate) or devalue (reduce the current, fixed exchange rate to a lower rate), a derivative market may begin to act as a gambling house for speculators on where the new rate will land. This is especially true in times of financial crises, because profits are available based on either good or bad information. The BOP imbalances of the country in question apply this pressure. Just like a gold standard, an economy that chooses fixed exchange rates must maintain its currency's value through monetary policy in reaction to new BOP data and market pressure.

Choosing to fix a currency's value is put into practice by a bilateral or multilateral agreement. All countries involved must agree to the fixed exchange rate and the international financial markets must observe the asking economy's willingness and ability to maintain that exchange rate. An example of an economy with a bilateral agreement is Saudi Arabia and the United States. Because the American economy purchases a large amount of oil from Saudi Arabia, a fixed currency value reduces the Saudi oil producers' risk of a currency fluctuation against the Saudi currency (the riyal). If Saudi Arabia has a BOP surplus, the riyal exchange rate will not rise but pressure will build for it to rise. To maintain the agreement, the Saudi central bank must act as if under a gold standard and expand the number of paper riyal available to reduce the appreciation pressure.

When a bilateral arrangement is in place, there is an anchor economy whose currency acts like gold. As the anchor economy's currency value fluctuates, there is some exposure to currency risk if other countries act as customers or financiers of the fixing country. For example, when Saudi Arabia chooses the dollar as its nominal anchor, there is a risk of fluctuations against other currencies not fixed to the dollar's value. Since 2003, the dollar has slowly fallen in value against the euro; beginning in late 2007, the dollar's slide became very quick due to a mix of policy expectations and American recessionary pressure. Those countries that are part of the euro area have enjoyed relatively less expensive oil imports from Saudi Arabia because oil is priced in dollars. This reduces the profits made by Saudi oil producers, and forces oil prices to rise. Not all goods enjoy that price flexibility. Further, the Saudi government must be careful not to raise oil prices too much as that inflation will affect American inflation and drag the Saudi currency down with it.

A hybrid choice is a managed float. As we have seen speculation and macroeconomic shocks have an ability to directly affect a currency's value. In the managed float, an economy can pick an exchange rate and attempt to manipulate it as the BOP naturally moves the rate. This stabilizes the exchange rate through direct intervention and signals to the international financial community that the economy in question is cognizant of problems that arise when exchange rates fluctuate too much. The managed float also has its problems. Exchange rate intervention can usurp and undermine monetary policy goals otherwise.

If an economy increases its money supply to reduce appreciation pressure on the currency, inflation pressure is increased at the price of a stable exchange rate. If the money supply is contracted due to a rapidly depreciating currency, domestic interest rates may rise and stifle an economy whose exchange rate was falling due to domestic economic growth. In countries such as Canada, Australia, and New Zealand, which are relatively small but advanced economies, exchange rate intervention has been necessary to avoid reducing exports. Exchange rates in these countries have been historically low to the dollar so as to not artificially lose comparative advantage.

The managed float has a sister policy when exchange rates are fixed, known as sterilization. Sterilization is the use of monetary policy for non-exchange maintenance purposes when in a fixed exchange rate regime. Suppose an economy chose a fixed exchange rate and experienced a domestic financial crisis that led to a monetary expansion from providing liquidity to domestic banks. This would put immediate depreciation pressure on the domestic currency. Under fixed exchange rates, this problem can be avoided if the domestic economy owns foreign reserves of its anchor currency. By purchasing the necessary domestic currency, call it pesos, from the international financial markets with holdings of its anchor, say dollars, there is initial pressure downward on the domestic currency. When the domestic central bank prints new currency, as if it were going to expand the domestic money supply, it purchases the foreign reserves back from the international financial markets, leaving the foreign money market unchanged. Domestically, the originally purchased pesos circulate as if a monetary expansion took place; internationally, the BOP pressure is relieved, or sort of relieved.

Sterilization has been abused in the past, and is not a simple process. A level of commitment must be shown by the domestic economy to reverse the money supply at a later date to relieve the ultimate depreciation pressure that will arise from domestic monetary expansion. Without that commitment, any mass purchase of currency by a central bank or government will send up red flags of a currency attempting sterilization of a domestic monetary expansion. A domestic monetary contraction is sterilized by reducing domestic currency levels by purchasing foreign currency. The purchase of foreign currency causes depreciation pressure on the peso while the domestic monetary contraction causes appreciating pressure, nullifying the net change in foreign markets.

In sum, the choice of fixed exchange rates is not a light one for the economy making that regime choice. While it mimics the first Bretton Woods system in fixing exchange rates to an anchor currency, the anchor is not necessarily tied to a value of a commodity such as gold. Remember that fixed rates come in two main forms, crawling and adjustable pegs. A managed float is much like a fixed exchange rate if the economy managing the rate does it against a specific currency and is credible in its commitment to long-term exchange rate stability. Sterilization takes place when domestic monetary change is sought under explicit exchange rate agreements, where the managing economy attempts to take short-term gains from monetary policy while understanding it must reverse its policy to eliminate the inevitable exchange rate pressure the policy causes.

Case study 13.2 The evolution of nominal anchors

In 1973, the world left the gold standard behind. The new system of floating exchange rates, mixed with the use of nominal anchors for those countries that wanted to remain fixed to a single currency or basket of currencies, was dubbed "Bretton Woods II". The dollar became a nominal anchor currency from the end of World War II onward. The amount of international transactions taking place in terms of US dollars grew annually and continues to grow. The theory behind choosing a nominal anchor is not conclusive by any means. Meissner and Oomes (2006) provide outstanding figures that show the evolution of nominal anchor choice since 1940, and break the choices down by developed and developing nations. Feenstra and Taylor (2008) provide an extended version to include the gold standard years (p. 764). From 1940 forward, the British pound gave way to the US dollar, which partially gave way to the euro once it was introduced. Independence in Africa and southern Asia over this period determined some of the shifting; the French franc was also a pegged currency, especially in western Africa, before the euro's introduction. Eastern Europe used the German mark after the Soviet Union's collapse.

One look at China's recent history with moving toward a basket of currencies and away from a strict US dollar peg provides some guidance for nominal anchor decisions (Obstfeld 2009). An economy such as China, whose trade portfolio has expanded in both breadth and depth since 1995, probably switched policies to match new trading partners and levels, as well as reduce the risk of being linked to one currency alone. Much has been made of this switch to a basket of currencies; the American government accused China of fixing its currency price versus pressure on it to naturally appreciate. The ideals of a well-operated, optimal currency area (OCA) may shift future choices toward monetary union rather than countries continuing to use volatile, individual currencies. Whether those choices lead to more consolidation in nominal anchor choice remains to be seen, but it is likely that the US dollar and the euro will continue to be the dominant currencies of choice. As finance and trade worldwide remains centered on the American and European economies, countries in transition or those emerging will probably stay tied to their chief export markets.

Currency unions and optimal currency areas

The euro's success against the dollar since 2003 has sparked both a reversal of initial agreement about modern monetary unions and a debate over whether or not other areas of the world may be candidates for similar policy amalgamation. Currency or monetary unions are agreements between countries to share central banking functions and currency, essentially abandoning individual forms of both. Fixed exchange rate regimes are different from currency unions because the countries involved do not explicitly share central banking functions. The countries that engage in monetary union agree to fix the value of their original currencies to a unit of the newly formed currency. In that way, currency unions are fixed exchange rate agreements between the countries involved; since they share a currency, there is no individual monitoring and derivative markets for the old currencies. Unless there are one-for-one exchange rates, this does not hold true in cases of economies choosing nominal anchors.

But giving up central banking is not easy; the European currency union was 50 years in the making. From the time that the European Union was conceived to the actual issuance of the euro, many changes took place in both world politics and economic theory concerning such agreements. Currency unions begin with small steps and cannot exist before other agreements are made. The first is to form a free-trade area (FTA), where the internal barriers to trade between FTA members are eliminated. Free-trade arrangements reduce the costs of trade between two countries and make international trade more competitive. This first step in combining markets is a necessary one for the next step, becoming a customs union. A customs union harmonizes trade barriers between all members. For example, if Canada and the United States have a customs union (which they do not yet), import tariffs that exist in the United States now exist for Canada and vice versa. This is a difficult change for many countries, as there are political implications when a strained relationship between an economy outside the customs union and only one country within it forces all countries to participate in trade barriers or handcuffs an antagonistic economy from using trade barriers as political devices. The European Common Market (ECM) was formed in 1977 as a customs union, not as a true common market.

A common market is when the free flow of labor and capital takes place, along with goods, across all member economies. In principle, a common market must be in place before a monetary union can operate correctly; current monetary unions exist where common markets are in name only. Goods flowing freely between the countries make their costs predictable and less volatile than with tariffs and other institutional costs. The free flow of capital makes interest rates more predictable and asset markets more stable. If both goods and capital can flow without impediment, a common currency's value will not be questioned between countries that have similar markets.

What has kept the European Common Market and ultimately the European Union from working smoothly is the actual freedom in the flow of labor. It is not easy for a resident of France to simply move to Germany and begin working, even though they have the same currency in both countries and the assumption of a common market. The lack of harmonized tax laws outside trade and financial flows keeps the common market aspects of the EU from working correctly. Why should this matter in the end? Robert Mundell and Marcus Fleming simultaneously began to answer this question in the early 1960s and initiated millions of pages of research on optimal currency areas (OCAs).

An optimal currency area is a group of countries that collectively have the characteristics to form a currency union where the differential effects of monetary policy are minimized. In the first Bretton Woods agreement, the EU countries presented a good case to have fixed exchange rates between them, and thus could issue common currency as if it were gold. Debates have raged over what those characteristics should be. Alesina and Barro (2002) provide a good overview of the Mundell (1961) model of optimal currency areas. How labor and capital move between two economies and how flexible prices are in each provide evidence as to optimal a currency union would be for a set of economies. Most research has focused on the economic characteristics of countries seeking to have a common currency, such as the integration of trade and financial flows. Others have sought to look at the conditions under which countries should not come together. Looking at a functioning currency area helps see these ideas more clearly.

The euro area and beyond: whither optimal currency areas?

Now that the euro area seems to be working as promised, many other currency unions are being discussed or expanded, where the first order of business is whether or not the group of economies constitutes an OCA. Some agreements are considered de facto unions because of their use of a nominal anchor. Groups of countries that claim to be good candidates provide some evidence of monetary union use in the future. We begin with the west African monetary unions which use the euro as their nominal anchor.

In western and central Africa, two economic zones came from the decolonization and eventual independence of several countries. The first zone is a collection of former French and Spanish colonies, called the CFA Zone, for "*Coopération financière en Afrique centrale*" in French. It is a monetary union that issues a currency called the CFA franc, which was anchored by the French franc before the euro came into existence. Its central bank is located in Cameroon. The CFA franc also circulates in western Africa, among a group of Anglophone and Francophone nations called "*Union Économique et Monétaire Ouest Africaine*" in French, or the West African Monetary Union (WAMU). There are 15 countries using the CFA franc currently, which now constitute the West African Monetary Zone (WAMZ) and are following the footsteps of the European Union. Those countries that speak English are likely to introduce a new common currency called the eco in 2009. Southern Africa is also investigating a common currency, and has already experimented with monetary union based on the South African Rand; not all of the countries in the Southern African Customs Union are part of the common monetary area; Botswana does not use the rand.

The history behind these African monetary unions follows the ideas of Robert Mundell and others concerning the reduction of transactions costs in trade between nations and facilitating financial flows. Another issue with currency unions is the differential effects of policy between the countries involved. MacKinnon (1963) extended the Mundell analysis by discussing issues of size and which countries would be poor candidates for a currency union. The future of currency unions is likely to involve larger countries, especially China and Japan in an East Asian currency union, and the United States, Canada and maybe Mexico in a North American currency union. The United States is in de facto currency unions with many countries, as some countries such as El Salvador and Ecuador have dollarized, or use the dollar as their currency explicitly.

When discussing an East Asian currency union, China and Japan look to be the dominant nations in such a union. A worry for countries such as South Korea, Thailand, Vietnam, Taiwan, and other smaller nations would be how monetary policy would affect China and Japan differently than the smaller nations. The Asian currency crises of 1997 provide a context for those countries wanting to amalgamate central banking and attempt to reduce the risk of any one currency's value driving down the region's exchange rates. Since the Asian flu, most of the Asian currencies, less Japan, have been pegged to the US dollar. The Chinese currency, the renminbi yuan, is now anchored to a basket of currencies to reduce its exposure to US dollar fluctuations, with the euro, South Korean won, and the Japanese yen as the other major currencies in the yuan's basket.

It is difficult to know the extent to which the Chinese economy would want to engage in a currency union with its East Asian neighbors. China's monetary policies are likely to be tested in the face of maintaining its peg as its economy continues to grow. For similar reasons why the British economy decided not to join the euro area, it is likely that the largest struggle to adopt an East Asian monetary union would be in Japan. Giving up partial control over monetary policy to China in part is likely to be a difficult social, cultural, and economic hurdle to eclipse. Monetary union is also likely to be stalled due to a lack of a free-trade area between China and Japan. However, it is likely that China and its smaller neighbors will take on some form of FTA or beyond in the near future.[1]

In South America, the formation of MercoSur in 1991 began the process of building a free-trade area and customs union. Most of the other nations in South America now have at least associate status in MercoSur. The countries that are the main members, Brazil, Argentina, Uruguay, and Paraguay, have all struggled since 1991 in maintaining their economic or financial health. Argentina is by far the most volatile, experiencing two separate currency crises since 1991. No true monetary union is set, though the "South American Bank" was launched in 2006 as a sign of further integration between the economies. Brazil is now poised to be the leader in Latin American economics and possible the strongest emerging market outside China in the world.

Summary

This chapter expands on the international finance themes in Chapter 12. Choosing a fixed exchange rate changes the way monetary policy is conducted, regardless of central banking structure or history. The central bank becomes dependent on the agreement between the economy in question and the international financial community, where policy now has a solitary focus: maintenance of an appropriate exchange rate. The exchange rate may move away from its initial pegged value, but does so as a result of a new negotiated agreement. History suggests that the promise of reduced inflation under the gold standard, which lasted longer than any other international financial system, was lost due to war and the hoarding of gold by larger nations. The movement from commodity money to fiat money began with the gold exchange standard, where a vehicle currency (the pound sterling) became like gold for international transactions. The Bretton Woods system centralized BOP clearing and formed an "international" currency known as the special drawing right (SDR). The world in practice used American dollars as a vehicle currency and as a result demanded the dollar en masse. As inflation crept into the American economy in the early 1970s, the dollar's value began to fall, also due to a shift of American consumption patterns toward more foreign-manufactured goods. This inflation displaced the gold standard; the major currencies of the world followed the American lead and allowed their currencies to float.

Many economies could not afford such a float and began to fix their currencies to major trading partners, forming de facto currency standards and unions. Some countries formed currency zones in Africa, and trade zones in South American and Asia as potential precursors of monetary union. The European nations began with the Common Market and continued toward a currency union throughout the 1970s and 1980s, culminating in the Maastricht Treaty of 1992. By 1999, the euro was born. As a result, the debate about optimal currency areas (OCA) and the differential effects of united monetary policy on certain regions of a currency union has grown. The North American Free Trade Agreement (NAFTA), which is slowly encompassing more countries, such as Chile and Colombia, may also be a precursor to monetary union. Since currency standards as de facto monetary unions are controlled by the currency chosen to be fixed, the American economy may face the huge challenge of being the central bank for much of the globe. However, it is likely that the euro and pound sterling will share some of that work in the future. The final chapter of this text explores the potential future of central banks and financial institutions.

Key terms

1 Bretton Woods system: an international agreement concerning the international financial system and the methods by which the balance of payments would be cleared struck in 1944 and continued in a modified form to the present time.
2 Common market: an economic bloc or agreement in which labor and capital move freely between the economies inside the economic bloc.
3 Carry trade: an investor borrows in a low interest rate currency, converts those funds into a high interest rate currency, and lends the resulting amount at the higher interest rate.
4 Currency union: an economic bloc or agreement in which the economies within share the same currency and central bank.
5 Customs union: an economic bloc or agreement in which internal trade barriers are eliminated and external trade barriers are harmonized.
6 Economic union: an economic bloc or agreement in which each member economy shares fiscal, legal, monetary, and trade policies with all other members. The United States is an example.
7 Free-trade area: an economic bloc or agreement in which the internal barriers to trade are eliminated.
8 Gold exchange standard: a modified gold standard in which a currency acts as equivalent

to gold in international transactions, such that the currency is considered a vehicle currency.

9 Gold standard: an international financial agreement in which gold is accepted as payment for all transactions within the international agreement at a par value of local currencies.

10 Managed float: a flexible exchange rate system where a central bank intervenes regularly to support the currency's value.

11 Monetary union: see currency union.

12 Nominal anchor: in a fixed exchange rate agreement, the host currency, or the currency which does not maintain the value of the fixed exchange rate in such an agreement.

13 Optimal currency area: a monetary union in which the effects of monetary policy are distributed proportionately among the member nations.

14 Sterilization: the process by which an economy engages in offensive monetary policies while under a fixed exchange rate without changing the agreed value of the currency.

Questions and problems

1 Provide thoughts about whether an economy should choose fixed or floating/flexible exchange rates and defend your case.

2 Explain the difference between a currency union and a fixed exchange rate agreement between two or more economies.

3 What did the gold standard attempt to do for economies using gold as money? Explain.

4 Why did the original gold standard evolve in to a "gold exchange standard"? Explain.

5 Explain the migration of an economy from a single nation with no free-trade arrangements to a monetary union.

6 What is an optimal currency area? What makes it optimal? Explain

Websites and suggested readings

Websites

Find the WAMZ website at: http://www.wama-amao.org/.
William Jennings Bryan's speech: http://historymatters.gmu.edu/d/5354.
For the text and breakdown of the Maastricht Treaty: http://europa.eu/scadplus/treaties/ maastricht_en.htm.

Suggested readings

"Does Europe's Path to Monetary Union Provide Lessons for East Asia?", Federal Reserve Board, San Francisco, *Economic Letters*, Number 2005–19, August 12, 2005.
Robert Mundell's Nobel Laureate speech: http://www.columbia.edu/~ram15/cema2000. html.

14   The future of banking, private and central

Introduction

Banking is facing a strange future internationally. The euro's recent success has put a new focus on currency unions and on consolidating monetary policy where possible. In the United States, credit unions do not face the same regulations as commercial banks but operate much like commercial banks and other depository institutions otherwise. The internet has changed the way banking does business and the way financial transactions are made worldwide. Many companies worldwide now have financial arms, including retail firms, where a bank supports but is not the sales force behind those products.

In the economic environment of this new century's first ten years, emerging and emerged markets will all be tested financially. This text is being written at a time of much upheaval and uncertainty in both private and central banking, where the dynamics between them are augmenting concern. For academics, it is a revolutionary time in both finance and banking, both private and central. Central banking is now under more scrutiny than ever before. Those who become central bankers face as much media pressure as a movie or pop music star in any country; their statements make front-page news and influence financial markets with the simplest of public comments. However, the focus of central banking is changing, with advances in economic theory as much as practice. Inflation-fighting as the primary goal of central banking is now an accepted practice worldwide, and has evolved in many countries into explicit rules and announcements as central banking's path. Also, how independent the central bank is from the fiscal policy-making portions of the government is changing and theory suggests it should change. The inflation bias of central banks that have employed dual mandates of output growth and inflation control may well be over. Does this mean the Phillips curve is no more and that Monetarism has won after all? Can output and employment growth be abandoned by central banks so easily?

The type of borrower is shifting from traditional borrowers to a more personal relationship around the world. The microfinance revolution, seen as a trifle in the major financial capitals of the world, has been posited as one of the main reasons why emerging markets in Asia and South America have emerged. The implications of microfinance on economic development have yet to be pondered fully by researchers, but, if the anecdotal evidence has any weight, financing small businesses with relatively small loans has helped economic development get off the ground in emerging markets. Will microfinance transcend development where traditional banking is probably better poised to take emerging market credit the rest of the way to convergence? The connections between central and private banks may become larger over time. The chapter and text conclude by discussing these linkages.

Private banking and its future

The future of private banking is likely to be one where classic depository functions and financial investment and management remain closely tied. Repealing portions of the Glass-Steagall Act in 1999 in the United States provided economies of scale and scope in banking, bringing investment banking back together with its cousin, the depository institution. Trends seem to be emerging in private banking and are likely to continue as a result of technological advances and the economies of scale in amalgamating all the financial aspects of people's lives. Some issues are microeconomic. The allocation of risk is specific to each bank. The way accounting is done, especially when and at what value mortgages are booked, has effects on the ability of banks to make loans and keep loans on their balance sheets, or slows down their sale to secondary markets.

Is it possible to track the fundamentals of a mortgage as if it was corporate debt? Increasing default risk in mortgages leads to changes in liquidity structure at a bank and thus changes the way banks use leverage. The bank's use of leverage, shifting from exposure in one type of leverage to another, does not affect financial markets when the shift is in a specific bank. When the entire market engages in a reallocation of assets and attempts to shift the risks of using leverage ("deleveraging"), it can change the way banks lend and create another credit channel, restricting the ability of monetary policy to relieve market pressure. In a recent article in *The Economist* (17 May 2008) about the future of international banking, the authors provided three reasons why banks are "fragile".[1] First, fragility is inherent in the business model of a bank. Second, the lending between banks is a large part of bank business, and a slowdown in interbank lending is generally a signal that the macroeconomy is beginning to slow down in its growth. Finally, an economic downturn can exacerbate problems in lending, and the credit markets are somewhat driven by the business cycle.

We should think deeply about these points. The first one is somewhat counterintuitive. The business model of a bank is only a problem if the bank itself faces a flattening yield curve. The fundamental model of a bank's profits, as we saw in Chapters 7 and 8, is dominated by the expectations theory of interest rates. So long as the yield curve remains upward sloping, private banks can make profits. This fragility characteristic is more about a bank's heightened ability to expose itself to risk rather than the business model itself. There is no doubt that the expansion of secondary mortgage markets through collateralized debt obligations (CDOs) and credit-default swaps (see Chapter 5) provided banks with an ability to lend in a more risky manner. However, if it were not for banking and financial markets being more risky, it is also unlikely that the expansion of world markets after 2002, especially housing in the United States and Europe, would have been as strong and fast as it was. When looking at the economics of this decade (2001–10), it is likely that economic historians will concur that growth exceeds losses.

The second and third points are more intuitive. The dependence of banks on each other to provide and demand interbank loans, funding arbitrage transactions from one bank to another, connects banks from a risk standpoint. As the riskiness of one bank which borrows from another rises, the interbank rate may not reflect the correct amount of risk in the lending bank's asset. If this perceived, risk-free market fails to deliver, one foundation upon which banking is built, diversification of risk, begins to crumble. Further, if private lending markets are more risky, and the demand for interbank loans is reduced, the revenue lending banks planned for, and depended upon somewhat for foundational cash flow, falls.

The third point assumes that loan demand is a function of economic growth or some measure of consumption and investment spending. The intuition behind this point is one of consumer and business confidence. The more confident the economy, the more likely loan demand will follow, as both consumers and firms have incentives to borrow while interest rates are relatively low, especially if they perceive the economy will continue to grow and the demand for goods, capital and loans will drive interest rates and prices up naturally.

Credit union and regional banking growth are likely to experience courting for a merger or acquisition by larger firms. Two reasons exist for this prediction. First, both credit unions and regional banks use their locations as a niche. Most of their customers are local merchants and households, and these firms provide service as a priority. Also, they may provide slightly larger rates on accounts such that these institutions attract more local customers who remain loyal to the bank by purchasing products offered beyond simple interest-bearing checking accounts. These regional depository institutions and thrifts also help to diversify risk for a larger bank or help to penetrate specific regions that are likely to experience growth. Smaller depository institutions pride themselves on more face time with customers, and have built good reputations in their local communities by having a community focus by design. For larger institutions, the current financial problems are likely to stimulate some acquisition activity to diversify both the firm's assets and their public perceptions.

The events of 2006 to the present concerning financial markets continue to affect the strategic plans of both depository and non-depository institutions. It is unlikely that the securitization of mortgages will go away, and in fact it is likely to come back strong with new regulations and some cleansing of firms who were in the industry simply for quick profits. Financial regulators worldwide face a major crisis of moral hazard with investment banks if these are not regulated in similar ways to depository institutions. Remember the definition of moral hazard in Chapter 5. Moral hazard is a problem of asymmetric information where the incentives of one party in the transaction are in question concerning their ability to complete the deal. In allowing investment banks to act like lenders for all purposes but holding deposits, does the economy (not only the central bank) face an incentive problem? Investment banks are in business to maximize the firm's profit and client wealth simultaneously, not to be low-risk structures where security of funding is the first priority. Depository institutions already serve that function. If investment banks are seen as originators of loans, or have the capability to take on that role, does that put an economy's financial system at greater risk? Is acting in the public interest not within the bounds of maximizing shareholder wealth? Central banking will find challenges in both policy and regulatory fronts.

Case study 14.1 Chinese banking: evolution as China's economy expands

After the Chinese revolution succeeded in 1949, the new government nationalized Chinese banks that had flourished before the Second World War. After stopping runaway inflation that came in the wake of both war and subsequent revolution, the People's Bank of China, the central bank formed during this time under the Ministry of Finance (in a similar system evolved in Japan), began its operations. This bank was not independent; it served as the treasurer of the Chinese government, providing monetary growth to help fund Chinese fiscal expenditures. Microfinance institutions sprung up in rural areas, called rural credit cooperatives, under the jurisdiction of The Agricultural Bank, an entity set up parallel to the People's Bank to facilitate rural credit. Urban credit cooperatives also began to facilitate loans to businesses in cities. This was a later development than the rural cooperatives; the urban cooperatives began alongside Chinese export growth and economic liberalization in the 1980s.

Before 1986, interbank lending and strong connections between all depository institutions in the banking system were somewhat non-existent. Regional financial networks began to grow as the 1980s ended; in 1986, the Chinese stock market began to operate again, albeit in small ways. Two major advances came with the opening of stock exchanges in Shanghai and other cities. First was further access to capital and diversification of portfolio assets. Before this, the Chinese economy was financially insulated. Second, major financial transactions were all done within the banking system prior to the mid-1980s. Because the Chinese people were strongly urged by both their government and culture to save, bank deposits were the main way people held their savings until equity markets began in earnest.

The expansion of banking and financial services in the 1980s also brought new technologies to Chinese banking. The issuance of debit cards began in 1985 and expanded greatly through the next two decades. In 1995, the People's Bank of China was declared the central bank of China over a larger system of private banking. This was after a history in Chinese banking where the People's Bank was the only bank (the state monopoly on banking services and control of currency) from 1949 to 1978. In 1998, a similar structure to the US Federal Reserve was established where nine "district" banks were set up and were outside the communist, local administrative structure. In 2003, further progress was made on the People's Bank supervising financial markets and currency values. The Bank of China (BOC), as a private operation, shows how banks have evolved. The BOC is cited as the leader in private Chinese banking, excluding banks that operated in Taiwan (Bank of China 2009). It is likely that Chinese banking will continue to evolve as it would in any developed economy, where the government will keep a watchful eye on banking practices in the wake of the global financial problems.

Central banking and its future

There is likely to be growing pressure on countries to amalgamate monetary policies and form regional monetary unions. As the first decade of the twenty-first century nears its end, the American economy will contend with rising inflation expectations due to multiple forces of demand-side economic growth, continued demand for primary products by most industries, and central bank policy shifting from inflation-fighting to inflation creation to stimulate growth. More central banks will use specific inflation rules regardless of monetary union formation or fixed currency regimes expanding beyond the current agreements. Monetary rules provide less misunderstanding as to the mission of policy, but come with lower growth rates due to shocks no longer being unexpected.

The role of the International Monetary Fund (IMF) in dealing with the current financial crisis is a major question. In the summer and fall of 2008, the country of Iceland came precariously close to bankruptcy as an economy. The banking industry in Iceland was highly leveraged in two ways. First, Icelandic banks used lending to foreign housing markets as a way of generating income and were domestically owned. Like other countries that experienced current account deficits, when the foreign credit market dried up for Iceland they suddenly had an inability to pay for their imports with borrowing, and had to use foreign reserves. When those quickly ran out, and the asset side of their major banks' balance sheets fell in value with changing housing and asset market prices, these banks were pushed toward insolvency. The IMF may have to broker a deal to salvage these banks, rather than producing the loan.

In late 2008, Hungary's central bank increased its lending rate by 300 basis points at one time to try and reduce pressure on its exchange rate due to a forecasted economic downturn. Hungary, much like Iceland, has current account deficits that have risen rapidly while Hungary grew, and it also had capital outflows to accumulate foreign reserves. These twin incentives to supply Hungarian forints into the international financial markets signaled major inflation in Hungary to come, which made Hungarian assets face a sell-off worldwide. To enhance the confidence of foreign investors, Hungary's central bank increased rates of interest in October 2008. Unless Hungary is immune to recession, and the threat of a global downturn, this move to adjust foreign investor confidence is likely to force recession onto the economy. The ECB is likely to lend Hungarian banks as much as $7 billion to revive its credit market.

South Africa is an economy that relies on export demand, and thus may be vulnerable to a major recession in industrialized nations. When commodity prices surged in 2007 and early 2008, demand for the rand followed. As commodity prices slowly fall, and oil prices very rapidly, the South African Reserve Bank (SARB) is faced with an interesting conundrum. With a discount rate of 12 percent in 2008, it is likely that SARB does not have a lot of room to move that rate up to stop the worldwide slide of the rand's value. An increase in interest rates further stagnates domestic investment, and may not draw any new foreign investment given commodity prices are a major source of export revenue for South Africa. On the other hand, to lower interest rates probably exacerbates the rand's sliding value and may not stimulate a great deal of consumption growth. It may provide some short-term advantages in exports. Much like Hungary and Iceland, South Africa faces a serious central banking puzzle; unlike those other countries, South Africa remains strong in the long term in its current account surplus. Its dependence is not on imports as much as capital inflows.

South Korea (ROK) is an economy whose central bank is likely to have a great deal of pressure on it in the coming years. In 2008, ROK has the largest loan to deposit ratio of all the developed Asian nations and faces a current account deficit, rapid growth of its foreign-held debt, and rising commodities prices due to import dependence. South Korea's exposure to foreign borrowing provides both a blessing and a curse for its central bank. With a large number of foreign reserves accumulated, it is somewhat insulated from a second round of Asian flu. Its domestic debt levels, rising due to economic growth through both household spending and residential investment during this decade, has exposed ROK's economy to a domestic recession led by a housing slowdown. What is the Bank of Korea to do here? Should it follow the American lead and begin a bailout plan of its banks using foreign reserves to buy some of the potentially bad debts without affecting the ROK won's value? Would interest rate adjustments downward now rather than later provide some continued spending or is inflation brewing? An increase of interest rates may stave off risk by re-pricing new loans (and old, adjustable ones) such that foreign investors and domestic banks see South Korea as a place of relative financial safety in Asia.

Brazil, Russia, India, and China have now become known as the "BRICs" developing nations. Each is somewhat exposed to the current economic turmoil, and each of their central banks is facing potential problems. Much like South Africa, declining commodity prices threaten that Brazil's historic growth period is coming to an end. For China, its real GDP growth is threatened by a global recession and so is its monetary policy stance long held to keep the yuan's value relatively high. If American and European imports continue to fall, it is likely the Chinese government will have little choice but to reduce the yuan's value in an attempt to continue export sales. In contrast, India is much more exposed in terms of services versus goods manufacturing.

India is probably the most exposed of these four countries to global recession of any length. India's growth has put inflation pressure into its economy, where the rupee is now suffering under the strain of large fiscal and current account deficits. Because India's economy is more reliant on services, it is more likely to face job cuts and outmigration. India's monetary policy faces a large question that is similar to other fast-growing, emerging markets. Can monetary policy reverse consumer-driven recessions without causing a great deal of inflation? What seems obvious about the future of central banking is that, if the world is truly flattening, and convergence of many economies may take place over the next 20 years in a similar way to Germany and Japan in the 1970s to the American economy, the battle between inflation and unemployment will continue regardless of the use of monetary rules.

Brazil and Russia are likely to emerge from these crises in relatively good shape. Their monetary policies have been to maintain inflation at a relatively high rate and to push exports as much as possible. Commodity prices retreating in both 2008 and early 2009 probably limit the growth of foreign reserves in these two countries and the possibility of foreign investment finding profitable opportunities. The major test of each of these countries is whether their central banks can navigate through the financial storm to come, specific to their local real estate and domestic savings markets. Neither country has had much success in the last two decades.

Case study 14.2 A Nobel Peace Prize to an economist: microfinance and the future of lending

Give an economist a simple idea, a bank and an entrepreneurial market and great strides can be made. Muhammad Yunus, an economist educated at Vanderbilt University in the United States, came from Bangladesh to study economics. He earned a PhD in economics in 1970 and briefly taught at Middle Tennessee State University before going back to Bangladesh to teach as an economist at Chittagong University. While a professor, Dr Yunus started a rural bank project called Grameen Bank. This bank was meant to reduce the dependence of both local businesses and entrepreneurs on usurious loans from loan sharks and other street lenders. Considering ways to fight poverty in rural Bangladesh, Dr Yunus provided a small loan to women in a small village making bamboo furniture. This small amount of lending provided funds for the women and their families to purchase bamboo, manufacture the furniture, and sell their wares without a large interest payment reducing profits. By sharing the profits, in a similar way to Islamic finance discussed in Chapter 6, the borrowers' ability to pay back was a function of their profitability and not necessarily their inherent risk. By engaging in "microfinance", lenders provide conditions to be profitable, meaning loan payback at relatively low rates of return to the lender, but high rates of return for relative prosperity and use of local resources.

Dr Yunus's vision is a large but simple one: eradicate the world's poverty problem by using the larger economies to finance the smaller ones in such a way that is not usurious and focuses on sharing profits. Consider this perspective of Dr Yunus also: everyone has a right to credit. We have seen this idea crumble developed countries' housing and financial markets because credit facilitated consumption rather than production. Western economies, assuming that credit was a fundamental right, engaged in innovations that made credit markets work more quickly, and provided money at a rapid rate for anyone willing to borrow. The consumer credit card is iconic concerning the proliferation of credit in Western society. Impoverished people can be lifted from poverty's burden simply by providing them with credit to produce that does not affect their ability to have profits in terms of fixed interest costs. Allow profitability to dictate the return to both the lender and entrepreneur. Consumption comes from that profitability.

From a banking standpoint, this idea flies in the face of classic banking tradition, and would have a difficult time becoming standard practice in the developed world. Microfinance assumes that the borrower's peer group provides the necessary pressure to facilitate payback. The peer group acts as a loan monitor in lieu of the lender monitoring the loan. This, in theory, should reduce moral hazard in lending and increase the incentives for borrowers to pay back and to use the loan to provide funding for payback. The adverse selection problem is also reduced in theory because the peer group members know each other and have a history together. Microfinance also has its roots in the savings and loan associations in the United States, where members would place money into an association and lend to each other.

Microfinance need not be only for poor economies. There are organizations in Canada and the United States, for example, providing peer group lending in a microfinance model. For Dr Yunus's bank, the Grameen Bank, providing lending in economic conditions such as those in Bangladesh was the true revolution. With limited educational, infrastructural and investment opportunities, the depth and breadth of poverty in Bangladesh are great in magnitude. Microfinance in that country can also help in times of flooding (which is common) and drought (also common). As in any other country, credit provides a bridge between consumption and income. Whether credit has the ability to solve the world's poverty issues remains a mystery, but this example shows the possibilities, as poverty levels have fallen since the inception of microcredit organizations in Bangladesh. Over 1000 non-governmental organizations provide these funds as of 2007. Whether microfinance transactions evolve beyond a pawn shop in Western finance is hard to know yet, but the success of Grameen Bank should be considered a possible model. Because this work was more of a humanitarian effort than economic, the Nobel Prize was for peace rather than economic sciences for Dr Yunus.

Summary

This text has discussed financial markets, banking as a business and the macroeconomics of money and monetary policy. To conclude such a text is difficult, but I leave the reader with three insights about these industries. First, depository institutions and classic banking will change and become more virtual. Many depositors currently do most of their banking online, and the need to carry cash is shrinking. As a result, banks will probably take on a model where there are few employees per branch and the branches are few and far between. If cash can be easily moved from one account to another, liquidity should become less of a factor.

Second, investment banks are likely to face regulations similar to depository institutions where they are more responsible for their client's funds. Issues of ethics and capitalism are very difficult to reconcile, but the new regulatory environment is unlikely to easily forget about the latest financial market downturn. For central banks and other regulatory agencies worldwide, it is difficult to truly know how to answer a question concerning the greed of financial institutions and stopping that greed. Greed is inherent in capitalism, and is also why command economies have ultimately failed when used as an alternative to capitalism. How can monetary policy and regulation do anything about this? Regulators must stand aside from innovation, while shaping and monitoring the practices and growth of new markets.

Finally, it is likely that central banking will become more rule-based for all economies. The violence with which markets move from one direction to the other in economies where monetary discretion is employed makes a case for shaping expectations through predictability. This third point is really connected to the other two. How can central banks, which must be careful not to interfere with growth patterns, be a constant force in the economy? Central bankers are now like rock stars, selling books about their time on boards of governors and testifying in front of legislative bodies. My hope is that you have more insight about monetary affairs after reading this text.

Questions and problems

1   Discuss three reasons why credit unions and regional banks rather than large, corporate depository institutions may become the focus of consumers.
2   Compare and contrast monetary discretion and rules in the context of the current financial problems. Would a monetary rule help shape the next business cycle? Explain.
3   Would penalizing central bankers (jail or lower salaries) make any difference in their performance? Explain why that could help or hurt economies.

Notes

1 Understanding money

1 See http://www.federalreserve.gov/Releases/h6/discm3.htm for the Federal Reserve's notice.
2 The financial crises of 2007–08 in the United States ignited widespread financial issues in many countries because of subsequent changes in the Federal Reserve's policies and the links of international financial markets to those in the United States. To date, the Federal Reserve has used both policy and regulation to quell these problems.

2 Interest rates and financial markets

1 See http://www.treasurydirect.gov/govt/charts/principal/principal_govpub.htm.
2 See http://www.investopedia.com/terms/b/bondrating.asp for more.
3 There is a difference between a bond that sells at a *discount* and another that sells at a *premium*. Most bonds sell at a discount in the primary market, while secondary market bonds may sell at either a discount or a premium, less or more than their par value.

3 Risk and risk aversion

1 See Post et al. (2008) for an academic look at "Deal or No Deal?"

4 Equity markets, stock markets and real estate

1 For a look at each stock in Table 4.1 and its recent price history, go to http://finance.yahoo.com and type in the relevant ticker symbol.
2 We will relax this assumption later when we talk about the difference between rational and adaptive expectations.
3 It is the covariance of asset **k**'s returns with the market return on average divided by the variance in the average market return. Regression coefficients generally are the ratio of the covariance between x and y with the variance in x.

5 Derivative asset and insurance markets

1 For more, see Schaede (1998), Volume 6, where papers discuss the Tokugawa monetary system, 1787–1868, and whether the Dojima rice **market** during the Tokugawa period qualifies as a financial *futures market*.
2 See *The Economist*, 8 November 2008, p.14.
3 See Akerlof (1970) for a seminal study in information (and all of) economics.

6 Financial intermediaries

1 Both the US commercial and thrift banking industries were hard hit in the 1980s due to a mix of regulatory failure, risky lending and economic downturn. Credit unions were small enough an industry at the time that they were less affected, if at all.
2 Moody (1971) has a long history of credit union development before 1970.

3   Social security systems worldwide are either fully funded, where the worker funding the account receives the benefits of that investment and it is not funded from any other source, or, as has happened to many social security systems, they become "pay as you go" systems. In this case, the funding source for current beneficiaries is paid by the young for the old, at least partially. There are many implications of this transition on world financial markets yet to be realized.

4   Costa (1998) has an outstanding history of both the financial choice to retire and of pensions as a way of funding that choice.

5   This is an extension of the famous "lemon" problem of Nobel Prize-winning economist George Akerlof (1970). Lowering the price of a used car usually reduces the number of good cars that remain, and the compensation for risk in a lower price leads to an "adverse selection" because no good cars are left.

7   The microeconomics of banking

1   See Lindert and Morton (1989) for an extensive, famous study of sovereign debt.
2   See Wall and Peterson (1990) for more on Continental Illinois.
3   See Gregorio and Valdes (2001) for more on the Asian flu of 1997.

8   Connections between commercial and central banking

1   While reserve requirements are rarely changed, they will be reaffirmed at 10 percent for banks with more than $44 million on deposit in the United States on January 9, 2009. A history of reserve requirements in the United States and in economic thought can be found at http://www.federalreserve.gov/monetarypolicy/0693lead.pdf.
2   See Fortune (2000) for more on margin loan history and regulation.
3   See Cecchetti et al. (2006) for more on policy and its efficiency.
4   See Freedman (1994) for a background on how Canadian monetary policy is structured, as well as the Bank of Canada website: http://www.bankofcanada.ca.
5   See Friedman (1971) for a seminal article on seigniorage.
6   See Kaminsky and Reinhart (2000) for more on financial contagions and crises.
7   It is important to remember the difference between economic and accounting costs; the cost of capital not only includes the accounting cost of capital acquisition, it also includes the opportunity costs of purchasing a specific piece of equipment. The inclusion of an opportunity costs is the difference.
8   See Friedman (2006) for a synopsis of how the Greenspan Federal Reserve performed.

9   The domestic market for money

1   See Cagan (1956) for a seminal article on money demand.
2   See Friedman and Schwartz (1963) for a treatise on American monetary history and its maturation internationally.
3   See Ireland (2008) for an outstanding review of transmission mechanisms.

10   Money, employment, inflation and expectations

1   See Jensen (2002) for a recent study on transparency in central banking.
2   See "Websites" section for the Reserve Bank of New Zealand's website.
3   See "Websites" section for the Bank of Canada's website.
4   See http://www.rbnz.govt.nz/monpol/about/2851362.html for New Zealand's monetary policy basics.
5   See Phillips (1958) for one of the seminal articles in empirical macroeconomics.
6   The natural rate is also the known as the non-accelerating inflation rate of unemployment (NAIRU), the long-run unemployment rate, and other monikers. The main idea is that represents the unemployment rate at which all unemployment is frictional, or the economy is in full employment. Please see the discussion below of the full employment Phillips Curve for more.
7   See Sheffrin (1996) for a history and survey of rational expectations theory.

8   See Chapter 12 for more on the IS-LM model and a full description of the interest rate channel of monetary policy.

11 Money and the macroeconomy

1   Hicks (1937) is one of the most famous interpretive articles in the economics canon. It has become the foundation of millions of pages of research.
2   Under a sticky price assumption, this inflation tax may be small.
3   Find any articles or reviews of fiscal versus monetary policy and the potential problems in the EU.
4   There have been recent developments in monetary theory and the pedagogy for the IS-LM model. The LM curve is now taking the form of a "monetary policy" curve (sometimes known as "MP") or a BP curve for open economy models. Because it is important for students to understand where these ideas originated, and the importance of people such as John Hicks to economic science, we stick with the traditional IS-LM set-up here.
5   The crowding-out effect can be exacerbated or lessened depending on the trade balance. In Chapter 13, the use of foreign financial markets to fund domestic fiscal deficits is explored more fully.
6   Is there a piece of research or book that has a list of central banks tied directly to law-making functions of government or more specifically fiscal policy-makers?

12 Monetary policy in the open macroeconomy

1   Mundell (1961) and Fleming (1962) are seen as simultaneous works on the same basic subject (optimal currency areas and monetary unions), thus both are given credit for the subject's genesis. McKinnon (1963) is also a classic.
2   Dornbusch (1976) is considered the beginning of the field of "New Open Economy Macroeconomics". It has become a seminal article in international finance.

13 The world economy and monetary policy choices

1   See Ng (2002) for a recent perspective on an Asian currency union.

14 The future of banking, private and central

1   See *The Economist*'s Special Report on international banking, 17 May 2008, pp. 1–14.

References

Akerlof, G. A. (1970) "The market for lemons: quality uncertainty and the market mechanism", *Quarterly Journal of Economics*, 84(3), 488–500.

Alessina, A., and Barro, R. (2002) "Currency unions", *Quarterly Journal of Economics*, 117(2), 409–36.

Algebra.com. (2008) *The Algebra of Finance*. Available at: <http://www.algebra.com/algebra/homework/Finance/>.

American Bankers Association (2008) *Consumers*. Available at: <http://www.aba.com/abaef/consumers.htm>.

American Stock Exchange (2008) *The AMEX*. Available at: <http://www.amex.com/>.

Bade, R. and Parkin, M. (1984) "Central bank laws and monetary policy". Department of Economics, University of Western Ontario, Canada.

Bank of Canada (2008) *Bank of Canada*. Available at: <http://www.bankofcanada.ca/en/index.html>.

Bank of China (2009) "About BOC". Available at: <<http://www.bank-of-china.com/en/aboutboc/>>

Bank of England (2008) *Interest and Exchange Rates*. Available at: <http://www.bankofengland.co.uk/statistics/>.

Bank of International Settlements (2009) Proposed enhancements to the Basel II framework. Available at:<http://www.bis.org/publ/bcbs150.htm>.

Barth, M. J. III, and Ramey, V. A. (2001) "The cost channel of monetary transmission", in *NBER Macroeconomic Annual 2001*, Cambridge, MA: MIT Press, 199–239.

Benessay-Quere, A. (2005) Africa Puts Forth its Eco. *Centre d'Etude Prospectives et Informations Internationales* working paper no. 243, March. Available at: <http://www.cepii.fr/anglaisgraph/publications/lettre/pdf/2005/let243ang.pdf>.

Bernanke, B., and Gertler, M. (1995) "Inside the black box: the credit channel of monetary policy transmission", *Journal of Economic Perspectives*, 9(4), 27–48.

Blinder, A. S., Ehrmann, M., Fratzscher, M., De Haan, J., and Jansen, D.-J. (2008) "Central bank communication and monetary policy: a survey of theory and evidence", *Journal of Economic Literature*, 46(4), 910–45.

Bordo, M. (2008) "Gold Standard", *The Concise Encyclopedia of Economics*. Available at: <http://www.econlib.org/library/Enc/GoldStandard.html>.

Bryan, W. J. (1896) *Cross of Gold Speech*. Available at: <http://historymatters.gmu.edu/d/5354>.

Cagan, P. (1956) "The monetary dynamics of hyperinflation", in Friedman, M. (ed.), *Studies in the Quantity Theory of Money*, Chicago: University of Chicago Press, 25–117.

Canada Mortgage and Housing Corporation (2008) Housing market outlook, Canada edition, fourth quarter 2008. Available at: <http://www.cmhc-schl.gc.ca/odpub/esub/61500/61500_2008_Q04.pdf>.

Carlstrom, C. L., and Fuerst, T. S. (2009) "Central bank independence and inflation: a note," *Economic Inquiry*, 47(1), 182–86.

Cavallo, M. (2006) "Interest rates, carry trades, and exchange rate movements", *Federal Reserve Bank of San Francisco Economic Letter*, 17 November.

Cecchetti, S. G., Flores-Lagunes, A., and Krause, S. (2006) "Has monetary policy become more efficient? A cross-country analysis", *The Economic Journal*, 116(511), 408–33.

Chan, N., Getmansky, M., Haas, S. M., and Lo, A. W. (2006) "Do hedge funds increase systemic risk?", *Federal Reserve Bank of Atlanta: Economic Review*, 91, 49–80.

Chicago Mercantile Exchange (2008) *The MERC*. Available at: <http://www.cme.com/>.

Chiu, S., and Newberger, R. (2006) "Islamic finance: meeting financial needs with faith-based products", *Federal Reserve Bank of Chicago: Research Review*, February, 8–14.

Cohen, B. (2008) "Bretton Woods system", *Routledge Encyclopedia of International Political Economy*. Available at: <http://www.polsci.ucsb.edu/faculty/cohen/inpress/bretton.html>.

Costa, D. (1998) *The Evolution of Retirement: An American Economic History, 1880–1990*, Chicago: University of Chicago Press.

Craig, V. V. (1998) "Japanese banking: a time of crisis", *FDIC Banking Review*, Summer 1998.

Cukierman, A. (2008) "Central bank independence and monetary policymaking institutions – past, present and future", *European Journal of Political Economy*, 24, 722–36.

Della Paolera, G., and Taylor, A. M. (2003) *A New Economic History of Argentina*, London: Cambridge University Press.

Di Tella, R., Pill, H., and Vogel, I. (2005) "Mexico: the tequila crisis, 1994–1995", *Institutions, Macroeconomics, and the Global Economy: Casebook*, Singapore: World Scientific, 83–108.

Dornbusch, R. (1976) "Expectations and Exchange Rate Dynamics", *Journal of Political Economy*, 84(6), 1161–76.

Economagic.com. Referenced on multiple occasions. Available at: www.economagic.com.

Economist, The (2004) "Playboys?", 21 August, 61.

—— (2007) "The English Patient", 10 November, 70–1.

—— (2008) "A report on international banking", Special Report, 17 May, 1–14.

—— (2008) "Giving credit where it is due", 8 November, 14.

—— (2009) "International: A unity government, at last; Zimbabwe", 14 February, 57.

—— (2009) "Good Sport: State-Owned Banking", 14 March, British Edition, 35.

Enron: The Smartest Guys in the Room. DVD. Directed by Alex Gibney. 2005, Los Angeles: Magnolia.

European Central Bank (2008) *Monetary Aggregates*. Available at HTTP: <http://www.ecb.int/stats/money/aggregates/aggr/html/index.en.html>.

European Union (2008) *Maastricht Treaty*. Available at: <http://europa.eu/scadplus/treaties/maastricht_en.htm>.

Federal Deposit Insurance Corporation (2008) Available at: <http://www.fdic.gov>.

Federal Reserve Board (2008) *Data download*. Available at: <http://www.federalreserve.gov/datadownload/>.

—— (2008) *Information about the Basel II Accords*. Available at: <http://www.federalreserve.gov/generalinfo/basel2/default.htm>.

—— (2006) *Notice about M3*. Available at: <http://www.federalreserve.gov/Releases/h6/discm3.htm>.

——(2006) *Reserve Requirements: History, Current Practice, and Potential Reform*. Available at: <http://www.federalreserve.gov/monetarypolicy/0693lead.pdf>.

Federal Reserve Board, Boston (2008) *Balance of Payments*. Available at: <http://www.bos.frb.org/economic/special/balofpay.pdf>.

Federal Reserve Board, New York (2008) *Foreign Exchange Markets*. Available at: <http://www.newyorkfed.org/education/fx/foreign.html>.

—— (2008) *Descriptions of Interest Rates*. Available at: <http://www.newyorkfed.org/education/diff_rates.html>.

Federal Reserve Board, Philadelphia (2008) *Describing the Federal Open Market Committee and its Operations*. Available at: <http://www.philadelphiafed.org/education/fomc.html>.

Federal Reserve Board, San Francisco (2008) *A History of The American Currency*, Available at: <http://www.frbsf.org/currency/index.html>.

—— (2008) *The Fed in Brief*. Available at: <http://www.frbsf.org/publications/federalreserve/fedinbrief/index.html>.

Feenstra, R., and Taylor, A. (2008) *International Economics*, New York: Worth Publishers.

Fisher, I. (1911) *The Purchasing Power Of Money: Its Determination And Relation To Credit Interest and Crises*, Whitefish, MT: Kessinger (reprinted 2006).

Fleming, J. M. (1962) "Domestic financial policies under fixed and under floating exchange rates", *Staff Papers, International Monetary Fund*, Vol. 9 (November), 369–79.

Fortin, C. (2008) "Chile 1973–1985: the failure of monetarism", *Development Policy Review*, 3(2), 137–46.

Fortune, P. (2000) "Margin requirements, margin loans, and margin rates: practice and principles for more on margin loan history and regulation", *New England Economic Review*, Sept/Oct, 19–45.

Freedman, C. (1994) "The use of indicators and the monetary conditions index in Canada", in Balino, T. J. T. and Cottarelli, C. (eds.), *Frameworks for Monetary Stability*, Washington DC: IMF Institute International Monetary Fund, Monetary and Exchange Affairs, 458–78.

Frexias, X., and Rochet, J. C. (2007) *Microeconomics of Banking*, 2nd ed., Cambridge, MA: MIT Press.

Friedman, B. M. (2006), "The Greenspan era: discretion, rather than rules", *NBER Working Paper Series*, 12118, March.

Friedman, M. (1970) The counter-revolution in monetary theory. First Wincott Memorial lecture, delivered at the Senate House, University of London, 16 September, London: Transatlantic Arts.

—— (1971) "Government revenue from inflation", *Journal of Political Economy*, 79(4), 846–56.

Friedman, M., and Schwartz, A. (1963) *A Monetary History Of The United States, 1870–1960*, New York: Princeton University Press.

Garcia-Swartz, D. D., Hahn, R. W., and Layne-Ferrar, A. (2006) "The move toward a cashless society: a closer look at payment instrument economics", *Review of Network Economics*, 5(2), 175–98.

Gerdes, G. R. (2008) "Recent Payment Trends in the United States", Federal Reserve Bulletin, October 2008, A75-A106. Available at HTTP: <http://www.federalreserve.gov/pubs/bulletin/2008/pdf/payments08.pdf>.

Gertler, M., and Bernanke, B. (1995) "Inside the black box: the credit channel of monetary policy transmission", *Journal of Economic Perspectives*, 9(4), 27–48.

Glick, R. (2005) "Does Europe's path to monetary union provide lessons for east Asia?" *Federal Reserve Board, San Francisco Economic Letters*, no. 2005–19, August 12.

Gregorio, J. D., and Valdes O. O. (2001) "Crisis transmission: evidence from the debt, tequila, and Asian flu crises", *World Bank Economic Review*, 15(2), 289–314.

Hicks, J. (1937) "Mr. Keynes and the classics", *Econometrica*, 5(2), 147–59.

International Monetary Fund (2008) *BOP Manual*. Available at: <http://www.imf.org/external/np/sta/bop/BOPman.pdf>.

Investopedia.com (2008) *Bond Ratings*. Available at: <http://www.investopedia.com/terms/b/bondrating.asp>.

Ireland, P. N. (2008) "Monetary transmission mechanism", in Durlauf, S. N. and Blume, L. E. (eds.), *The New Palgrave Dictionary of Economics*, 2nd ed., New York: Palgrave Macmillan.

Islamic Bank of Britain. Home page. Available at: <http://www.islamic-bank.com/islamicbanklive/GuestHome/1/Home/1/Home.jsp>.

Jarrow, R. A. (1999) "In honor of the Nobel laureates, Robert C. Merton And Myron S. Scholes: a partial differential equation that changed the world", *Journal of Economic Perspectives*, 13(4), 229–48.

Jensen, H. (2002) "Optimal degrees of transparency in monetary policymaking", *Scandinavian Journal of Economics*, 104(3), 399–422.

Kaminsky, G. L., and Reinhart, C. M. (2000) "On crises, contagion, and confusion", *Journal of International Economics*, 51(1), 145–68.

Kashyap, A., and Stein, J. C. (1994) "Monetary policy and bank lending", in N. Gregory Mankiw (ed.), *Monetary Policy, Studies in Business Cycles*, vol. 29, Chicago: University of Chicago Press, 221–56.

Keynes, J. M. (1924) *A Tract on Monetary Reform*, London: Macmillan.

—— (1936) *The General Theory of Employment, Interest and Money*, London: Macmillan (reprinted 2007).

Kwan, S. (2006) "Safe and sound banking: 20 years later", *Federal Reserve Board, San Francisco Economic Letters*. Available at: <http://www.frbsf.org/publications/economics/letter/2006/el2006–26.pdf>.

Laidler, D. (1993) *The Demand for Money: Theories, Evidence and Problems*, New York: Norton.

Lindert, P., and Morton, P. (1989) "How sovereign debt has worked", in J. Sachs and S. M. Collins (eds.), *Developing Country Debt and Economic Performance: The International Financial System*, Chicago: University of Chicago Press, 39–106.

MacDonald, R. (2003) *Derivative Markets*, New York: Prentice Hall.

Malkiel, B. (2003) *A Random Walk Down Wall Street*, New York: Norton.

Masson, P., and Pattillo, C. (2005) *The Monetary Geography of Africa: Africa, Macroeconomics, Global Economics*, Washington DC: Brookings Institution Press.

McCallum, B. T. (2008) "Monetarism", *The Concise Encyclopedia of Economics*. Available at: <http://www.econlib.org/library/Enc/Monetarism.html>.

McKinnon, R. M. (1963) "Optimal currency areas", *American Economic Review*, 53(Sept.), 717–25.

Meissner, C.M., and Oomes, N. (2006) "Why do countries peg the way they peg? The determinants of anchor currency choice", Cambridge Working Papers in Economics 0643, Faculty of Economics, University of Cambridge.

Mills, P. F., and Kiff, J. (2007) "Money for nothing and checks for free: recent developments in U.S. subprime mortgage markets", *International Monetary Fund, IMF Working Papers*, No. 07/188.

Mishkin, F. S. (1999) "Lessons from the tequila crisis", *Journal of Banking and Finance*, 23(10): 1521–33.

—— (2006) "Monetary policy strategy: how did we get here?", *NBER Working Paper Series*, no. 12515, September.

Moody, J. C. (1971) *The Credit Union Movement: Origins And Development, 1850–1970*, Lincoln: University of Nebraska.

Mundell, R. (1961) "A theory of optimal currency areas", *American Economic Review*, 51(4), 657–65.

—— (2008) *Nobel Laureate Speech*. Available at: <http://www.columbia.edu/~ram15/cema2000.html>.

Mushinski, D., and Phillips R. J. (2008) "The role of Morris plan lending institutions in expanding consumer microcredit in the United States", in Yago, G. and Barth, J.R. and Zeidman, B. (eds.), *Entrepreneurship in Emerging Domestic Markets*, in *The Milken Institute Series on Financial Innovation and Economic Growth*, vol. 7, Berlin: Springer, 121–39.

New York Mercantile Exchange (2008) *The NYMEX*. Available at: <http://www.nymex.com/index.aspx>.

Ng, T. H. (2002) "Should the Southeast Asian countries form a currency union?", *The Developing Countries*, 40(2), 113–34.

Norges Bank (2009) "Monetary policy in Norway". Available at: <http://www.norges-bank.no/templates/article_12345.aspx>.

Obstfeld, M. (2009) "International finance and growth in developing countries: What Have We Learned?", *NBER Working Paper Series*, no. 14691.

Obstfeld, M., and Rogoff, K. (1995) "Exchange rate dynamics redux", *Journal of Political Economy*, 103(3), 624–60.

Ojo, M. O. (2004) "The challenges of introducing the eco currency", for The Zonal Workshop For The Mass Media In The West African Monetary Zone, Conakry, Republic Of Guinea, 8 June. Available at: <http://www.wami-imao.org/english/doc/IntroducingEcoCurrency.pdf>.

People's Bank of China (2008) *Statistics*. Available at: <http://www.pbc.gov.cn/english/diaochatongji/tongjishuju/>.

Phillips, A.W. H. (1958) "The relation between unemployment and the rate of change of money wage rates in the United Kingdom, 1861–1957", *Economica*, 25, 283–99.

Post, T., Van den Assem, M. J., Baltussen, G., and Thaler, R. H. (2008) "Deal or no deal? Decision making under risk in a large-payoff game show", *American Economic Review*, 8(1), 38–71.

Rai, A., Seth, R., and Mohanty, S. K. (2007) "The impact of discount rate changes on market interest rates: evidence from three European countries and Japan", *Journal of International Money and Finance*, 26, 905–23.

Ravenna, P. and Walsh, C. (2005) "Optimal monetary policy with the cost channel", *Journal of Monetary Economics*, 53(2), 199–216.

Reserve Bank of Australia (2008) *Financial system statistics*. Available at: <http://www.rba.gov.au/FinancialSystemStability/Statistics/index.html>.

Reserve Bank of India (2008) *Database*. Available at: <http://www.rbi.org.in/scripts/Statistics.aspx>.

Reserve Bank of New Zealand (2008) *Reserve Bank of New Zealand*. Available at HTTP: <http://www.rbnz.govt.nz/>.

—— (2008) *Monetary policy accountability and monitoring* Available at: <http://www.rbnz.govt.nz/monpol/about/2851362.html>.

Santomero, A. M. (1984) "Modeling the banking firm: a survey", *Journal of Money, Credit and Banking*, 16(4), Part 2: Bank Market Studies (Nov), 576–602.

Saxton, J. (2003) *Argentina's Economic Crisis: Causes and Cures*. Joint Economic Committee, United States Congress. Available at: <http://www.house.gov/jec/imf/06-13-03long.pdf>.

Schaede, U. (1998) "Forwards and futures in Tokugawa-period Japan: a new perspective on the Dojima rice market", in M. Smitka (ed.), *The Japanese Economy in the Tokugawa Era, 1600–1868 (Japanese Economic History, 1600–1960)*, vol. 6, London: Routledge.

Sheffrin, S. M. (1996) *Rational Expectations*, 2nd ed., London: Cambridge University Press.

Shin, H. S. (2009) "Reflections on modern bank runs: a case study of Northern Rock", *Journal of Economic Perspectives*, 23(1), 101–19.

Speedwell Weather (2009) "Weather trading". Available at: <http://www.speedwellweather.com/pages/market/market_home.aspx>.

Stiglitz, J. E., and Weiss, A. (1981) "Credit rationing with imperfect information", *American Economic Review*, 71(3), 393–410.

United States Treasury Department (2008) *Intragovernmental and Public Debt Holdings*. Available at: <http://www.treasurydirect.gov/govt/charts/principal/principal_govpub.htm>.

Wall, L. D., and Peterson, D. R. (1990) "The effect of Continental Illinois' failure on the financial performance of other banks", *Journal of Monetary Economics*, 26(1), 77–99.

Walsh, C. and Ravenna, P. (2005) "Optimal monetary policy with the cost channel", *Journal of Monetary Economics*, 53(2), 199–216.

West African Monetary Agency (2008) *WAMA*. Available at: <http://www.wama-amao.org/>.

World Council of Credit Unions (2004) "News releases". 15 February. Available at:<http://www.woccu.org/press/releases?id=802>.

Yahoo!.com (2008) *Yahoo! Finance*. Available at: <http://finance.yahoo.com>.

Index

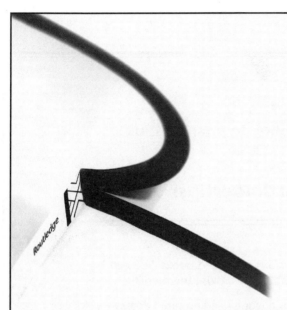